READINGS, CASES, AND STUDY GUIDE FOR

PSYCHOLOGY OF ADJUSTMENT
AND HUMAN RELATIONSHIPS

READINGS, CASES, AND STUDY GUIDE FOR

PSYCHOLOGY OF ADJUSTMENT
AND HUMAN RELATIONSHIPS

Third Edition

JAMES F. CALHOUN
University of Georgia

JOAN ROSS ACOCELLA

McGraw-Hill Publishing Company
New York   St. Louis   San Francisco   Auckland   Bogotá   Caracas
Hamburg   Lisbon   London   Madrid   Mexico   Milan   Montreal
New Delhi   Oklahoma City   Paris   San Juan   São Paulo   Singapore
Sydney   Tokyo   Toronto

Readings, Cases, and Study Guide for Psychology of Adjustment and Human Relationships

Copyright © 1990, 1983, 1978 by McGraw-Hill, Inc. All rights reserved. Printed in the United States of America. Except as permitted under the United States Copyright Act of 1976, no part of this publication may be reproduced or distributed in any form or by any means, or stored in a data base or retrieval system, without the prior written permission of the publisher.

1234567890 MAL MAL 9543210

ISBN 0-07-009761-5

This book was set in Times Roman by Laser Type Technology.
The editors were Barry Ross Fetterolf and Tom Holton; the production supervisor was Frank P. Bellantoni.
The cover was designed by Katharine Hulse.
Malloy Lithographing, Inc., was printer and binder.

Contents

Preface	vii
Acknowledgments	ix
1 Adjustment: A Way of Handling Problems	1

UNIT I/*Self*

2 The Self: What It Is and How to Analyze It	14
3 The Self-Concept: What It Is and How It Develops	24
4 The Self-Concept: How to Change It	32
5 Self-Control: What It Is and How It Develops	43
6 Self-Control: How to Change It	54
7 Three Self-Control Problems: Diet and Exercise, Study Habits, and Anxiety	65

UNIT II/*Others*

8 The Social Self: How We Interact	76
9 Social Perception: What It Is and How It Operates	86
10 Social Perception: How to Change It	96
11 Social Influence: What It Is and How It Operates	105
12 Social Influence: How to Change It	114
13 Three Social Problems: Making Contact, Becoming Assertive, and Fostering Intimacy	126
14 The Environment: How It Affects Us and How We Can Affect It	137
Application Chapter A Intimate Adjustment: Love, Sex, and Marriage	147
Application Chapter B Adjustment and Maladjustment in Adulthood	157

Preface

The purpose of this guide is to assist you, the student, in understanding and learning the material in *Psychology of Adjustment and Human Relationships*, 3rd edition. The materials in the guide are designed to do this based upon the method of study described in Chapter 7 of the text. You may find it helpful to read that discussion of studying at the beginning of the course in order to facilitate your use of this guide.

Chapter Outline

Each section in this guide begins with the chapter outline from the corresponding chapter in the text. The purpose of the outline is to give you a brief overview of the chapter and to draw your attention to important points to be discussed. You should look over this outline to get a clear picture of what the chapter is about *before* you read it. In doing this, you will have in your mind a structure of the material into which you can insert the specific points made by the chapter.

Readings

In order to illustrate further the material in the text, this guide contains a set of three readings for each chapter. The first reading is an article concerning a topic of particular relevance to the chapter material and of potential interest to you. The second is a summary of a research study illustrating some of the research done in the area discussed in the chapter. The final reading in each set is a case vignette about some person who has encountered a problem of adjustment described in the chapter. Each reading has with it a set of questions to help guide you and focus your attention on the important issues raised by the readings. Not only will you find the readings interesting, but you will also find that they improve your understanding of the text material.

Self-Test Items

After you have read the material in a chapter, you should evaluate how much you understand and what you have learned. To assist you in doing this, the guide contains a variety of multiple choice, true-false, completion, and essay questions for each chapter. Use them to test yourself after first reading the material and again when you study for your exams. Answers to all but the essay questions are provided at the end of each guide chapter to facilitate your self-evaluation.

Studying

As noted previously, Chapter 7 in the text gives a detailed picture of how to study. You are encouraged to read this section at the beginning of the course. However, there are several points from that material that deserve to be summarized here.

1. Learning is the input, processing, and storage of information for retrieval at some later time. Therefore, learning takes time and effort. Give yourself that time and be prepared to exert that effort.
2. Choose a regular time for studying. Put yourself on a schedule so that you spend some time each day and each week studying. Do not try to study too much or too long at one time.
3. Establish a special place for studying. Have a particular, quiet place in which to do your studying. Avoid places where there are distractions. Only study in that special place. A library, an empty classroom, for example, can serve this purpose.
4. Develop a method of studying. Have an approach to your work that is regular and systematic, one in which you know if you are learning. Such a method is presented in Chapter 7: the SQ3R method. It consists of five steps:
   a. Survey: Using your outline, look over the chapter material in order to understand the structure of the material to be learned.
   b. Question: Develop and write out questions to ask yourself concerning the chapter material based on the outline for that chapter. (Simply turn these statements into questions, such as: What are . . . ?)
   c. Read: Read the material in order to answer these questions. Make sure that you can fully and completely answer all questions by the time you finish the chapter.
   d. Recite: After reading, go back and ask yourself the questions and then recite the answers to yourself. For any questions that you cannot answer, go back over the material and locate the answer.
   e. Review: Periodically, go back over your questions for the material and test your ability to answer them. This regular review will increase the likelihood of your retaining the information you have learned, and allow you to avoid cramming.

Acknowledgments

Russell W. Belk, "My Possessions, Myself," from *Psychology Today* magazine, July 1988. Copyright © 1988 (PT Partners, L.P.). Reprinted by permission of the publisher.

Jane B. Burka and Lenora M. Yuen, "Mind Games Procrastinators Play," from *Psychology Today* magazine, January 1982. Copyright © 1982, Jane B. Burka and Lenora M. Yuen. Reprinted by permission of the Wallace and Sheil Agency, Inc.

Colin Campbell and M. Brewster Smith, "Are You an Iceberg, A Mirror or an Island: Our Many Versions of the Self," from *Psychology Today* magazine, February 1976. Copyright © 1976, (PT Partners, L.P.). Reprinted by permission of the publisher.

Thomas Cash and Louis Janda, "The Eye of the Beholder," from *Psychology Today* magazine, December 1984. Copyright © 1984 (PT Partners, L.P.). Reprinted by permission of the publisher.

Sheldon Cohen, "Sound Effects on Behavior," from *Psychology Today* magazine, October 1981. Copyright © 1981, (PT Partners, L.P.). Reprinted by permission of the publisher.

Bob Considine, "Lessons Learned," from *They Rose Above It*. Copyright © 1976, 1977 by Millie Considine, Executrix of the Estate of Robert Considine. Reprinted by permission of Doubleday & Company, Inc.

Richard Driscoll, "Their Own Worst Enemies," from *Psychology Today* magazine, July 1982. Copyright © 1982, (PT Partners, L.P.). Reprinted by permission of the publisher.

Thomas J. D'Zurilla, from "Reducing Heterosexual Anxiety," from *Behavioral Counseling: Cases and Techniques,* edited by John D. Krumboltz and Carl E. Thoresen. Copyright © 1969 by Holt, Rinehart and Winston. Reprinted by permission of the publisher.

Israel Goldiamond, from "Self-Control Procedures in Personal Behavior Problems," from *Psychological Reports, 17* (1965), 851–868. Reprinted by permission of the author and publisher. Monograph Supplemental 3-V17. Available as a separate from the journal. Reprinted by permission of the author and publisher.

Stephen M. Johnson, "Frank's Prison," and "Ken's Dating Games," from *First Person Singular.* Copyright © 1977 by Stephen M. Johnson. Reprinted with permission of Harper & Row, Publishers, Inc.

George Kaluger and Meriem Fair Kaluger, "Murder on the Street," "Falling out of Love," "An Open Relationship," "Boot Camp," and "Self-Image of Four Girls," from *Profiles in Human Development.* Copyright © 1976 by The C. V. Mosby Co., St. Louis. Reproduced with permission of the authors and the publisher.

David Kipnis and Stuart Schmidt, "The Language of Persuasion," from *Psychology Today* magazine, April 1985. Copyright © 1985 (PT Partners, L.P.). Reprinted by permission of the publisher.

Elizabeth Loftus, "Eyewitnesses: Essential but Unreliable," from *Psychology Today* magazine, February 1984. Copyright © 1984 (PT Partners, L.P.). Reprinted by permission of the publisher.

Jo Loudin, "Some Personal History," from *Act Yourself.* Copyright © 1979 by Prentice-Hall, Inc., Englewood Cliffs, N.J. Reproduced by permission of the publisher.

John E. Martin and David A. Sachs, "The Effects of a Self-Control Weight Loss Program on an Obese Woman," from *Behavior Therapy and Experimental Psychology,* Vol. 4 (1973), 155–159. Copyright © 1973 by Pergamon Press, Ltd. Reprinted by permission of the publisher.

Jeff Meer, "Loneliness," from *Psychology Today* magazine, July 1985. Copyright © 1985 (PT Partners, L.P.). Reprinted by permission of the publisher.

Ayala M. Pines and Elliot Aronson, with Ditsa Kafry. "Too Much Stress," from *Burnout: From Tedium to Personal Growth.* Copyright © 1981 by Ayala M. Pines, Elliot Aronson, Ditsa Kafry. Reproduced by permission of the Macmillan Publishing Company, Inc.

Maya Pines, "Psychological Hardiness: The Role of Challenge in Health," from *Psychology Today* magazine, December 1980. Copyright © 1980, by Maya Pines. Reprinted by permission of the author and publisher.

John Rempel and John Holmes, "How Do I Trust Thee?" from *Psychology Today* magazine, February 1986. Copyright © 1986 (PT Partners, L.P.). Reprinted by permission of the publisher.

Laurel Richardson, "Another World" from *Psychology Today* magazine, February 1984. Copyright © 1984 (PT Partners, L.P.). Reprinted by permission of the publisher.

Stanley Schachter, "Don't Sell Habit-Breakers Short," from *Psychology Today* magazine, August 1982. Copyright © 1982 (PT Partners, L.P.). Reprinted by permission of the publisher.

R. L. Spitzer, A. E. Skodol, M. Gibbon, and J. B. W. Williams, *DSMIII Casebook,* American Psychiatric Association, Washington, D.C., 1981, "Dressing Up." " The Workaholic."

Barry Stevens, "I," from *Person to Person.* Copyright © 1967 by Real People Press. Reprinted by permission.

"The Nine-to-Five Dilemma" from *Psychology Today* magazine, February 1986. Copyright © 1986 (PT Partners, L.P.). Reprinted by permission of the publisher.

Lois Timnick, "Now You Can Learn to Be Likable, Confident, Socially Successful for Only the Cost of Your Present Education," from *Psychology Today* magazine, August 1982. Copyright © 1982, (PT Partners, L.P.). Reprinted by permission of the publisher.

Claire Warga, "You Are What You Think," from *Psychology Today* magazine, September 1988. Copyright © 1988 (PT Partners, L.P.). Reprinted by permission of the publisher.

1 Adjustment: A Way of Handling Problems

CHAPTER OUTLINE

MODERN LIFE: A NEW CHALLENGE
Increased Knowledge
Higher Expectations
Increased Freedom
Stress and Burnout
ADJUSTMENT
What Is Adjustment?
Controlling Your Adjustment
WHAT IS GOOD ADJUSTMENT?
Factors in Evaluating Adjustment
   The situation
   Values
PSYCHOLOGICAL THEORIES OF ADJUSTMENT
Psychodynamic Theory
   Sigmund Freud: Id, ego, and superego
   Modern psychodynamic theory
Behavioral Theory
   Cognitive behaviorism
Humanistic Theory
   Abraham Maslow: The hierarchy of needs
   Carl Rogers: The self theory
Existential Theory
Viktor Frankl: The will-to-meaning
The Psychological Theory of This Book

READING

Psychological Hardiness: The Role of Challenge in Health

MAYA PINES

It's true, stress researchers will tell you, that tax accountants become particularly susceptible to heart attacks around April 15th—the deadline for tax returns. It is also true that air-traffic controllers, who have to make split-second decisions affecting many lives, develop hypertension with four times the frequency of people in other occupations. And it's true that the death of a close relative statistically increases one's own chances of becoming ill or dying soon afterward; in England, for instance, some 5,000 widowers who were studied for six months after the death of their wives had a mortality rate 40 percent higher than the average for men of their age.

Dozens of studies in the past two decades have shown that people who are in high-stress occupations or who have suffered a major setback in their lives run an unusually high risk of disease. Despite the increased risk, however, such disease is not inevitable. As a small group of researchers is now emphasizing, large numbers of people do not fall sick under stress.

Thus, many people work night and day at high-powered jobs without becoming ill, even while others who have seemingly easier occupations develop ulcers, colitis, hypertension, or heart disease. Some people survive even the horrors of a concentration camp, while others cannot cope with everyday problems without falling apart, mentally or physically.

What distinguishes the people who stay healthy? This is one of the most absorbing questions in medical science today. A good heredity surely helps. But investigators in the field of behavioral medicine are only starting to learn how various kinds of behavior, such as the restless striving and impatience of so-called Type A's, are related to such illnesses as hypertension or coronary disease. Though the research is in its infancy, we now have a few clues to the psychological qualities and social circumstances that may account for resilience to stress.

At the University of Chicago, Suzanne C. Kobasa and Salvatore R. Maddi have defined some of the characteristics of what they call "hardiness." Stress-resistant people, they say, have a specific set of attitudes toward life—an openness to change, a feeling of involvement in whatever they are doing, and a sense of control over events. In the jargon of psychological research, they score high on "challenge" (viewing change as a challenge rather than a threat), "commitment" (the opposite of alienation), and "control" (the opposite of powerlessness). These attitudes have a profound effect on health, according to the two psychologists, who have been studying the incidence of life stresses and illnesses among hundreds of business executives, lawyers, army officers, and retired people.

Unlike researchers in psychosomatic medicine in the 1950s, who attributed much illness to patients' inner conflicts, Kobasa and Maddi have been looking at how people interact with specific aspects of their environment. In this sense, they follow in the footsteps of Richard S. Lazarus of the University of California at Berkeley, the psychologist whose 1966 book, *Psychological Stress and the Coping Process*, emphasized that stress resides neither in the person nor in the situation alone, but depends on how the person appraises particular events. (See "Positive Denial: The Case for Not Facing Reality," *Psychology Today*, November 1979.) Kobasa and Maddi have been trying to find out what determines such appraisals—as well as the consequences of these appraisals. Interestingly, their subjects' answers vary somewhat according to the unwritten rules of behavior within different occupations.

Kobasa's work began with a study of 670 middle- and upper-level managers at an Illinois public utility —all of them white Protestant males, college graduates, between 40 and 49 years old, married, with two children. As part of her doctoral dissertation, Kobasa first asked them to describe on checklists all the stressful life events and illnesses they had experienced in the previous three years. Next she picked out two groups for comparison: 200 executives who scored above average both on stress and on illness, and another 126 with equally high total stress scores who had scored below average on illness. Members of both groups filled out detailed personality questionnaires.

Kobasa had defined the three criteria of hardiness in advance as a working hypothesis; her premises were drawn from existential psychology, whose principal exponents in the United States include Maddi, Rollo May, and Viktor Frankl. Existential psychology postulates that a feeling of engagement and of control over one's life is essential to mental health. Both Maddi and Kobasa practice a form of psychotherapy based on it.

When Kobasa analyzed the Illinois utility managers' answers in 1977, she found that the high-stress/low-illness men stood out in all three categories of hardiness: they were much more actively involved in their work and social lives than those who became sick under stress; they were more oriented to challenge; and they felt more in control of events. Those were exciting findings. As Kobasa explained, "The mechanism whereby stressful life events produce illness is presumably physiological. Yet whatever this physiological response is, the personality characteristics of hardiness may cut into it, decreasing the likelihood of breakdown into illness."

Nevertheless, this study was open to question. Might not the executives' negative view of themselves and their lives be a *result* rather than the cause of the illness? "What we were seeing was just the tip of the iceberg," recalls Maddi, who was Kobasa's thesis adviser. To get more reliable answers, various groups of persons would have to be studied *before* they became ill and then followed for a few years to see what happened to them.

Maddi joined forces with Kobasa in a longitudinal project of this sort. He was deeply interested in the problem because he felt that much of the advice being given to people on the basis of existing stress research was misleading. He had been particularly upset by an article appearing in a women's magazine in 1972 that reported on the widely used stress scale developed by psychiatrists Thomas Holmes and Richard Rahe called the Schedule of Recent Life Events. Used with their Social Readjustment Rating Scale, the Holmes-Rahe test measures and gives specific weight to all the recent changes in a person's life—and assumes that any major change is stressful. Marriage, for example, rates 50 points on their scale, halfway up the scale from 0 to 100. The most severe stress of all, the death of a spouse, rates 100. The magazine published a checklist with which readers could add up their own stress scores. What incensed Maddi was the advice that came with it.

"It said that if your stress score is above 200, you have a 60 percent probability of being ill within the following year," Maddi recalls angrily. "And if your score is above 300, you have an 80 percent chance of falling sick. So if you want to stay healthy, avoid further stress. Don't even drive on the Los Angeles freeways, and don't have a confrontation with your spouse, because it might kill you!"

This baleful view of change contradicted some of Maddi's own research, which focused on the beneficial effects of novelty and surprise. He had not studied extreme circumstances, such as a death in the family or being sent to a concentration camp. But he had evidence that minor changes in people's routines were stimulating and led to growth. Maddi continues to believe that whether novelty is good or bad for a person depends on how it is experienced. He remains adamantly opposed to the theory that stress should be avoided whenever possible.

In this view, he would be supported by the father of stress research, Hans Selye, who has argued that certain kinds of stress—which he calls "eustress"—are good for people. Selye, who practically invented the concept of stress about 40 years ago, has described the body's physical response to it in numerous experiments. But since then, he has pointed out that the racing pulse, the quickened breathing, and the accelerated heart rate that betray stress also occur during times of great joy. A certain amount of stress is essential to well-being, though people's requirements will vary, Selye argues. In a 1978 interview ("On the Real Benefits of Eustress," *Psychology Today*, March 1978), Selye suggested that there are two main types of human beings: "race horses," who are only happy with a vigorous, fast-paced lifestyle, and "turtles," who need peace, quiet, and a tranquil environment. The trick is to find the level of stress that suits one best, he said.

Longitudinal studies of stress and disease are very rare. Most studies rely almost entirely on subjects' recollections of events and illnesses that occurred in the past. The few studies that look forward generally focus on college students and follow up on them for only a few weeks— hardly enough time to allow much stress to develop, let alone a related illness (according to Kobasa and Maddi, such illnesses often follow stress after a six-month lag). Furthermore, these studies seldom try to relate personality traits to the stress and disease, as Kobasa and Maddi did.

In their longitudinal study, Kobasa and Maddi collected information on 109 executives at three different times over a period of two years. They first analyzed the men's personalities and hardiness, based on questionnaires that pulled together a number of items which they had developed; plus some items from other scales relating to challenge, commitment, and control. They then asked the men to fill out a version of the Holmes-Rahe test and another questionnaire that asked for information on serious illnesses. To score high on the illness survey, a person would have to report far more serious illnesses than headaches or colds. A cold rated only 20 points, and even six colds a year would add up to only 120 points. By contrast, an ulcer rated 500 points, and a heart attack 855 points.

The results at the end of two years showed clearly that people whose attitudes toward life could be rated high on challenge, commitment, and control remained healthier than the others. Despite a high score on stressful life events, they had a total illness rating of only 510 for two years, compared with an illness rating of 1,080 for men who scored low on hardiness. "You see the striking degree to which a personality of the hardy type protects people who are under stress," says Maddi. "It could decrease your chance of being ill by 50 percent."

The healthier group's attitude towards change (challenge) appeared to be their most important protective factor, closely followed by commitment. When a man loses his job, for example, he can see it either as a catastrophe—an irreplaceable loss that shows he is unworthy and predicts his downfall—or as an experience that falls within the range of risks he accepted when he took the job. In some cases, he may even view it as an opportunity to find a new career that is better suited to his abilities. Similarly, when an elderly couple is forced to sell their home because it has become too expensive and too difficult to keep, they can view the change either as a tragedy or as a chance to find housing that is safer and perhaps closer to their children.

To rate people on challenge, Kobasa and Maddi asked them to what extent they agreed with statements such as "Boredom is fatal," "A satisfying life is a series of problems; when one is solved, one moves on to the next problem," or, "I would be willing to give up some financial security to be able to change from one job to another if something interesting came along." People who strongly agreed with those statements would rate high on the challenge scale. However, those who agreed with the following statements would rate low: "I don't believe in sticking to something when there is little chance of success," or, "If a job is dangerous, that makes it all the better." The first of these two statements reflects a lack of persistence in the face of challenge. The second represents what Kobasa calls "adventurousness," a form of excessive risk-taking that is typical of people who cannot feel really involved in anything unless it is extreme—for example, a fascist movement. Those who score high on challenge are willing to take some risks, but not excessive risks, she explains.

Kobasa points out that such differences in cognitive appraisal can make an enormous difference in how people respond to events. Those who score high on challenge are much more likely to transform events to their advantage and thus reduce their level of stress. In contrast, people who are low in hardiness may try avoidance tactics—for example, distracting themselves by watching more TV, drinking too much, taking tranquilizers or other drugs, or sleeping more. These are self-defeating tactics, since the real source of stress does not go away. Instead, says Kobasa, "it remains in the mind unassimilated and unaltered, a likely subject matter for endless rumination and subconscious preoccupation"—and it continues to exert its debilitating effects.

The healthy group also rated high on commitment, meaning—as Kobasa and Maddi define the word—that they *engaged* life rather than hanging back on the fringes of it. On Kobasa's tests, the hardy men strongly disagreed with statements such as, "Most of life is wasted in meaningless activity," or, "I am better off when I keep to myself." They took an active role in their work and family lives and believed that their activities were both interesting and important. The executives in the healthy group also believed they could have a real impact on their surroundings. They disagreed with such statements as, "No matter how hard you work, you never really seem to reach your goals," or, "This world is run by a few people in power, and there's not much the little guy can do about it." This gave the healthy executives a high score on control, the third aspect of hardiness.

In order to see whether the same psychological characteristics are equally protective for other kinds of people, Kobasa has also conducted similar studies of 157 lawyers and 75 army captains—all white Protestant males, college graduates, and married with two children, just like the business executives. She is now following up on 2,000 women patients reached through their gynecologists, as well as a group of men who are early retirees.

To her surprise, in the sample of lawyers there was no relationship whatever between stressful events and physical illness. The men who fell sick were often those who had scored lowest on stress, and vice versa. Some of the lawyers did show a relationship between high stress and a variety of psychiatric symptoms: they had trouble sleeping, suffered anxiety, or became severely depressed. Nevertheless, out of the 157 lawyers who had stress scores above 300 (which Holmes and Rahe would call evidence of a major life crisis), 24 reported no psychiatric illness. In line with Kobasa's previous findings, these 24 lawyers were distinguished by higher scores on the commitment scale.

In trying to explain why the lawyers did not become physically ill under stress while the business executives did, Kobasa examined the two groups' contrasting views of stress. Lawyers tend to believe that they perform best under pressure. Their whole training—as advocates, adversaries, and cross examiners—conditions them to produce, confront, and deal with stress. And despite all the stresses they are exposed to, they are reputed to lead very long, productive lives. The myth that lawyers thrive under stress seems to become a self-fulfilling prophecy.

Business executives, on the other hand, are constantly told that stress can kill them. As Kobasa puts it, the up-and-coming executive who is felled by a heart attack before the age of 50 is described as "the classical stress victim." Unfortunately, she says, "many business corporations, in their eagerness to set up stress-management programs, gyms on their top floors, and cardiac units in the medical department, seem to be buying into this negative, narrow view of stress. The executive is told that stress is harmful and that attempts will be made to reduce it; but in the meantime, use biofeedback or the exercise machine to ready your body for the assault." According to Kobasa, the executive's social group thus provides little support for a view of stress as positive or controllable. While a lawyer handling a difficult case might be congratulated for it by colleagues ("Gee, it must be really exciting to work on; it'll move you up in the firm"), a business executive who feels under pressure may receive only sympathy or be advised to work out frustrations in the gym.

Another professional difference came to light in Kobasa's study of army officers. In response to stress, these officers fell ill, mentally or physically, far more frequently than the business executives. Kobasa speculates that this might be because the army is a total institution, from which there is little escape; for military officers, the stresses that occur at work cannot easily be isolated from the rest of their lives. She also found that the army officers scored lower on commitment than either the business executives or the lawyers.

One aspect of hardiness that had proved particularly protective for the business executives—openness to change and challenge—actually led to more physical illness among the army officers. Again, Kobasa can only speculate on the reason. In the post-Vietnam army, she suggests, there is no room for people who have a taste for novelty or challenge. "It may be that to want interesting experiences is to want what the peacetime army is not providing right now," she adds. In this environment, those who seek only security appear to be healthier.

Such differences suggest complexities in the question of what produces stress resistance. As Hans Selye was the first to point out, many factors affect one's reaction to stress: physiological predispositions, early childhood experiences, personality, and social resources. Kobasa's findings imply that specific aspects of personality interact with specific aspects of the social environment in many ways, leading to more or less resilience. For that reason, researchers need to know a great deal more about the expectations and social pressures within different groups.

Meanwhile, other investigators have been studying the role of social supports such as family, friends, colleagues, and wider networks in protecting people from illness. The strength of these supports is closely tied in with one's personality and commitment. According to some studies, the most potent protection of all may be the closeness of a spouse.

Recently 10,000 married men who were 40 years of age or older were followed for five years in Israel. The researchers, Jack H. Medalie and Uri Goldbourt, wanted to find out how new cases of angina pectoris—a form of heart attack—developed. They assessed each man's medical risk factors for heart disease and then asked, among other items on a questionnaire, "Does your wife show you her love?" The answer turned out to have enormous predictive power. Among high-risk men—men who showed elevated blood cholesterol, electrocardiographic abnormalities, and high levels of anxiety—fewer of those who had loving and supportive wives developed angina pectoris than did those whose wives were colder (52 per 1,000 versus 93 per 1,000). It remains unclear, however, to what extent such love and support depend on the husband's personality characteristics.

Another Israeli researcher, Brooklyn-born Aaron Antonovsky, a professor of medical sociology at Ben Gurion University of the Negev, became interested in resistance to disease as a result of his work with survivors of Nazi concentration camps. Originally, he was only trying to find out how 1,150 women of different ethnic origins had adapted to menopause. In the course of this study, he happened to include the following question: "During World War II, were you in a concentration camp?" Of the 287 central European women who participated in the study, 77 said yes. This presented Antonovsky with an unusual, randomly selected subgroup of women whom he could compare with controls.

Not surprisingly, he found that the concentration-camp survivors, as a group, were more poorly adapted than the others on all his measures of physical and emotional health. What struck him, however, was another observation: a number of women among the concentration camp survivors were well adapted by any standard, even though their proportion was relatively small. "Despite having lived through the most inconceivably inhuman experience," Antonovsky wrote, "some women were reasonably healthy and happy, had raised families, worked, had friends, and were involved in community activities."

Whence their strength? he asked. And what about the countless members of minorities or immigrants who have survived atrocious conditions in many countries? What about the poor everywhere? "Despite the fact that the poor are screwed at every step of the way, they are not all sick and dying," he noted. In fact, the human condition is inherently stressful. Stress cannot be avoided by human beings ("the bugs are smarter," he comments). Then how do any of us manage to stay healthy?

To answer this question, Antonovsky shifted his research focus from specific stressors to what he called "generalized resistance resources"—characteristics of the person, the group, or the environment that can encourage more effective tension management. Knowledge and intelligence offer such a resource, he believes, for they allow people to see many ways of dealing with their difficulties—and to choose, when possible, the most effective means. A strong ego identity is another vital resource, he postulates. And so is commitment to a stable and continuing social network.

Antonovsky cites a nine-year study of 7,000 persons in Alameda County, California, which showed that people with many social ties—such as marriage, close friends and relatives, church membership and other group associations—have far lower mortality rates than others. The study, by Lisa Berkman, an epidemiologist now at Yale University, found that even men in their fifties who seemed to be at high risk because of a very low socioeconomic status, but who scored high on an index of social networks, lived far longer than high-status men with low-social-network scores.

Similarly, the social support provided by life in a kibbutz seems to protect children against the anxiety that one would expect as a result of prolonged bombardment. In 1975, at a time of heavy Arab shelling in certain parts of the country, an Israeli researcher compared the anxiety levels of children in several kibbutz and urban communities, in both bombed and tranquil areas. Although urban children who had lived through prolonged bombardment had higher anxiety levels than those from urban areas who had been spared, the kibbutz children did not show any such difference: their anxiety levels were low whether or not their kibbutz had been shelled. The researcher reported that at times of shelling, the kibbutz children were calmly led to shelters that were familiar to them, where educational programs and social life went on pretty much as usual. On the other hand, the urban children, accustomed to living in family units, were suddenly taken to alien and somewhat disordered community shelters; their daily routine was upset. Their higher anxiety level could be explained by the disruption of their normal social network.

In extreme cases, the loss of one's social ties can kill, Antonovsky points out. The phenomenon of voodoo death among tribes in Australia, Central Africa, and the Caribbean is probably the best illustration. When the tribe decides to punish one of its members for breaking a taboo, a witch doctor points a magic bone at him and recites some incantations which place him under a spell of death. "The man who discovers that he is being 'boned' is a pitiable sight," wrote an explorer in Australia, as quoted by the Harvard physiologist Walter Cannon. "He sways backwards and falls to the ground . . . he writhes as if in mortal agony and, covering his face with his hands, begins to moan. After a while he becomes very composed and crawls to his wurley [hut]. From this time onward he sickens and frets . . . his death is only a matter of a comparatively short time."

In Cannon's view, the primary factor in the victim's disintegration is the withdrawal of tribal support. Once the bone is pointed, his fellow tribesmen give him up for dead—and in his isolation, he has no alternative but to die. His heart becomes exhausted by overstimulation, his blood pressure drops calamitously, and his vital functions cease. Much the same appears to happen to some old people in this country when they are consigned to dismal nursing homes or back wards of hospitals, abandoned by the rest of the members of their "tribe."

A different approach to social ties, stress, and personality comes from the eminent Harvard psychologist David C. McClelland. People establish social ties for a variety of reasons, McClelland points out. Some are driven by a deep need for friendship, while others want prestige and power. McClelland and his associates have been studying the need for power for the past 30 years. Recently, they have examined its links to various kinds of stress and to illness.

The people who are most vulnerable to illness under stress, McClelland has found, are those who have a strong drive for power coupled with a high degree of inhibition about expressing it. Such persons "control their assertiveness in a socialized way and make good managers of people," McClelland says. But when they encounter difficulties, they become good candidates for hypertension and heart attacks. McClelland compares them to monkeys that were both enraged and restrained in an experiment by two British researchers; the monkeys developed heart disease as a result. "The equivalent at the personality level would appear to be a strong disposition to act assertively which is simultaneously checked by an inner desire for control and restraint," McClelland writes.

Last year, McClelland and John B. Jemmott III compared the effects of various types of stress on 82 male and female college students who were rated according to their need for power, their degree of inhibition in expressing this need openly, their need for friendship (called "affiliation"), and their need for achievement. First, the students were given projective tests in which they wrote stories about six pictures that were presented to them (one shows a ship captain explaining something to someone, another a man and a woman seated at a table in a nightclub). These stories were then coded, according to criteria developed by McClelland, for the frequency with which they contained "power thoughts" (of having impact on others through aggression, persuasion, or helping, or of seeking prestige and recognition); "achievement thoughts" (of performing better or of unique accomplishments); "affiliative thoughts" (of establishing, maintaining, or repairing friendly relations with others); or evidence of inhibition, such as the frequency of the word "not," which McClelland has found to be a powerful indicator of restraint. (He believes his scoring methods are statistically reliable and permit him to measure such characteristics "objectively, much as one would identify leukocytes in a blood sample, to avoid the self-serving biases that distort the self-reports of motivations obtained from questionnaires.")

Next, the students filled out a Schedule of Life Change Events for the previous six months, a checklist of mood states, and an illness inventory. The researchers then classified the lifechange events according to the type of stress they represented: power/achievement stress (events that challenged or threatened the student's ability to perform powerfully or to impress others), affiliative stress (such as loss of a loved one), or other changes (such as a change in residence).

When all the information was analyzed, it turned out that the students' health or illness depended largely on whether the kinds of stress they had been exposed to impinged on their basic motivations. For example, a high degree of power/achievement stress had disastrous effects on students who scored high both in need for power and in inhibition. When students were motivated more by a need for affiliation, however, the same high degree of power/achievement stress was *not* associated with severe illness. "Generally speaking, when the stress is related to the dominant motive disposition in the individual, it is more likely to be associated with illness," McClelland concluded. He also found that students who were high in need for power but not too inhibited about expressing it seemed relatively protected against power/achievement stress: their illness score was less than half that of students who could not express their power urge openly. The less-inhibited students may have been much like the business tycoon who said, "I don't *get* ulcers, I *give* them."

According to McClelland, men who have a strong need for power are generally "more argumentative and aggressive; they engage more often in competitive sports; they are sexually more active; they accumulate prestige supplies, like fancy clothes and cars; and they tend to join organizations and ally themselves with others who have influence." This sounds suspiciously like the hard-driving, hostile, and aggressive Type A's who began to make headlines a few years ago. The Type-A pattern was popularized by cardiologists Meyer Friedman and Ray H. Rosenman. In their 1974 book, *Type-A Behavior and Your Heart*, they reported on an eight-year study which showed that men with a Type-A pattern were twice as likely as the less-aggressive Type B's to develop coronary heart disease. McClelland has concluded that "the kind of behavior that has been described as Type A looks very much like that of persons who are high in the need for power, whose power motivation is inhibited, and who are also under power stress"—in other words, those he has found to be at greatest risk of stress-related illnesses.

McClelland is now running several experiments to find out how these men differ physiologically in their reaction to stress. One indication may come from an increase in the level of catecholamines and other hormones released by the sympathetic nervous system of Type A's under stress. Another clue may be that some of McClelland's subjects have smaller numbers of certain white cells in their blood—the NK (natural killer) cells that are part of the immune system—and therefore may be more prone to infections and tumors.

Meanwhile, Kobasa and Maddi have started to analyze the actual health records of the executives in their study, so they need not rely entirely on self-reports of illness. The public utility involved gives its managers a free medical exam every year, including some 40 lab tests, and the two psychologists are now working with physicians from the University of Chicago Medical School and the company's medical department to sort out this treasure trove of records.

As behavioral scientists begin to ally themselves with physicians, both groups are becoming more aware of the intricacy of the processes that lead to health or disease. Much of the information about the effects of stress in the existing research literature is still fragmentary—or even contradictory. Depending on circumstances, for example, fear can make one's heart beat either faster or slower (as when the heart "stands still"). Even more surprisingly, some kinds of stress will make breast cancers grow in mice, but the same stresses will slow down or actually prevent the growth of breast cancers in rats.

Eventually, with more research, we may be able to mitigate some of the dangerous effects of stress. Meditation techniques and biofeedback appear to help some people. Behavioral methods can, within limits, assist in breaking certain habits that lead to stress. For instance, Type-A individuals have been taught to allot more time to each activity in their lives, thus slowing down their pace and reducing tension. But these approaches are palliatives that do not deal with the basic causes of stress—or with the way stress is appraised by different people.

More fundamental kinds of reeducation are also possible, Maddi and Kobasa believe. They place their confidence in existential psychotherapy. Whether this form of therapy, however sophisticated, can give people the sense of challenge, commitment, and control that they may need in order to maintain their physical and mental health remains to be proved. It is obviously far more difficult to change one's underlying character structure than to learn a few behavioral techniques. Nevertheless, Maddi remains optimistic. He hopes to show that people of all ages can be taught hardiness.

"People's attitudes and outlooks are largely learned

from experience," he maintains, and "therefore, they can be altered."

Reading Questions

1. Briefly describe the characteristics of stress-resistant people according to Kobasa and Maddi.
2. In extending the findings of the earlier studies of stress-resistant people, Kobasa found differences for lawyers, army officers, and business executives. What were these differences, and what explanation did Kobasa give for them?
3. David McClelland and John Jemmott have taken a different approach to hardiness. What psychological processes have they focused on, and what have they found?

RESEARCH STUDY

Investigators:	Mark S. Pittman and B. Kent Houston.
Source, date:	"Response to Stress, Cognitive Coping Strategies, and the Type A Behavior Pattern," *Journal of Personality and Social Psychology*, 1980, *39*, 147-157.
Location:	University of Kansas.
Subjects:	218 male college students.
Materials:	brief measure of Type A behavior, Jenkins Activity Survey, physiograph, MAACL, eleven statements of responses to stress conditions, and digit span subtest.

The behavior pattern referred to as Type A tends to be related to a high incidence of heart disease and other cardiovascular disorders. This pattern is characterized by competitiveness, aggressiveness, and being under time pressure. Persons who display this pattern have been the focus of a good deal of research because of their tendency to develop heart disease. By contrast, the behavior pattern referred to as Type B is characterized by the absence of competitiveness and aggressiveness.

This study investigated how certain conditions affect Type A and Type B individuals. First, the authors suggested that the responses of Type A individuals to the physical threat of shock would be different from their responses to the psychological threat of failure. Second, the authors suggested that Type A persons more than Type B persons would tend to use denial when faced with a threatening situation.

Male undergraduates were separated into groups of Type A and Type B persons and then placed in conditions in which they were given failure feedback or threat of shock in accordance with their performance on a particular task. Their task was to recall a series of numbers. Those in the failure situation were told that they were not doing well. Those in the threat-of-shock situation were told that if they did not do well, they might be shocked (none were). Before and after the test situation, the subjects were asked to indicate their feelings on the MAACL and how they coped with the stress. Their pulse rate and blood pressure were recorded before, during, and after the test situation.

The researchers found that Type A individuals showed an increase in blood pressure over Type B individuals in the condition involving the psychological threat of failure but not in the condition involving the physical threat of shock. In addition, the Type A's used denial to cope with the stressful situation more frequently than did the Type B's. The Type A's denied the unpleasantness of the situation and consequently experienced less subjective distress than did the Type B's. Thus, in certain stressful situations, both the cognitive and physiological responses of Type A persons differ from the responses of Type B persons.

Research Study Questions

1. What behavior pattern did Pittman and Houston investigate, and what questions about this behavior pattern were raised in their study?
2. How did the investigators study this pattern of behavior?
3. What results were found in the study?

CASE STUDY

Too Much Stress

AYALA M. PINES AND ELLIOT ARONSON

Sue was 32, bright, warm, sensitive. She wanted to "help people" and to "make the world a better place," but, although she received a master's degree in social welfare, nothing in her background or her formal training prepared her for the stresses she would face in her work.

Sue's first job was in a residential program for psychiatric patients who were making the transition from hospital life back into the community. After three years Sue felt she had to leave the job. "I got tired of working with chronic patients," she said. "I was still interested in being a therapist but there was a limit to the amount of therapy that could be done with these patients. Work with them involved mostly maintaining them on medication and helping them to manage in the community. They were very needy people, very dependent, and it was draining. I did see some changes with a few of the young clients, but for the most part the improvement I saw was minuscule." Sue felt she was ready for a change.

Sue accepted a job as family counselor for a police department. Her unit was responsible for responding to domestic disturbance calls and for training police officers in family crisis intervention. "In the beginning it was really fascinating. It was exciting, pioneering territory. We had a lot of publicity. There were T.V. shows, newspaper articles, and a film. But there were also many problems."

Sue felt that she needed to distance herself from some of the situations she worked with. "Part of it was in self-protection because some of the things were so grim. I saw so much horrible stuff. Not only domestic violence, but child abuse and horrible ways that people lived, going into filthy homes, seeing so many crazy people who weren't coping. It was just too much. After a while I had to shut some of it off." Sue felt a sense of frustration and futility.

> The situations started looking so much alike to me. I could never see changes. It was always the same people, in the same situations. I would get angry when I'd go in. After a while, I stopped listening. I stopped being empathetic. I had to lose my compassion in order to survive emotionally. It wasn't a job where you got many thanks from the clients. It was a vicious circle; because the more angry I became, the less I felt like putting out in the counseling sessions, so of course the less happened with the clients.

Sue also felt isolated and frustrated on her job. She felt there was no flexibility and no encouragement of personal development by the department or by her boss. The atmosphere in the office was one of suspicion; staff members were reporting each other and Sue felt betrayed by people she had been fond of. "I was so upset I got to the point that I refused to associate with anyone on the staff. I saw things that were wrong and unethical, things that had to do with basic values that were more important to me than anything else. It was very disturbing to me, but I was getting no support from within the staff or the department. I felt alone in it. That was the hardest part."

After two years Sue noticed the signs of burnout. Her response was to work harder. She started teaching at a community college one course each quarter. "I had to get some rewards so I could feel like I was competent in some way. I derived a lot of gratification from my teaching." Teaching involved much time, little money, and no security, but there were intrinsic rewards. "I could see students learning and getting excited. I was teaching things that I enjoyed talking about." Sue tried to balance these rewards against the stress of her job. But with two jobs she had little time off. "One of the patterns I always had was that when things are going on that I can't cope with, or don't want to face, I get even busier. I would work the whole day, teach from seven to ten, and get back home at eleven at night too tired and too depressed to sleep."

Living this way increased Sue's burnout. "I didn't want one more person to ask anything of me. Instead of listening to my friends and trying to be helpful I would feel like screaming. It seemed like I cried the whole time. I was really depressed."

In her work Sue tried to avoid contact with her clients.

> Sometimes I would be late for home appointments. I would make stops on my way to home visits and do my errands just to have time that had nothing to do with my work. I sometimes spaced out during interviews with clients and I started referring people to other agencies or counselors. I would have a negative attitude before I even went in; I would be very curt, with no warmth at all. In retrospect I think that I was fighting to create this distance so the clients wouldn't like me. I thought that if I wasn't helpful and I wasn't sympathetic, when I asked if they wanted another appointment, they would say no.

One of the ways Sue dealt with her burnout was humor. "I felt that if I couldn't at least laugh at myself and my work, I was really in trouble. So I did a lot of it. I would make fun of the clients, not maliciously, but as a kind of catharsis. This constantly got me into trouble."

Sue felt she could not take any more, and after four years with the police department she quit her job. She had to sort what she wanted to do with her life. She knew she was burned out as a public servant. "I don't have any more to give to needy, dependent, victimized people. I have done my stint as a 'do-gooder.' I have really paid my dues." Sue wanted to use her teaching and analytical skills. She wanted to work in pleasant surroundings with people who enjoyed their work. She looked for work in a company that encouraged creativity and was both supportive and challenging. After a long search, she found such a job.

Case Study Questions

1. Name some of the stresses that Sue experienced in her first and second jobs.

2. How were the external stresses that Sue faced compounded by her reaction to them?
3. What were the consequences of these stresses for Sue?

SELF-TEST

Multiple Choice

1. Which of the following has been called a classic case of the mixed blessing?
   a. our increased freedom
   b. our increased knowledge
   c. our high economy
   d. our high expectations
2. Humans depend on which guidelines to tell them how to behave?
   a. instinct
   b. brains and culture
   c. friends
   d. psychologists
3. Imporvements in what areas offer us rich information, as well as opposing views and values, to choose from?
   a. communication and travel
   b. computer technology
   c. agronomy
   d. none of the above
4. Adjustment is something we tend to engage in:
   a. only when troubled
   b. very seldom
   c. only on occasion
   d. every day
5. Upon which of the following do the judgments you make about your own behavior depend?
   a. your values
   b. your situation
   c. both a and b
   d. either a or b
6. Which of following is said to be the moral code of personality?
   a. the id
   b. the ego
   c. the superego
   d. the libido
7. On what principle does the ego operate?
   a. pleasure principle
   b. moral principle
   c. reality principle
   d. none of the above
8. Which of the following is a state of extreme physical and emotional fatigue brought on by stress?
   a. psychosis
   b. adjustment
   c. maladjustment
   d. burnout
9. The social aspects of adjustment are emphasized by which theoretical perspective?
   a. Freudian
   b. modern psychodynamic
   c. humanistic
   d. social learning
10. Modern psychodynamic theorists define adjustment as whether one can:
    a. remain true to the id
    b. form intimate, loving relationships
    c. remain rational and moral
    d. remain true to the superego
11. Modern psychodynamic theorists' major objection to Freud's theory is his emphasis on the role of:
    a. sex
    b. the id
    c. the libido
    d. the conscious
12. Erikson differentiates developmental stages not by anatomical zone but by:
    a. "crises" involving relationships with others
    b. age
    c. experiences of early childhood
    d. growth of intellectual functioning
13. According to behaviorists, people engage in certain behaviors because:
    a. the behaviors are instinctive
    b. they learned to associate these behaviors with rewards
    c. they see others engaging in these behaviors
    d. the behaviors have been punished
14. In which of the following theories does adjustment mean that the individual develops all of his or her human capabilities to the fullest?
    a. humanistic
    b. existential
    c. social learning
    d. psychodynamic
15. In what way(s) do humanists differ from both psychodynamic and behavioral theorists?
    a. Humanists see humans as free shapers of their own destinies.
    b. Humanists stress the uniquesness of each person's experience.
    c. Humanists believe that early experience has no bearing on present behavior.
    d. a and b
16. Humanists view individuals as:
    a. inherently selfish

    b. inherently evil
    c. inherently brilliant
    d. essentially loving and good
17. Like the humanists, the existential theorists in the field of psychology:
    a. hold a pragmatic view of the personality
    b. hold a spiritual view of the personality
    c. hold a dynamic view of the personality
    d. do not try to evaluate the personality
18. Which of the following theories would "becoming" be most closely associated with?
    a. humanistic theory
    b. existential theory
    c. social learning theory
    d. neo-Freudian theory
19. Viktor Frankl is most often associated with which psychological theory?
    a. humanistic
    b. existential
    c. social learning
    d. psychodynamic
20. According to existential psychology,
    a. self-actualization is automatic
    b. individuals' perceptions are unique
    c. self-actualization is a struggle
    d. b and c

True-False

1. Traditionally, people could choose what they would become.
2. Our high expectations are an example of a mixed blessing.
3. Adjustment can be defined as a continuous rather than a discrete process.
4. For the most part, problems arise when the adjustment process starts to work against us.
5. Psychology is the study of human emotions and thoughts.
6. According to Freud, only a small portion of our thoughts and actions emerges from conscious mental processes.
7. The aspect of the personality that, according to Freud, operates in the unconscious is the id.
8. According to Freud, the well-adjusted person is able to resolve id-superego conflicts with a strong ego.
9. The post-Freudians see adjustment in social terms.
10. According to social learning theory, the well-adjusted person is one who has learned behaviors necesssary to deal successfully with life's demands.
11. Social learning theory suggests that psychology should be studied in quantifiable, objective terms.
12. Humanistic psychologists disagree entirely with the behaviorists' pragmatic approach to human existence.
13. Humanists stress the universality of experience.
14. The existential theorists hold a dynamic view of the personality.
15. The existentialists view behavior as the result of free choice.

Completion

1. The process whereby we handle our problems-in-living is called _____.
2. For the most part, citizens of industrialized nations are faced with _____ problems.
3. Whatever values we choose to embrace, they must survive constant exposure to _____ values.
4. Our high expectations have been regarded as a classic case of a mixed _____.
5. Human beings, unlike other animals, have very few _____ to tell them how to behave.
6. In deciding what to do and what to be, young people today must rely on two sources of guidance: well-developed brains and their _____.
7. Unsuccessful psychological self-treatments may be harmful as they can be blows to _____ _____.
8. Coping with problems in an effective way to avoid psychological crises is _____.
9. _____ is anything that requires one to adjust.
10. The sum total of what you already are is called your _____ .
11. The science of _____ can intervene to change your adjustment.
12. Our values concern how we think people _____ behave.
13. Evaluations of human adjustment are _____.
14. According to Sigmund Freud, the major influence on our behavior is the _____.
15. According to psychodynamic theory, the _____ is the thinking part of the personality.

Essay Questions

1. Briefly define the term "adjustment" and discuss the three factors of adjustment that are constantly influencing our lives. (p. 12–13)
2. Define the term "psychology," and briefly discuss how adjustment draws upon the subfields of psychology. (p. 17)
3. What two original ideas served as the basis for Freud's theory of personality? What are Freud's three branches of personality? (pp. 18–19)
4. Compare and contrast psychoanalytic theory and post-Freudian theory with regard to "good adjustment." (pp. 19–22)
5. Discuss how existential and humanist views differ from other views of psychological growth. (pp. 24–27)

SELF-TEST ANSWERS

Multiple Choice

1. d (p. 8)
2. b (p. 10)
3. a (p. 5)
4. d (p. 13)
5. c (p. 16)
6. c (p. 18)
7. c (p. 19)
8. d (p. 12)
9. b (p. 19)
10. b (p. 19)
11. b (pp. 19–20)
12. a (p. 20)
13. b (p. 22)
14. a (p. 23)
15. d (p. 25)
16. d (p. 25)
17. c (p. 26)
18. b (p. 26)
19. b (p. 27)
20. d (p. 27)

True-False

1. false (p. 7)
2. true (p. 8)
3. true (p. 13)
4. true (p. 13)
5. false (p. 17)
6. true (p. 18)
7. true (p. 18)
8. true (p. 19)
9. true (p. 19)
10. true (p. 20)
11. false (p. 22)
12. true (p. 23)
13. false (p. 25)
14. true (p. 26)
15. true (p. 27)

Completion

1. adjustment (p. 4)
2. existential (p. 5)
3. opposing (p. 5)
4. blessing (p. 8)
5. instincts (p. 10)
6. values (p. 10)
7. self-esteem (p. 11)
8. adjustment (p. 13)
9. stress (p. 11)
10. self (p. 13)
11. psychology (p. 17)
12. should (p. 17)
13. relative (p. 17)
14. unconscious (p. 18)
15. ego (p. 18)

2
The Self: What It Is and How to Analyze It

CHAPTER OUTLINE

WHAT IS THE SELF?
The Self as a Construct
Five Aspects of the Self
The Unity and Continuity of the Self
The Dynamic Quality of the Self

SELF-ANALYSIS
Description
  Object of description
  Methods of description
  Preliminary rules for description
  Further suggestions for description
Functional Analysis
  Finding correlations
  Pitfalls in looking for correlations
  Forming a hypothesis
  Testing the hypothesis
The Rewards of Self-Analysis

READING

Our Many Versions of the Self

M. BREWSTER SMITH TALKS WITH COLIN CAMPBELL

Colin Campbell: For several years now you've been thinking about the self, about how human beings define themselves and others, and especially the ways modern psychologists have described the great mystery of the self. There's the iceberg self of the psychoanalysts, who say that most of the person lies beneath the surface of consciousness. And there's the mirror self, a thing defined partly by our reflections about the world and other people. There's the onion, the vacuum, the chooser. It seems to me we could invent metaphors forever. Do you think we'll reach any conclusion?

M. Brewster Smith: Maybe you're overestimating my project. What I'm trying to do is sort out the major images of the self. We are partly creatures of our own images. Our theories of self affect what we theorize about. Are they impoverished, or simplistic, or incoherent? It makes a difference.

Those metaphors are powerful figures of speech. It makes a difference to me how I think about myself. Am I free or not free? Do I control my life? Do I have a core worth searching for? There's a growing body of evidence in psychology that the answers people give to such questions make a tremendous difference in terms of their happiness, the decisions they make, the way they treat other people—how they live, how they die.

Campbell: But are we in a position to determine what the self really is?

Smith: For different people at different times, the self has meant really quite different things. We can at least spell out our assumptions. That's what the iceberg and the mirror and so on really are. They're preconceptions, prescientific models. They're the notions psychologists assume before they walk into the laboratory or the clinic. It would be a scandal if it weren't so understandable, if the self weren't so elusive.

Campbell: How do the preconceptions of scientists influence how I think about myself?

Smith: Oh, in many ways. They change language. They filter down. Scientific models have shaped our images of who we are for centuries. They tell how we fit into the universe. Think of Copernicus, who made the sun the new center of things and the earth a small suburb, or Darwin, who rewrote our family history. It was another revolution when Freud started dredging up all those primitive urges beneath the surface of polite society.

In any case, these intellectual doctrines about the self don't just sit around in unreadable scholarly journals. They wind up in people's heads. They turn into folk philosophies and ideologies and even common sense. Most educated Americans probably assume, for instance, that the experiences of infant children leave a deep mark on their personalities as adults. People haven't always taken that for granted.

These metaphors of self become part of the world view of students who hear about them from their teachers, and of patients who listen to their doctors—and of all kinds of people who are searching around our culture in order to understand themselves. Some of these same ideas wind up in the heads of journalists, politicians, artists, bureaucrats. Think of Don Campbell's work on evaluating Government programs. That's a fairly serious entry of the social sciences into real life, and presumably those scientists are going to work with a certain image of man, certain notions of what a human being is all about—whether they know it or not.

Campbell: Do you feel that images of the self can sometimes be pernicious?

Smith: I do. I'd put the extreme Skinnerian position—what I've labeled the vacuum self—in the pernicious category. I don't think Skinner is a fascist, as Noam Chomsky seems to, but his way of talking above his work confers a blessing on the irresponsible manipulation of people. The powerful doctor above and the patients below. The experimenter and his subjects. I've become very suspicious of experts.

Campbell: Hannah Arendt once claimed that the trouble with modern behaviorism isn't that its theories are wrong but that they could become true—that they really do reflect certain obvious and dangerous social trends.

Smith: She puts it well. Many students of behavior simply have no use for any concept of the self, or even of personality. They say the self is illusory, illegitimate, a ghost in the machine. To the most urgent questions, "Who am I?" they answer, "There is no you." And this nonself is a familiar, if frightening, caricature of some human beings today.

I also think it's a caricature of science, by the way—physics, probably— and I'm getting quite tired of that. Academic psychologists made a big mistake, I think, when they decided to model their discipline on physics. We weren't ready for such hardness, and we still aren't, and we never will be, probably. We haven't done enough observation, enough natural history and careful analysis of the ways human beings think and feel in real life.

Besides, there's no counterpart in physics for the way in which human beings take their own understanding and appraisal of themselves into account. This brings in degrees of freedom beyond anything Heisenberg imagined.

Campbell: How exactly can an image of the self as vacuum harm an individual? After all, even Skinner doesn't say the self is empty. He says it's a black box, unknowable.

Smith: Maybe unknowable is another way of saying, "We won't think about it. We can understand human beings without the self." That's like saying, "forget it."

This idea can be bad for the health, dangerous to a person's self-sufficiency. It says that we're not free men but a bundle of conditioned responses. And yet the idea of freedom, the belief in it, changes the way we act and feel about ourselves. Certain images of ourselves tend to *make* us relatively free, relatively competent and self-sufficient.

You can see this phenomenon in politics all over the world today. That's partly what liberation movements are all about. Start telling people they're free agents rather than subjects, and behold, they start acting like free agents. Or maybe start telling them they are programmed dupes but could be free agents. It's quite remarkable. Anticolonialism, women's liberation, ethnic power—these political movements live off the sense that people are capable of great things.

Campbell: And on a more private level?

Smith: It's the same story. The psychologist Richard DeCharm, for instance, has examined the differences between people who feel like "pawns" and those who see themselves as "origins of causation." The pawns end up being traded off in life. Robert White has emphasized personal competence, and Julian Rotter has talked about people's sense of internal control. A whole stream of research seems headed for a much more *active* sense of psychological well-being than our older notions of adjustment.

I'm afraid it sounds like Norman Vincent Peale and the power of positive thinking, which is hogwash, but it goes much deeper than just conning yourself. I think it's pretty obvious that some people are more free than others. Some people take the initiative, whether at work or in their marriages or wherever. They create or select their own environments. Certain others, by contrast, feel and appear as though their lives were living them.

Free will isn't an absolute, in other words. It's more like an empirical fact, which varies with the individual. And degrees of freedom aren't just arbitrary, they have causes. One becomes a pawn as a result of bad luck, a certain kind of childhood and education and social milieu. There can be a deterministic science of freedom.

Campbell: Metaphors of the self, I gather, involve other matters besides freedom.

Smith: They do. I first tried to sort them out, in fact, when I realized that I had overemphasized the importance of personal freedom. There was too much achievement, too much instrumentality in my picture of the well-made person. He—or she—might be incredibly competent, but he was lopsided and probably headed for an ulcer. Too much *he*, probably.

So I started reading the humanistic psychologists in earnest, to see what they could tell me about the elements of personality I had slighted, things like emotion and expression and affection. And I'm still interested in that side of human nature, although I've been disappointed in the humanists.

Campbell: How so?

Smith: Well, I'm thinking of Abraham Maslow and his followers, of whom there seems to be millions. He's an attractive nuisance—like one of those old refrigerators that children keep locking themselves into. He encouraged people to think lazily and wishfully about matters that are really very hard. According to Maslow, you plant the acorn, and you water it, and it flowers into a tree, and the process of human growth is supposed to be the same.

I don't believe it. It doesn't do justice to the role of human action and choice, not to speak of the old problem of evil, which real humanists have always been attentive to. Maslow set himself up as a humanist, but his basic metaphors and assumptions were actually more biological than humanistic, and there's a tremendous difference between an organism and a human being.

Campbell: You think his metaphor of the self was foolish.

Smith: Pollyanna-optimistic, I'd say. But the main thing was that his basic image of the self remained always in the background. I kept asking myself, *what* self is going to be actualized? The question troubled me a lot more than it troubled Maslow, who liked to point to Albert Einstein and Eleanor Roosevelt as examples of self-actualization—the people he liked, in other words. I like them too, but there are other ways of actualizing oneself that I don't happen to like. Maslow make things too easy.

The truth of the matter is more complicated. For instance, if you think of the self as something rich and valuable, yet hidden from everyday consciousness, then some sort of openness to those hidden depths might be the surest route to self-actualization. Some sort of extreme spontaneity.

Campbell: This is the iceberg self?

Smith: Yes. Or maybe a better image would be the Jungian notion that each human being is an island joined to other islands by deep connections under the sea. These connections are the collective unconscious, and each island rises above the water like a volcano, which sometimes allows what lies below to erupt into consciousness. I think it's a good image, and it's gained an extra measure of plausibility from the recent discovery of mankind's incredibly old age, perhaps 3,000,000 years.

Campbell: Do you think a belief in psychic depths necessarily makes people spontaneous? Some people probably picture a gray monster out of *Jaws* down there.

Smith: That's true. The point, in any case, is that it all depends on what you think is down there, or whether you think there is a "down there." It matters what you think, or feel deeply, because these images have practical consequences. Maslow saw sweetness and light: hence spontaneity was the order of the day.

Campbell: A genuine heretic.

Smith: Yes. Sort of the flip side of the self as sinner.

Campbell: There is something speculative about all of these metaphors of the self, even the materialistic ones.

Smith: I think that's true. Remember, these are *pre*scientific assumptions. They may not be speculative, but they're not scientific either. Skinner's assumptions about what he *should* think about people are just as value laden as Jung's. Their main thing is to look at them and think about them and not just assume them.

Campbell: Tell me about mirror self.

Smith: Well, obviously, it's very different from the depth psychology of the iceberg or the island. The mirror self is much more concerned with intellect, much less concerned with dreams, childhood, sex. For example, it's very mirrorish of me to want to bring all these metaphors of the self up to the surface for discussion.

Years ago in Chicago, George Herbert Mead proposed that essential human nature emerges in the process of interaction with others. Selfhood develops with the ability to communicate, and we communicate not only with others but with ourselves, through inner dialogue. This all sound very philosophical, but it's an important image. A good many thinkers, even William James, have taken the mirror metaphor quite seriously. And so do I. There's something about self-awareness, about reflection, that's particularly human.

Campbell You think the mirror is true to life?

Smith: The image captures something essential about what's human—not everything, though. The mirror metaphor, with its emphasis on communication and social development of self-consciousness, tells us very little about the life of impulse. It ignores the whole range of things examined by Freud and Jung, those pressures from within, from the past and toward the future. There's something not quite biological enough about the mirror self.

The mirror also makes me wonder what self-actualization might be, in *its* terms. Presumably it's something like the Socratic maxim, "The unexamined life is not worth living." Examination, reflection, dialogue, introspection, rationality: these are what matter to the mirror self. These and the ability to act according to principles. And I think these things do matter, but there are other things that matter, too. I don't believe art, for instance, springs from the mirror self. It is too irrational.

Campbell: Tell me about the onion.

Smith: The metaphor comes from Ibsen's poetic drama *Peer Gynt*, whose hero is constructed like an onion, all layers and roles and facades, but no substance. No core. He's a kind of organization man. Modern role theorists, and some social-learning theorists as well, seem to be saying we're *all* like that, simply creatures of our social roles. Erving Goffman has shown how often we act out standard rituals in everyday life. We are in cahoots with each other to support each other's roles.

Campbell: Like actors in a film, never the director.

Smith: Right. Jobholders, consumers, conformists. Participants in a con game where we are both players and victims.

Campbell: How is this different from the mirror self, where everything is very conscious or social?

Smith: How is Socrates different from H. R. Haldeman? The mirror is an image of communication, of lucidity. The onion is just a ball of stereotypes.

This way of looking at people drives the humanistic psychologist right up the wall, and they say, "No, you've got it all wrong, we're not all onions, we're all agents and selves." Or, "we are shadows of a transcendental, transpersonal selfhood." But again, the squabble strikes me as too absolute. It's the old argument between free will and determinism, and as I've said, I think some people are more like onions than others.

Campbell: Maybe role theory in the social sciences has developed as a response to some recent bumper crops of onion.

Smith: I'm afraid that's true. David Riesman said that in *The Lonely Crowd*, when he described the historical transition from the inner-directed self to the more contemporary "radar" personality—people tuned in to whatever's going on outside. The onion is a plausible psychological model for large numbers of people.

Campbell: So if the shoe fits . . .

Smith: The point is that the shoe doesn't *have* to fit. A person constructed like an onion is a failure. If people are nothing but layers of roles, then we can stop worrying about trifles like other people's inner qualities, real interests, abilities to think and choose for themselves. All these ideas become meaningless. We might as well become contemptuous and manipulative in the worst sense, in the manner of propagandists and the most cynical political regimes. The Nixon administration was a bastion of onionism. It reflected the basic orientation of one very cynical segment of our culture, the segment that sees mass communications as a weapons system and an alternative to open discussion.

It's no coincidence that Haldeman was an ad man.

Campbell: You've written about at least one other metaphor, the self as chooser.

Smith: The notion of man as chooser seems to have grown both from the work of writers like Erik Erikson—psychologists interested in identity—and from the existentialist philosophers, who have focused on the arbitrariness and essential humanness of choice. The chooser is a rich metaphor, especially since our recent history has bombarded us with choices, and since most standards seem to be in chaos.

But I must add that the existentialist perspective tends to view free will as a philosophical gift, and I don't see how that makes much sense. Neurotics, cripples, prisoners—these people aren't essentially choosers. At lease they're less so than others.

Campbell: What is to prevent us from inventing hundreds of these metaphors?

Smith: I'm sure there are other images of the self besides the ones I've mentioned—but not hundreds.

Campbell: What about the self as pilgrim or godhead—metaphors that have been powerful images of what a human being is all about.

Smith: I think they're worth studying. And yet many of those religious metaphors, such as the idea that man is the child of God, have collapsed within my lifetime. And this collapse has left an empty space that various secular images are trying to fill.

A lot of my students are turned on to "transpersonal psychology," which looks to me like the old mysticism in psychologists' clothing. Read William James on *The Varieties of Religious Experience*—he's deeper and sounder than Assagioli, or Watts, or Maharishi. So many people seem to want to escape from selfhood.

As for inventing new metaphors of the self, what often happens is that we create grotesques and caricatures. And some of these grotesques are taken very seriously, such as the self as digital computer and several others we've talked about. They take a little part of man for the whole, and that's absurd, It's dangerous, because we're talking about a science of man complete with various technologies. We're not just talking about half a dozen clever but vaporous figures of speech.

Here's another one: The self as calculator of self-interest, the metaphor that economists have always believed in. Even that hoary old halftruth seems to be having a revival, and among psychologists of all people, who ought to know better.

Some of the strangest metaphors are still possible. People can be marvelously inventive in their beliefs about themselves. But you see, that inventiveness makes me pause. It's as scary as it is wonderful. We can be so stupidly reductive sometimes, thinking that we've captured the essence and the range of every man and woman in a phrase.

What counts right now, I think, is that we recognize what images we're living by

Reading Questions

1. In what ways do the preconceptions of scientists influence how we think about ourselves?
2. What does M. Brewster Smith mean by the statement that "there can be a deterministic science of freedom"?
3. What are our many version of the self?

RESEARCH STUDY

Investigators:	William B. Swann and Stephen J. Read.
Source, date:	"Acquiring Self-Knowledge: The Search for Feedback That Fits," *Journal of Personality and Social Psychology,* 1981, *41,* 1119-1128.
Location:	University of Texas at Austin.
Subjects:	243 undergraduate students and 33 graduate students.
Materials:	self-report measure of self-conceptions and lists of questions.

It has been found repeatedly that people's views of themselves are extremely stable. In their efforts to help clients change their negative views of themselves clinical psychologist have found that clients' self-views are highly resistant to change. Similarly, researches have found that people's self-ratings remain stable over long periods of time.

Why are individuals' views of themselves so stable? For one thing, research has shown that people pay more attention to information that supports their self-view than to information that does not. For another, people will actively seek out evaluations of themselves that fit with their own self-view. Finally, people prefer information that confirms, rather than disconfirms, their self-views.

The present study was designed to determine whether people actively seek information that confirms their views of themselves and to see whether they view that confirmatory feedback as more informative than feedback that does not confirm their view of themselves.

The participants in the study were first asked to fill out a measure of how they viewed themselves in terms of their assertiveness and their level of emotionality. Next they were told that someone else was going to evaluate them and that they could indicate which questions they wanted that person to ask them about their assertiveness and emotionality. The questions were designed to focus on high or low levels of each of these two characteristics. Finally, the participants were asked to rate how informative each of the questions would be.

The results indicated that the participants preferred to be asked questions that focused on those levels of assertiveness and emotionality that were consistent with their own views of themselves. Further, they felt that those questions that did focus on levels consistent with their own self-view would be more informative than questions that were inconsistent.

The results of this study indicated that we tend to look for and consider informative information about ourselves that is consistent with the view that we already have of ourselves. In doing this, we tend to verify and maintain our self-view.

Research Study Questions

1. Discuss the general concern of this study and the specific focus of the issues it raised.
2. Describe how the investigators studied these issues.
3. What were the results of the study, and what do these results indicate about our view of ourselves?

CASE STUDY

"I"

BARRY STEVENS

In the beginning, I was one person, knowing nothing but my own experience.

Then I was told things, and I became two people: the little girl who said how terrible it was that the boys had a fire going in the lot next door where they were roasting apples (which was what the women said)—and the little girl who, when the boys were called by their mothers to go to the store, ran out and tended the fire and the apples because she loved doing it.

So then there were two of I.

One I always doing something that the other I disapproved of. Or other I said what I disapproved of. All this argument in me so much.

In the beginning was I, and I was good.
Then came in other I. Outside authority. This was confusing. And then other I became *very* confused because there were so many different outside authorities.

Sit nicely, Leave the room to blow your nose. Don't do that, that's silly. Why, the poor child doesn't even know how to pick a bone! Flush the toilet at night because if you don't it makes it harder to clean. DON'T FLUSH THE TOILET AT NIGHT— you wake people up! Always be nice to people. Even if you don't like them, you mustn't hurt their feelings. Be frank and honest. If you don't tell people what you think of them, that's cowardly. Butter knives. It is important to use butter knives. Butter knives? What foolishness! Speak nicely. Sissy! Kipling is wonderful! Ugh! Kipling (turning away).

The most important thing is to have a career. The most important thing is to get married. The hell with everyone. Be nice to everyone. The most important thing is to have money in the bank. The most important thing is sex. The most important thing is to have everyone like you. The most important thing is to dress well. The most important thing is to be sophisticated and say what you don't mean and don't let anyone know what you feel. The most important thing is to be ahead of everyone else. The most important thing is a black seal coat and china and silver. The most important thing is to be clean. The most important thing is to always pay your debts. The most important thing is not to be taken in by anyone else. The most important thing is to love your parents. The most important thing is to work. The most important thing is to be independent. The most important thing is to speak correct English. The most important thing is to be dutiful to your husband. The most important thing is to see that your children behave well. The most important thing is to go to the right plays and read books. The most important thing is to do what others say. And others say all these things.

All the time, *I* is saying, live with life. That is what is important.

But when I lives with life, other I says no, that's bad. All the different other I's say this. It's dangerous. It isn't practical. You'll come to a bad end. Of course . . . everyone felt that way once, the way you do, but *you'll learn!*

Out of all the other I's some are chosen as a pattern that is me. But there are all the other possibilities of patterns within what all the others say which comes into me and become other I which is not myself, and sometimes these take over. Then who am I?

I does not bother about who am I. I *is*, and is happy being. But when I is happy being, other I says get to work, do something, worthwhile. I is happy doing dishes. "You're weird!" I is happy being with people saying nothing. Other I says talk. Talk, talk, talk. I gets lost.

I knows that things are being played with, not possessed. I likes putting things together, lightly. Taking things apart, lightly. "You'll never have anything!" Making things of things in a way that the things themselves take part in, putting themselves together with suprise and delight to I. "There's no money in that!"

I is human. If someone needs I gives. "You can't do that! You'll never have anything for yourself! We'll have to support you!"

I loves. I loves in a way that other I does not know. I loves. "That's too warm for friends!" "That's too cool for lovers!"

"Don't feel so bad, he's just a friend. It's not as though you loved him." "How can you let him go? I thought you loved him?" So cool the warm for friends and hot up the love for lovers, and I gets lost.

So both I's have a house and a husband and children and all that, and friends and respectability and all that, and security and all that, but both I's are confused because others say, "You see? You're lucky," while I goes on crying. "What are you crying about? Why are you so ungrateful?" I doesn't know gratitude or ingratitude, and cannot not argue. I goes on crying. Other I pushes it out, says "I am happy! I am very lucky to have such a fine family and a nice house and good neighbors and lots of friends who want me to do this, do that." I is not reasonable, either, I goes on crying.

Other I gets tired, and goes on smiling, because that is the thing to do. Smile, and you will be rewarded. Like the seal who gets tossed a piece of fish. Be nice to everyone and you will be rewarded. People will be nice to you, and you can be happy with that. You know they like you. Like a dog who gets patted on the head for good behavior. Tell funny stories. Be gay. Smile, smile, smile . . . I is crying . . . . "Don't be sorry for yourself! Go out and do things for people!" "Go out and be with people!" I is still crying, but now, that is not heard and felt so much.

Suddenly: "What am I doing?" "Am I to go through life playing the clown?" "What am I doing, going to parties that I do not enjoy?" "What am I doing, being with people who bore me?" "Why am I so hollow and the hollowness filled with emptiness?" A shell. How has this shell grown around me? Why am I proud of my children and unhappy about their lives which are not good enough? Why am I disappointed? Why do I feel so much waste?

I comes through, a little. In moments. And gets pushed back by other I.

I refuses to play the clown any more. Which I is that? "She used to be fun, but now she thinks too much about herself." I lets friends drop away. Which I is that? "She's being too much by herself. That's bad. She's losing her mind." Which mind?

Case Study Questions

1. Describe the distinguishing features of each of the selves as described by Barry Stevens.
2. Which "I" seems to be dominant in the narrative? What conflicts did the dominant "I" encounter?
3. Which "I" would the author have wanted most to identify with? Which "I" was losing its mind in the end?

SELF-TEST

Mulitiple Choice

1. What hypothetical construct refers to the complex physical, behavioral, and psychological processes characteristic of the individual?
   a. the soul
   b. the self
   c. the id
   d. the libido
2. What word describes the unifying principle tying together the many aspects of an individual's personality?
   a. self
   b. libido

c. id
d. soul
3. Which one of the following would not be considered an aspect of the self?
   a. social self
   b. psychological self
   c. self-as-process
   d. physical self
4. Which aspect of the self controls what we show to others as we role-play?
   a. social self
   b. physical self
   c. ideal self
   d. self-concept
5. The aspect of the self that describes what you would like to be is the:
   a. self-concept
   b. ideal self
   c. social self
   d. physical self
6. When we wish to direct or change the future self, we must first analyze the:
   a. ideal self
   b. future self
   c. past self
   d. present self
7. The methodical process of self-analysis involves what two basic steps?
   a. description and statistical analysis
   b. description and functional analysis
   c. statistical and functional analysis
   d. correlational and functional analysis
8. The research method in which the researcher simply asks the individual to say how he or she feels or thinks is the:
   a. performance measure
   b. simple observation
   c. self-support
   d. MMPI
9. Which of the following is a preliminary rule for self-description?
   a. simplicity
   b. objectivity
   c. specificity
   d. all of the above
10. Self-analysis will be much easier if you break down your:
    a. tolerances into small units
    b. resistances into manageable units
    c. complex behaviors into equal units
    d. complex behaviors into small, simple units of behaviors
11. There are very few human motives as powerful as the motive to:
    a. protect ourselves from unpleasant thoughts
    b. become self-actualized
    c. become self-aware
    d. reach economic stability
12. If, through the process of self-analysis, you discover that increases in your cigarette consumption are accomplished by decreases in your food consumption, what can you infer about the two factors?
    a. They are inversely related.
    b. They are positively related.
    c. They are negatively related.
    d. They are directly related.
13. Which of the following characterizes the "distributed practice" study method?
    a. studying for eight hours straight the day before an exam
    b. studying in two four-hour segments the day before an exam
    c. studying in eight one-hour segments the day before an exam
    d. studying in eight one-hour segments over several days before an exam
14. What pitfalls have you run up against if you find a positive relationship between studying and grades but that neither one causes the other?
    a. third-variable problem
    b. correlation inequality problem
    c. factorial problem
    d. matched-error problem
15. If you hypothesize that studying is an important cause of your low grade, then studying is what type of variable?
    a. hidden
    b. third
    c. independent
    d. dependent
16. In the hypothesis of question 15, "low grades" would be which type of variable?
    a. hidden
    b. third
    c. independent
    d. dependent
17. When testing the accuracy of your hypothesis through experimentation, you usually manipulate which variable?
    a. concurrent
    b. dependent
    c. independent
    d. constant
18. A person is more likely to be confident that he or she is dealing with a genuine cause-and-effect

relationship if he or she observes the desired changes in which variable?
a. hidden
b. third
c. dependent
d. independent

19. Repeated practice with self-analysis helps people to perceive the structure:
a. of their experience
b. of their world
c. of their knowledge
d. of their psyche

20. When individuals attempt to understand why they do what they do, they are using which process?
a. dream work
b. free association
c. insight
d. learning

True-False

1. Unlike physical and behavioral events, the psychological processes of higher organisms, such as humans, are more difficult to understand.
2. A construct is something that is said to exist but cannot be detected by our five senses.
3. The dynamic quality of the self refers to the self as a fixed, finished product.
4. The goal of self-analysis, to understand ourselves, is achieved by creating a framework within which we can organize our experiences of ourselves.
5. Behavioral problems are considered much easier to analyze than are physical attributes.
6. Typically, the method of self-report is considered to be less precise than is a performance measure.
7. Behavioral problems are those that involve specific, overt actions that disturb the individual or someone else.
8. Since the time of Ben Franklin, the method of behavioral self-monitoring has been considered a fairly thorough method.
9. Like simplicity and objectivity, the rule of subjectivity is basic to self-description.
10. Self-analysis is usually much easier to accomplish with large units of behavior than when dealing with small units.
11. The technique of graphing has been found to be effective enough to replace the "description of behavior" that it charts.
12. It is important to remember that correlations, whether positive or negative, do not indicate cause-and-effect relationships.
13. Although internal events are not observable, they can still have a potent effect on behavior.
14. The statement "variable X is an important cause of variable Y" is stating that "variable Y is dependent upon variable X."

Completion

1. A _____ is something that is said to exist but cannot be detected by our five senses.
2. It is possible when a young girl must undergo cosmetic surgery for medical reasons, her sense of _____ may become threatened.
3. The _____ self consists of many different roles that we show to others in various situations.
4. With regard to its dynamic quality, the self is not considered to be a finished product but is a set of _____.
5. The act of studying something by examining its essential features and their relationships to each other is referred to as _____.
6. Our habit of adjusting our words and behavior in such a way as to produce a desired impression on the people observing us is called _____.
7. The methodological process of self-analysis involves the two basic steps of _____ and functional analysis.
8. The simplest and most accurate method of self-description is _____.
9. To get a more precise description of recurrent feelings of depression, it is best to self-monitor depressive _____.
10. When two variables tend to increase or decrease at the same time, then they are said to _____.
11. Functional analysis is the examination of behaviors and the events and situations surrounding them in order to discover _____ and _____ relationships.
12. If, in the process of self-monitoring, you find that an increase in your food consumption accompanies an increase in your emotional stress, you say that there is a _____ between these two variables.
13. A _____ is a proposed explanation of what is causing the target behavior.
14. When testing your proposed explanation of what is causing the target behavior, you will manipulate the _____ variable.
15. The chicken or the egg relationship is referred to as a _____ relationship.

Essay Questions

1. The "self" is said to be composed of several interrelated aspects. What are they and how do they differ? (pp. 34–37)
2. Briefly define the term "analysis." Include in your description what its goals are and how to keep it "scientific." (p. 39)
3. Briefly describe the basic skills involved in self-description. Why are they important? (pp. 44–46)
4. Functional analysis and correlations seem to go hand in hand in self-analysis. Briefly describe each, telling how they are important in the formation of hypotheses. (pp. 46–51)
5. Once you have come up with a plausible hypothesis, how do you go about testing it? (p. 51)

SELF-TEST ANSWERS

Multiple Choice

1. b (p. 34)
2. a (p. 34)
3. b (p. 35)
4. a (p. 35)
5. b (p. 37)
6. d (p. 39)
7. b (p. 39)
8. c (p. 42)
9. c (p. 44)
10. d (p. 44)
11. a (p. 44)
12. c (pp. 48–49)
13. d (p. 47)
14. a (p. 50)
15. c (p. 51)
16. d (p. 51)
17. c (p. 51)
18. c (p. 51)
19. a (p. 52)
20. c (p. 52)

True-False

1. true (p. 34)
2. true (p. 34)
3. false (p. 38)
4. true (p. 39)
5. false (p. 41)
6. true (p. 42)
7. true (pp. 42–43)
8. true (p. 43)
9. false (p. 44)
10. false (p. 44)
11. false (p. 46)
12. true (p. 50)
13. true (p. 49)
14. true (p. 51)

Completion

1. construct (p. 34)
2. self (p. 34)
3. social (p. 35)
4. processes (p. 38)
5. analysis (p. 39)
6. impression management (p. 38)
7. description (p. 39)
8. physical measurement (p. 42)
9. behavior (p. 44)
10. correlate (p. 46)
11. cause, effect (p. 46)
12. correlation (p. 46)
13. hypothesis (p. 51)
14. independent (p. 51)
15. circular (p. 50)

3
The Self-Concept: What It Is and How It Develops

CHAPTER OUTLINE

DIMENSIONS OF THE SELF-CONCEPT
Knowledge
Expectations
Evaluation

THE NEGATIVE AND THE POSITIVE SELF-CONCEPT
The Negative Self-Concept
The Positive Self-Concept

THE DEVELOPMENT OF THE SELF-CONCEPT
Childhood Development: The Conceptual Anchor
Sources of Information for the Self-Concept
    Parents
    Peers
    The society
Learning
    Association
    Consequences
    Motivation
Learning Problems and the Self-Concept
    Insufficient or inconsistent feedback
    Forbidden feeling: Rogers' self theory
Cognitive Consistency and Cognitive Dissonance
    Self-schemata
Self-Efficacy and Prophecy

READING

My Possessions, Myself

RUSSELL W. BELK

Burglary victims often say that they feel they have been personally polluted, even raped. Since they never had any personal contact with the burglar, what has been violated is the sense of self that exists in their jewelry, clothing, photographs and other personal possessions.

The feeling of violation goes even deeper since the burglar has also wounded the family's sense of identity by penetrating its protective skin, the family home. Clearly, the sense of self is not only individual. Heirlooms, for example, can represent and extend a family's sense of identity, while public buildings, monuments and parks help us develop regional and national identities. Although we Americans think of ourselves as highly individualistic, aggregate identity is important to us, as the willingness to preserve and restore symbols such as the Statue of Liberty shows.

What we possess is, in a very real way, part of ourselves. Our thoughts and our bodies are normally the most central part of our self-concept. But next in importance are what we do—our occupations and skills—and what we have—our unique set of possessions. The fact that jewelry, weapons and domestic utensils are found in prehistoric burial sites is evidence that we have long considered possessions as part of the person, even after death.

We find the same identification of people with possessions in examples as diverse as the reverence religions pay to relics of saints and prophets, the intensity of autograph hounds, the emphasis auctioneers place on the previous ownership of objects up for bid and the difficulty secondhand stores have in selling used underwear and garments worn close to the body. In each case a sense of the prior owners is thought to remain in the things that touched their lives.

We generally include four types of possessions in our personal sense of self: body and body parts, objects, places and time periods, persons and pets. Body parts are normally so well integrated into our identities that we think of them as "me" rather than merely "mine." But several studies have shown that body parts vary widely in their importance to us.

Recently, doctoral student Mark Austin and I gave 248 adults a group of cards, each of which listed a single item in one of the four categories: body parts such as kidneys, hearts and knees; objects such as a favorite dessert or the contents (other than money) of your wallet; places and times such as a favorite city or time of life; and particular people or pets.

We asked people to put the 96 cards in two piles, things they considered self and nonself. They then sorted each of these into two piles representing a little or a lot of self or nonself. We then gave each pile a "self" score (1, 2, 3, 4) and calculated average scores for each card. This gave us a rating of how central each item was to the sense of identity.

Eyes, hair, heart, legs, hands, fingers, genitals and skin were the most important body parts, while throat, liver, kidneys, chin, knees and nose were least essential to the sense of self. In general, women saw their bodies—particularly external parts such as eyes, hair, legs and skin—as more central to their identities then men did to theirs. In interviews, we found that many willing donors, men and women, believed that having part of themselves live on in someone else's body promised a kind of immortality.

Objects were somewhat less central than body parts to the sense of self. Not surprisingly, the most important material possessions were dwellings, automobiles and favorite clothes—each a kind of second skin that embellishes the self we present to others. Automobiles were particularly important to the identities of the men.

For both houses and cars, the more recently they had been acquired and the better the condition, the more important they were to someone's sense of self; and the more important they were, the better care they got—dusting, painting and remodeling in the case of houses; washing, waxing and oil changing for the cars. The similarities stopped when it came to the possession's age. Here, older houses and newer cars were considered more important parts of the self. It may be that houses are looked on as heirlooms, for which age is a virtue, while new cars run and look better.

Other objects important to a sense of self included favorite rooms, artwork, jewelry and clothing—all meaningful attachments to the body and the home. We found that academics were especially likely to cite books as favorite possessions, perhaps because they represent the knowledge on which their work is based. For other people, sporting goods represent what they can or could do, while the contents of wallets or purses were important because they indicated central characteristics such as age, sex and organizational memberships, as well as personal power to spend (credit cards) and travel (driver's license).

For some, collections were a significant part of their extended selves—possessions that had been acquired through considerable personal effort. For others, heirlooms were vital parts of family self, providing a sense of the past and of continuity with prior generations.

The third category of possessions important to the extended self is the less tangible one of time and place. To most of the people in our study, and others we interviewed, childhood was an especially important time of life. They tended to cherish memories, accurate or otherwise, of this period. We found that older people were most likely to name nearby cities, states and countries as important to their sense of self, while younger ones generally named places farther away.

Our interviews showed that people can be as acquisitive of places they visit as they are of objects they collect. We even found a sedentary form of place acquisition. An Amish man whose religion forbids him to drive a motorized vehicle collected the hometowns of people who visited his community. While speaking to us, he reeled off a list of their states and countries much as other people mention the places they have visited personally.

There were few surprises in the final major category of possessions—people and pets—that individuals used to define themselves. The most important people were generally parents, spouses, siblings, children and favorite friend of the same sex. Prominent political figures and favorite stars of movies and television were usually at the opposite end of the "selfness" continuum, unrelated to the sense of identity.

The common idea that some people consider their pets part of their family (and therefore of themselves) was supported by a series of interviews with people who owned dogs, cats, ferrets, birds and various other animals. While not all owners identified strongly with their pets, some felt closer to them than to their immediate families.

Is the fact that we are what we possess desirable or undesirable? There is no simple answer, but certain advantages and disadvantages seem evident. Among the advantages is that possessions provide a sense of the past. Many studies have shown that the loss of possessions that follows natural disasters or that occurs when elderly people are put in institutions is often traumatic. What people feel in these circumstances is, quite literally, a loss of self. Possessions also help children develop self-esteem, and learning to share possessions may be important in the growth of both individual and aggregate senses of self.

Incorporating possessions deeply into the sense of self can also have undesirable consequences. Too much attachment to pets can reflect an unhealthy drive to dominate and possess power and result in less devotion to family and friends. Investing too much of the self in collections and other possessions may displace love from people to things. Regarding other people as parts of our self can lead to jealousy and excessive possessiveness. Or by identifying too strongly with a spouse or child, we may end up living vicariously, instead of developing our own potential. As Erich Fromm asked in his book *To Have or To Be*, "If I am what I have and if what I have is lost, who then am I?"

Reading Questions

1. According to Russell Belk, there are four types of possessions included in one's personal sense of self. Name the four types and give examples of each.
2. Discuss the differences with regard to possessions and sense of self for males and females.
3. Discuss the positive and negative outcomes associated with the statement "We are what we possess."

RESEARCH STUDY

Investigators:	Russell H. Fazio, Edwin A. Effrein, and Victoria J. Falender.
Source, date:	"Self-Perceptions Following Social Interaction," *Journal of Personality and Social Psychology*, 1981, *41*, 232-242.
Location:	Indiana University.
Subjects:	42 undergraduates.
Materials:	10 index cards, tape recorder, Snyder and Swann trait inventory.

Research findings have supported the notion of the self-fulfilling prophecy. Essentially this is the idea that one's expectations of another person will influence that other person to act in ways consistent with expectation. For example, if a teacher expects a student to do poorly, the student is likely to be influenced by that expectation to perform poorly and to fulfill it.

In an attempt to add to our understanding of self-perceptions and the self-fulfilling prophecy, Fazio, Effrein, and Falender asked whether the student (or anyone) not only acts according to the expectation of the teacher but also internalizes this expectation and begins to see himself or herself in ways that are consistent with the expectation. In other words, does the original expectation of the teacher about the student become part of the student's self-perception? If so, it can be seen how social interactions contribute to the development of self-conceptions.

To answer this question, the investigators created an interview situation in which the study participants were asked a set of questions that were biased toward either extroversion or introversion. Then the participants completed a self-report questionnaire in which they indicated their degree of introversion and extroversion. Next they were put in a social situation in which they were observed to determine whether they acted in an introverted or an extroverted manner.

The results indicated that after the subjects participated in the interview that was biased toward introversion or extroversion, their behavior and perceptions of themselves corresponded with the particular bias of the interview. Thus expectations conveyed in the interview not only caused the participants to perceive themselves in accordance with those expectations but also caused them to act in accordance with them in a totally different situation. Such a finding shows how detrimental negative expectations may be for one's self-concept, especially for the mentally ill, the handicapped, and other stigmatized persons.

Research Study Questions

1. What is the "self-fulfilling prophecy," and what aspect of this prophecy did this study investigate?
2. How did the investigators study the process of internalizing others' expectations?
3. Discuss the results of the study and the implications of negative expectations for the self-concept of stigmatized persons.

CASE STUDY

Some Personal History

JO LOUDIN

I remarried a man who had as few expectations of me as I had of him. We had a baby girl when I was thirty-nine. I admit I had a few expectations of her, out of ignorance. I thought having the baby was the hardest part! I soon learned that raising her was tougher!

I no longer try to be a "good wife"; actually I have no idea of what that is. If I do not have time to cook, I ask him to do it. I often do not have time to do the dishes; recently he has been doing them more than I. Fortunately both my husband and I believe that household tasks need to be shared. We also believe that we are both capable of doing all kinds of work. He can do more than I can because he is stronger, but there are certain things he will not do, like iron or sort clothes. And I can do some things he cannot because my physiology is different and my hands are smaller, but there are things I will not do, like mow the lawn or take out the garbage. At times one of us may feel put upon, but it usually does not last because we express it. We do not have a perfect marriage because neither one of us is perfect. But it is very satisfying at times, sometimes fun and sometimes a drag, sometimes happy and sometimes a bore. And each of us feels it is okay to be who we are without being expected to be more or less; what else is there?

Nor do I try to be a "good mother." I soon found out that I did not like staying home every day with my little girl. When she was an infant, I was too tired to do anything other than stay home. I felt exhausted, trapped, and resentful much of the time. Somehow all the advertised pleasures of the homemaker did not alleviate my negative feelings. I got no pleasure out of waxing my floors (I remember being so tired my husband had to vacuum the floors for a year) or having the shiniest windows. Housework has always seemed futile to me. I do not get jollies from baking; I know that if I bake it I eat it and then I get fat, so why bother? I do not knit or crochet or watch soap operas. I do like outdoor sports, travelling, and oil painting—none of which I was able to do when my child was a baby. When my daughter was about two-and-a-half years old, I remember spending many hours washing the walls with a sponge mop to work out my frustrations on something inanimate. I knew then as I know now that I will never be satisfied while staying home with no outside interest.

So I do not try to be a "good mother" and devote my life to my child. I do enjoy doing things with her. We go to movies and plays, to the zoo and to fairs. We go boating in summer and skiing in winter. We play games together and if I bake at all it is because she likes to do it. But I have my own life as does she. I teach and do therapy; she goes to school. We enjoy each other when we are together. When we get bored with each other, we are able to pursue our separate lives.

I have not only stopped trying to be a "good" wife and mother, I do not even attempt to be a "nice" person anymore. I have discovered that being "nice" is a trap. I remember years ago when I would feel angry and show it, a voice in my head would say "Nice girls don't act that way." I would mentally whip myself for days or weeks until I managed to depress myself. Now I seldom whip myself. When I am angry I permit myself to express it. I went through a phase of believing that I was rotten when I got angry. I would have to tell myself "I'm okay even though I got angry." Now I no longer have to console myself. I simply believe it is okay to express anger directly and verbally. So I do not limit my behavior with the "nice" label. Sometimes I am warm and friendly and outgoing; other times I am cold and angry and withdrawn.

I have the feeling now that I am "real" most of the time, rather than the "nice" plastic caricature of a person I was in years past. I was such a nice, adaptive child. I tried so hard I naturally displeased others. I remember that when I was eight years old I went to a new school. The teacher, in a attempt to spread her favors, gave me a nickel and asked me to go to the lunchroom and get a carton of milk. It did not register with me that she wanted to drink the milk, and drank it myself. I felt humiliated when I realized that she had wanted the milk for herself. For years afterwards I experienced feelings of humiliation whenever I thought about the incident. I was so very, very nice!

I feel far more comfortable now. I think other people feel more at ease with me too. When I was nice, others did not really know me. I did not dare let them know me because I was afraid they could not possibly like me if they saw what was underneath the nice exterior. Consequently people felt I was cold and distant. They were right—I was. Now that I am no longer nice I feel comfortable letting people know me as I really am. If they do not like me that is okay too. I don't expect everyone in the whole world to like me. To those who do not I say "That's your problem. You have missed knowing a neat person."

I am still much the same person I was before I started to change my attitudes. I do not deliberately hurt people because I have stopped thinking of myself as nice, nor do I blow myself up to put other people down. On the contrary, I think more highly of other people because I think more highly of myself. I give others more options to feel because I do the same for myself. I am aware that when I criticize others, whether or not I verbalize my criticism, I am also criticizing myself. Conversely, when I allow others to exist as they are in the here and now, then I am allowing myself to be as well.

I realize that in many other ways I am really the same person I was before. Despite my good feelings and good days, I still have bad days. They just do not occur as frequently, nor do they last as long. I feel angry, hurt, scared, lonely, and sad at times, but now I feel happy feelings more of the time. The difference now is that I accept the bad feelings along with the good ones. I accept myself for what I *am* rather than for what I *should* be.

I also accept the way I was a child, understanding that my feelings as a little kid were okay too. It was very appropriate for me to feel lonely and small and afraid when I was little. I was small in proportion to the big people around me. I was afraid because I could not comprehend what was going on around me. Actually, I was right-on to feel lonely and small and afraid; any other feelings would have meant that I was not in touch with the reality I was experiencing. I was also smart to act nice, hold my angry feelings in, and behave like a miniature adult. That is the behavior pattern my parents and society expected of me. I must have been smart and right-on; I managed to survive my childhood!

Now that I am a "big person" with a child of my own I understand that I no longer need those childhood feelings or behavior patterns. I no longer need to feel small or helpless because I am not small anymore and I am capable of helping myself. I do not need to feel afraid unless there is something in the here and now to fear. Of course, there are still times when I do have those childhood feelings. I think perhaps that I always will, albeit in diminishing amounts, because I am not and never will be perfect. But now when I feel my archaic childhood feelings I can usually dispel them quickly by saying, "I am okay, I am okay, I am okay—whatever I am feeling and thinking." Excuse the repetition, but repetition helps stick it in my brain. Sometimes when I am feeling shaky I have to repeat, "I'm okay" a dozen times before it sticks! Or, "I am, therefore I'm worthwhile." I do not have to do anything or be anybody or have anything to prove I am worthwhile. I am worthwhile, okay, and perfect with myself because I exist—because I have survived!

Now I allow myself to feel whichever way I am feeling in regard to what is happening in the world around me, and I give others the same right. When I was little I had very limited options. My parents, my society, did not permit me to feel angry or resentful or hateful or rebellious or silly, so I did not express those feelings. I buried them alive inside of me and carried them around for years. And because my angry, negative feelings acted like a cork, bottling up any positive feelings inside me, for years I felt scared and depressed and sad and sick and lonely and tired. These were not enjoyable feelings; I was miserable, aching inside much of the time. But the feelings were familiar, and I did not have permission to feel any other way. People told me I *should* be happy, but how could I feel happy when I was *de*pressing myself with *re*pressed anger? Nor did I know I could change. When I found out that I could, it was a revelation to me, then a lot of hard, sometimes scary work, then pure joy.

When I was feeling very not okay I remember a sense of actually being two people. Sometimes I had the feeling of looking down on myself, watching the way I behaved, and criticizing myself severely for not acting the "right" way. When my upper self came down on the other me too harshly, I actually got a stiff neck and an aching back from tensing myself against the criticism. As I began to feel more okay I began to integrate my two selves. Now I no longer have a critical me above myself. I have become whole in a very real sense.

Case Study Questions

1. What were some of the notions of how a woman should be that this woman was trying to get away from?
2. How was she seeking to view herself now?
3. What things was she doing to reinforce her "new" way of looking at herself?

SELF-TEST

Multiple Choice

1. The self-concept is considered to be composed of which of the following:
    a. knowledge, experience, and expectations
    b. expectations, experiences, and evaluation
    c. experience, knowledge, and evaluation
    d. expectations, evaluation, and knowledge
2. Information about ourselves is organized in what way?
    a. intuitively
    b. subjectively
    c. conceptually
    d. randomly
3. The relationship between the expectations that constitute the ideal self and the self-concept is characterized as:
    a. essential
    b. unimportant

3/THE SELF-CONCEPT: WHAT IT IS AND HOW IT DEVELOPS

    c. important
    d. somewhat related

4. An individual's self-esteem is the measurement of all of the following *except*:
    a. "I-am"
    b. "I-could-be"
    c. "I-must-be"
    d. "I-should-be"

5. An individual who is not living up to his standards and expectations of himself will probably have:
    a. a high self-esteem
    b. a low self-esteem
    c. an inconsistent self-esteem
    d. an altered self-esteem

6. Which of the following is not true of the child at birth?
    a. She or he has no knowledge of herself or himself.
    b. She or he has no awareness of the environment.
    c. She or he has no expectations for herself or himself.
    d. She or he has no evaluation of herself or himself.

7. For the developing child, the conceptual anchor is influenced by the notions surrounding:
    a. only pleasurable events
    b. only painful events
    c. both pleasurable and painful events
    d. the development of the ego

8. The greatest spurt of progress in the development of the self-concept is indicated by which event?
    a. the transition to the anal stage of development
    b. the ability to manipulate the environment
    c. the use of language
    d. the formation of concepts

9. According to sociologist Charles Horton Cooley, the notion of the "looking-glass self" refers to:
    a. how we see ourselves in others
    b. the transparency of mankind
    c. the vanity of mankind
    d. how we see ourselves in a mirror

10. Which of the following has the most influence on our self-concept?
    a. our peers
    b. our religion
    c. our society
    d. our parents

11. The study of the Ashanti tribe of West Africa demonstrated that:
    a. naming children by the day of their birth is extremely efficient
    b. expectancies are directly related to self-concept
    c. expectancies are quite unrelated to self-concept
    d. a person's self-concept is unrelated to parental attitudes

12. Which of the following is not considered to be an important factor in the learning of the self-concept?
    a. motivation
    b. consequences
    c. intelligence
    d. association

13. An infant learns to value his parents as very special features of the environment because the infant:
    a. is taught to "honor thy mother and father"
    b. associates his parents with fear
    c. associates his parents with sexual pleasure
    d. associates his parents with physical gratifications

14. Which of the following indicates the dictum held by the "perfectionist"?
    a. "I must try not to make mistakes"
    b. "I should try not to make mistakes"
    c. "I should never make mistakes"
    d. "I cannot make mistakes"

15. The effectiveness of a consequence in "stamping in" a particular behavior depends upon:
    a. the value attached to the consequence
    b. the motivation of the behavior
    c. the consequence having followed the behavior
    d. all of the above

16. According to Carl Rogers' theory, the key to emotional health is the development of:
    a. a self that is congruent with the organism
    b. conditional positive regard
    c. efficient means of screening out experiences that do not fit in with the self
    d. conditions of worth

17. According to the theory of cognitive dissonance, an individual will do which of the following when confronted with inconsistent information?
    a. He will automatically resort to distortion.
    b. He will automatically resort to denial.
    c. He will automatically change his ideas.
    d. He will probably ignore it completely.

18. How would a person with a negative self-concept be most likely to explain his success at a task?

a. attribute success to skill
   b. attribute success to luck
   c. become angry
   d. refuse to explain
19. Self-concept is often described as:
   a. an objective evaluation of ourselves
   b. a totally fictional picture of ourselves
   c. a self-fulfilling prophecy
   d. totally dependent on feedback from others
20. If Mr. X has a negative self-concept, Mr. Y will respond negatively toward him because:
   a. Mr. X lets Mr. Y treat him that way
   b. Mr. Y believes that Mr. X should have a negative self-concept
   c. Mr. X communicates to Mr. Y his negative self-concept
   d. Mr. Y hates Mr. X

True-False

1. Mettee's experiment indicated that past performance has little bearing on future performance.
2. The self-concept is a mental portrait of yourself.
3. People tend to organize information about themselves in an objective manner.
4. Our self-esteem is the end result of our everyday self-evaluations.
5. The conceptual anchor is usually formed prior to the use of language.
6. The notion of the "looking-glass self" refers to how we use other people in evaluating ourselves.
7. The self-concept is considered to be a social creation.
8. With respect to the study of the Ashanti tribe of West Africa, expectations were shown to be of little importance.
9. Since virtue is seldom its own reward, the consequences of our actions play an important role in the establishment of self-esteem.
10. The state of arousal that we experience when straining toward a goal is referred to as the need to achieve.
11. According to cognitive dissonance theory, people tend to accept those ideas most similar to their own.
12. People will distort information in order to avoid challenging their beliefs.
13. Other people will tend to respond to us in ways that are consistent with the way we see ourselves.
14. The feedback about ourselves that we receive from other people is usually organized into the self-concept.
15. The theory of cognitive dissonance suggests that adults tend to perceive reality in ways that conform to their self-concepts.

Completion

1. The rock bottom of our self-concept is what we _____ about ourselves.
2. The vast number of social groups with which we identify make up our list of self- _____.
3. The "I-am" in the self-concept is constantly being measured against the "_____ _____ _____."
4. If a student's standard for her or his academic performance is at least a B, then a B+ average will probably create a _____ self-esteem.
5. As the newborn infant develops, she or he begins to form an idea of the relationship between the "_____" and the "_____ _____."
6. The discovery of your physical self as separate from the environment and the discovery of the importance of other people were basic to the notions that formed the _____ _____.
7. The major source of information for the self-concept is our _____ with other _____.
8. According to sociologist Charles Cooley, we use other people as _____ to show us who we are.
9. A relatively permanent psychological change that occurs as a consequence of experience defines _____.
10. Recent studies have suggested that black children are no longer invariably burdened with low self-esteem. This change is due not to the children but to the _____ as defined for them by their parents and peers.
11. One of the most crucial steps in the development of the self-concept is the infant's learning to value his or her _____ as very special features of his or her _____.
12. The standards against which we evaluate ourselves are simply the _____ and _____ of the past.
13. _____ is defined as the state of arousal that we experience when straining toward a goal.
14. According to psychologist Leon Festinger, one of the most powerful motives in human life is the drive for _____ _____.

15. The _____ that we receive from others is eventually organized into a self-concept.

Essay Questions

1. Discuss the experiment in which high school girls were given tests to measure "psychological sensitivity." What was the experiment designed to predict and what did it actually show? Why would someone want to "undo" a success? (pp. 59–60)
2. With specific reference to the self-concept, describe what the conceptual anchor is and where it comes from. What function does it seem to serve? (pp. 68–69)
3. Sociologist Charles Horton Cooley has introduced the notion of the "looking-glass self." To what does it refer? How does it relate to George Mead's idea of a two-stage development of the self? (pp. 70–71)
4. Discuss the relationship of the theory of cognitive dissonance for individuals with negative and positive self-concepts. In what ways do people distort reality for the sake of cognitive consistency? (pp.78–82)
5. With respect to the person having a positive and negative self-concept, discuss the three divisions of the self-concept. (pp. 65–67)

SELF-TEST ANSWERS

Multiple Choice

1. d (p. 60)
2. b (p. 61)
3. a (pp. 61–65)
4. c (p. 65)
5. b (p. 65)
6. b (p. 68)
7. c (p. 69)
8. c (p. 69)
9. a (p. 70)
10. d (p. 70)
11. c (p. 71)
12. b (p. 73)
13. d (p. 73)
14. c (p. 73)
15. d (p. 73)
16. a (p. 78)
17. a (p. 78)
18. b (p. 80)
19. c (p. 82)
20. c (p. 82)

True-False

1. false (p. 60)
2. true (p. 60)
3. false (p. 61)
4. true (p. 65)
5. true (p. 69)
6. true (p. 70)
7. true (p. 70)
8. false (p. 71)
9. true (pp. 74–75)
10. false (p. 74)
11. true (p. 78)
12. true (p. 78)
13. true (p. 82)
14. true (p. 76)
15. true (p. 78)

Completion

1. know (p. 61)
2. labels (p. 61)
3. I-could-be (p. 65)
4. high (p. 65)
5. me, not-me (p. 68)
6. conceptual anchor (p. 69)
7. interaction, people (pp. 70–71)
8. mirrors (p. 70)
9. learning (p. 71)
10. society (p. 71)
11. parents, environment (pp. 72–73)
12. rewards, punishments (p. 74)
13. Motivation (p. 74)
14. cognitive consistency (p. 78)
15. feedback (p. 76)

4
The Self-Concept: How to Change It

CHAPTER OUTLINE

ANALYZING THE SELF-CONCEPT
Description
   Isolating the problem
   Situational description
Functional Analysis
   External variables
   Internal variables
   Negative self-talk and irrational beliefs

HOW YOU WERE FOUND GUILTY: A REVIEW IN THE COURT OF APPEALS
Distortions and Denials
Faulty Categorizing
Old Standards
   Perfectionism
   Conventionality
   What the other guy thinks

CHANGING THE SELF-CONCEPT
Setting the Goal
Getting New Information
Cognitive Restructuring: New Self-Talk
   Listen to self-talk
   Talking back
   Acting on your back-talk
   The results

THE SELF-CONCEPT UNDER REVISION: A SAMPLE SCRIPT

READING

You Are What You Think

CLAIRE WARGA

Albert Ellis is cocky—a man who knows he's wearing a white hat. He'll be 75 this month and he's still riding herd on the bad guys: the irrational ideas that cripple people's emotional lives. Called Al by all, he's accessible nearly every Friday night (when he isn't out of town training psychologists) to anyone who drops into his nonprofit Institute for Rational-Emotive Therapy in New York to watch him shoot down the illogical beliefs of audience volunteers. He plans to keep working "until—preferably at the age of 110—I die in the saddle," and he shows no sign of slowing down his intense pace. On one such recent Friday, a devilishly beaming and enthusiastic Ellis, sporting a plaid shirt and a denim cowboy jacket, was gunning down people's self-destructive ideas just six weeks after he had major stomach surgery.

He's a born outsider, a man of quirky individualism, essentially self-made, despite his Ph.D.; he overthrew his orthodox Freudian training to create his own radically different brand of therapy and his own institute, with his own trainees—at one time all outside the academic establishment.

What better person to start a revolution in psychotherapy—one based on rationality, individualism and self-sufficiency. His Rational-Emotive Therapy (RET) teaches people how to evaluate critically their own thought processes to solve their own emotional problems, and to trust in their own reason, not the perfectionistic standards and moral imperatives with which society has overburdened them. It is based on the power of people to transform their lives by examining and challenging their current beliefs. Forget about toilet training, your parents, your traumas, the stifling "shoulds" of your childhood, he says. You are not the captive of your past experiences. Here and now you can change what you think, and thus, how you feel. You are what you think. As Ellis put it in a parody of *Old Folks at Home*:

4/THE SELF-CONCEPT: HOW TO CHANGE IT

Though my past was rather stinking
I'm now free to roam.
So let me change my nutty thinking—
And leave the old folks at home.

In 1985, the American Psychological Association (APA) gave Ellis one of its highest accolades, its Award for Distinguished Professional Contributions. It recognized him as one of the first psychologists to research love and sexuality and to practice marital and sex therapy. But it stressed another, even more important, facet of Ellis's career: his "profound effect on the professional practice of psychology."

As a therapist and theorist Ellis has given his field a new and enduring appreciation of the importance of cognitions—ideas, beliefs, assumption, interpretations, thinking processes—in the origins and treatment of emotional disturbance. By gaining scientific acceptance for his new form of therapy, Ellis helped pave the way for many other cognitive therapies that, like RET, are now part of the mainstream of clinical practice. He is, as the award's biography put it, "the pioneering practitioner and grandfather of cognitive behavior therapy." And he has helped turn psychotherapy into a powerful force behind today's new autonomy.

Even before the APA award, a survey of 800 clinical and counseling psychologists had already attested to his impact on the field: Ellis was ranked as the second-most influential psychotherapist, after humanist Carl Rogers (Freud placed third).

This was the same, once-scandalous Ellis who almost three decades earlier had outraged his professional colleagues with his outspoken sexual liberalism in such before-their-time popular books as *Sex Without Guilt* (1958), *The Art and Science of Love* (1960), and *Nymphomania: A Study of Oversexed Women* (1964).

How did a "semi-illegitimate," sickly boy with a Bronx accent turn the scorn of his professional colleagues into sweet repute—in his own lifetime? Largely, it seems by being an intellectual cowboy: by being self-directed, by doing excellent, innovative work and by not giving a damn about how others viewed him.

Sitting in his office in the imposing Beaux Arts building that is home both to Ellis and his institute, Ellis laughs, recalling the discovery of his "semi-illegitimacy." "For years, my mother told me that I was a sixth-month child," he says, "until one day I found out that there was no such thing." (At least not in 1913, when he was born.) "Even though my mother and father had dated for 10 years, they got married because of me." (They divorced when he was 12.)

When Ellis was 4, the family moved to the Bronx. Here, for the next three years, he was repeatedly hospitalized. But as an avid self-taught reader he later managed to skip two grades and catch up. Those years, Ellis says, taught him that, although not as strong as other boys, he could overcome the handicaps of illness.

At around age 12, Ellis decided he was good at writing and wanted to become a novelist or poet, but he realized he would need a trade to support his writing interests. That trade turned out to be accounting, which he studied at New York's High School of Commerce and at Baruch College of the City University of New York.

As a college freshman in an informal study group that "read all the philosophers and criticized them," Ellis was impressed by the psychological insights of Epictetus, the first-century philosopher who said, "What disturbs men's minds is not events but their judgment on events." That idea later became central to Rational-Emotive Therapy.

At 19 Ellis became active in a political group but was hampered by his terror of public speaking. Confronting his worst demons in the first of many "shame-attacking" exercises he would devise, Ellis repeatedly forced himself to speak up in any political context that would permit it. "Without calling it that, I was doing early desensitization on myself," he says, "Instead of just getting good at this, I found I was very good at it. And now you can't keep me away from a public platform."

After mastering his fear of public speaking, Ellis decided to work on the terrors of more private communication. "I was always violently interested in women," he says. "I would see them and flirt and exchange glances, but I always made excuses not to talk to them and was terrified of being rejected.

"Since I lived near The New York Botanical Garden in the Bronx, I decided to attack my fear and shame with an exercise in the park. I vowed that whenever I saw a reasonably attractive women up to the age of 35, rather than sitting a bench away as I normally would, I would sit next to her with the specific goal of opening a conversation within one minute. I sat next to 130 consecutive women who fit my criteria. Thirty of the women got up and walked away, but about 100 spoke to me—about their knitting, the birds, a book, whatever. I made only one date out of these contacts—and she stood me up.

"According to learning theory and strict behavior therapy, my lack of rewards should have extinguished my efforts to meet women. But I realized that throughout this exercise no one vomited, no one called a cop and I didn't die. The process of trying new behaviors and understanding what happened in the real world instead of in my imagination led me to overcome my fear of speaking to women." But, Ellis notes, he still had to overcome his fear of telling them "I love you" and "I want to sleep with you."

By the time Ellis graduated from college at age 20, the Depression was in full swing. After four years of unemployment and odd jobs, and a failed five-month marriage to an erratic 19-year-old actress, he finally landed a position as assistant to the president of a wholesale gift novelty house. Remarkably, in light of his later achievements, he worked there for 10 years. "I did anything from sweeping the floors to working as controller," he says.

He also wrote, churning out 20 manuscripts (novels, plays, comic verse, serious poems) by age 28, but none were published. "I spent my lunch money on stamps to send away manuscripts," says the now-published author/editor of more than 50 books and 600 articles.

Ellis eventually decided to switch to writing nonfiction—and on a new topic: love, sex and marriage. The man who later helped launch the sexual revolution of the '60s says, "I saw then that human beings were not monogamous but screwed around and liked to have sex before marriage. I was going to prove to the public that it was OK by writing a five-volume book called *The Case for Promiscuity*." It was written, but not published at the time.

"For it," Ellis says, "I read practically everything that had ever been written on the topic of sex, six books a day. I started with sexologists such as [Richard] Krafft-Ebing and Havelock Ellis, most of whom described their cases in detail. After a while I got to be pretty knowledgeable on the topic myself. Friends would tell me about their sex problems, and I'd tell them, from my reading of psychology and sexology, how to overcome them. I used all this stuff on myself, too, and saw that anxiety, as we know it today, was at the root of many sexual problems.

"Seeing that I was good at helping people and enjoyed it, I decided to get into this field as a counselor rather than just writing about it. So I set up the LAMP (Love and Marriage Problems) Institute, but after I had the stationery printed, my lawyer suggested that I go out and get some degrees if I wanted to go this route."

Ellis, approaching 30, took his lawyer's advice and enrolled in a clinical psychology program at Columbia Teacher's College. He did research on the emotion of love in college women for his dissertation. But after it was written he had to ditch it, he says, because a jittery post hoc committee at Columbia Teacher's College feared adverse publicity if news of this seemingly flighty research leaked out.

A determined Ellis proceeded to research and write a second dissertation on the validity of personality questionnaires. This respectable research, acclaimed after its publication in the prestigious *Psychological Bulletin* and *Psychological Monographs*, launched the 34-year-old Ellis as an authority in his field.

After receiving his doctorate, Ellis worked at the New Jersey Diagnostic Center, becoming within two years chief psychologist of the New Jersey Department of Institutions and Agencies. At the same time, he began training with a psychoanalyst from the Karen Horney Institute, preparing to become a psychotherapist.

By 1952 he had established a full-time practice in Manhattan, doing psychoanalytic psychotherapy and counseling patients with sex or marital problems. The fledging therapist also published popular books on sex, which inevitably led to media interviews, increasing name recognition and a wealth of patients. But his growing publicity in the puritanical '50s led to sneering disregard from fellow psychologists. "I was very much opposed in and out of the American Psychological Association for my sexual liberalism at the time," Ellis says. Others suggest that his use of salty language in public presentations also did little to endear him to his professional peers. Ellis, however, believes his earthly language helps establish a "no pretenses honored here" atmosphere with clients.

Ellis gradually became disillusioned with psychoanalysis as a form of treatment. "I was, I think, a good psychoanalyst, and people liked what I did and wanted more sessions. But I just didn't feel it was an efficient form of treatment. Clients temporarily felt better from all the talk and attention, but they didn't seem to get better; the insights it took them so long to arrive at didn't change things for them in significant ways.

"I began to wonder why I had to wait passively for weeks or months until clients showed that they were ready to accept my interpretation. Why, if they were silent most of the hour, couldn't I help them with some pointed questions or remarks? So, unlike the Freudian model, I became much more eclectic, exhortative-persuasive, activity-directing king of therapist. Also unlike Freud, I do not believe that early sexual issues cause all emotional problems and that parents are responsible for all that comes later. Infantile sexuality in my view is very rarely related to emotional disturbance.

"As I see it, psychoanalysis gives clients a cop-out. They don't have to change their ways, or their philosophies; they get to talk about themselves for

10 years, blaming their parents and waiting for magic-bullet insights."

Ellis began scouting for new therapeutic approaches, drawing upon his own self-help experiments and on what he deemed the best of psychologists and philosophers such as Alfred Adler, Karen Horney and John Watson. The result was RET. By 1955 he had developed the first incarnation of this new form of psychotherapy. Four years later he established the Institute for Rational-Emotive Therapy as a center for treatment and training.

As director of his own treatment-oriented institute, Ellis was an outsider to the influential realms of university-based academic psychology. He tried for years to storm these ramparts and gain acceptance for his theories and therapy by extensively writing and by lecturing at universities. By the late 1960s his efforts finally began to pay off. Academic researchers who were interested in behavioral forms of treatment realized the explicit and testable nature of his work and began to mine its ore.

A flood of research assessing the efficacy of RET and related forms of treatment began to flow and continues unabated. Most studies support the effectiveness of Ellis's cognitive form of treatment. The favorable research results boosted the therapy's scientific credibility and helped launch the popularity of RET and related forms of cognitive therapy, such as the somewhat similar types independently developed by psychiatrist Aaron Beck at the University of Pennsylvania.

Ellis is now widely acknowledged as a major force in the cognitive-therapy revolution that has been gaining ascendancy within clinical practice and government-funded clinical research since the late 1970s. Referring to the declining preeminence of psychoanalysis, Ellis wryly observes, "Some of my colleagues nowadays like to say that psychoanalysis is self-discovery cognitive therapy. You wait for the patients to get it on their own."

As an innovator of new forms of therapy (sex and marital) and of new psychoanalytical techniques, Ellis has earned a bouquet of awards from his colleagues and an enduring niche in the history of psychology. Among his new therapeutic techniques are: having the therapist be talkative and interactive; teaching clients through repetition the ABCs of analyzing and countering their emotional upsets; and emphasizing cognitive/behavioral "homework" —exercises and assignments designed to try out and establish new ways of being and behaving. Ellis also pioneered in using imagery exercises to help clients gain mastery in reducing disturbing emotions; in having them tape-record therapy sessions for later use; in providing "bibliotherapy" and "audiotherapy" (therapeutic self-help in printed and taped material for home study); and in offering clients a distinct variant of group therapy.

In summing up Ellis's impact on his field, Paul Wachtel, psychology professor at the City University of New York, says, "Prior to Ellis, behaviorists and psychoanalysts tended to disregard the cognitive domain in therapy.

"Ellis was one of the first to bring together a cognitive and behavioral emphasis and to encourage behaviorally oriented therapists to consider how their patients' ideas led them from behavior pattern A to pattern B. He also influenced therapists to focus systematically on new experiences for patients as the center of therapy and on prodding patients to develop as active experimenters in their own lives."

Today Ellis, despite long-term diabetes, remains a vigorous, iconoclastic, single-minded cowboy-psychologist, riding the full range of psychological practice (albeit often in a recliner with his shoes off). He works from 9 A.M. to 11 P.M. six days a week, seeing some 80 patients a week in individual and family therapy in addition to running five group-therapy sessions and supervising psychologist-trainees at the institute. "Over the last 40 years," says Ray Di Giuseppe, director of training and research at Ellis's institute, "Al's probably done more psychotherapy sessions than any psychologist has ever done, some 90,000 hours worth. And at $90 per hour he's probably the most affordable famous therapist."

Why work this hard and long? "I'm not compulsive," Ellis says. "I do it out of choice, I love my work. It's the same reason that I get involved at a party or on a plane when people tell me their problems. I like problem-solving. I like helping people."

Ellis's associate executive director at the institute, Janet Wolfe, a psychologist some 30 years his junior with whom he has lived for more than 23 years, confirms that "Al hasn't taken a vacation in 35 years. But," she explains, "there is simply nothing he enjoys more than his work."

Reading Questions

1. Briefly summarize Albert Ellis's major contributions to the field of psychology.
2. Why did Ellis depart from his early training as a psychoanalyst? In what ways does RET differ from this psychoanalytic perspective?
3. Explain how the statement "What disturbs men's minds is not events but their judgment of events" became central to RET.

RESEARCH STUDY

Investigators: Cory Newman and Marvin Goldfried.
Source, date: "Disabusing Negative Self-Efficacy Expectations via Experience, Feedback and Discrediting," *Cognitive Therapy and Research*, 1987, *11*, 401-417.
Location: State University of New York at Stony Brook.
Subject: 48 males.
Materials: situation questionnaire, survey of heterosexual interactions, social interactions self-statement test, role-play scoring sheet.

The preconceived notion of one's own abilities has been shown to effect how information about the self is processed. This bias in processing can occur in a highly generalized or situationally specific manner. In the latter case, studies have shown that once formed, perceptions of the self are difficult to change. Bandura (1977, 1982) has focused on the self-efficacy aspect of self-perception, suggesting that an individual's efficacy expectations are based on four sources of evidence: performance accomplishments, vicarious experience, verbal persuasion, and emotional arousal. Of these Bandura theorizes that performance accomplishments are most influential while verbal persuasions are weaker. The present study looked at the power these two variables: performance accomplishments and verbal persuasion, both independently and in combination and added another variable: "feedback."

The subjects, 48 undergraduate males, took part in a series of role-playing situations that involved first meeting with a member of the opposite sex. Following the role play, the subjects were given predetermined negative ratings. They were then divided into four separate groups, each using a different strategy to attempt to alleviate the efforts of the initial negative evaluation. The first group was provided with a second series of role-playing situations but provided no feedback. The second group was provided a second series of role-play situations without feedback but were told that the initial feedback was bogus. The third group participated in a second set of role-play situations and were given positive feedback only. And the fourth group did not participate in another role-play situation but were told that the initial feedback was bogus.

Results indicated that the group that was given no feedback showed significantly less recovery than the other groups on two of three efficacy measures. The positive feedback group and both experimenter-discrediting groups showed comparable showing on all efficacy measures.

Research Study Questions

1. What aspect of self-perception does this study investigate?
2. What were the results of the study?
3. What do the results suggest about feedback and self-efficacy?

CASE STUDY

Self-Image of Four Girls

The Image of Self: Debbie

I. Describe your physical self. How do you see yourself physically: size, shape, attractiveness, etc.? How do think others see you?

> I'm about five feet, six inches with light brown hair and blue eyes. I'm a little bit overweight, but not too much. I feel that I'm fairly attractive. One of the most noticeable things about me is my eyes. They can express, a lot, so I try to bring out their expressions with my makeup. I'm fairly certain that others see me about the same way I see myself. They'll tell me if I look good or bad on certain days and in general I feel they approve of my looks.

II. Describe your mental self. How do you see yourself intellectually: how do you think, learn, study, etc.? How do you think others see you?

> I find when it comes to thinking I sometimes have difficulty in applying myself. Usually, I have to be in a proper frame of mind before I can actually "get into" something. I can learn things easily depending upon my interest in them. As far as studying, it's a very static process for me. I can't apply myself when I don't want to—it's a useless function! But when an idea hits me, then I can come right out with it in a very short period of time. Others have tried to get me to open up, but I think they're tried the wrong way. It takes me a while, but if they have some patience I feel their wait will be worthwhile.

III. Describe your emotional self. How do you see yourself in terms of your disposition, moods, temperament, etc.? How do you think others see you?

> My temperament is passive. I try to understand people by thinking there is a reason why someone does or says different things. When I get in a bad mood, I become quiet and withdrawn rather than releasing it.

My parents say I let people walk over me a lot. I guess this is true in some ways because I lack nerve to say "no" or to let people know how I feel about certain things. I tell myself that in an hour things will look different, so control your temper—and try to rationalize what motivated and made a person the way he is.

IV. Describe your social self. How do you see yourself in a large group, a small group, with individuals of the same sex, the opposite sex, your relatives and family, etc.? How do you think others see you?

Socially, I get along with just about everyone. I can react best in a small group where I can get to know everyone. I like to get to know individuals and I can feel much closer to a guy than another girl. I guess guys are sort of that "big brother" that I never had. Relatives and family are more difficult to communicate with because I feel that they don't understand the world which I'm living. They see things the way they are around them and often don't consider other possibilities. Others must like me for I feel I have many close friends and many more acquaintances. I try not to forget names and faces for I feel that a friendly "Hi" is always welcome in any situations.

V. Describe your moral or spiritual self. How do you see yourself in terms of values, standards, etc.? How do you think others see you?

Morally, I guess you could say I'm not a naive kid. I see and understand much of what is going on around me. I try as much as I can to be myself although at times this proves to be quite difficult. Spiritually, I feel alienated from the idea of a church at this time. I've come to believe that I want to find myself first and then from there I can believe much more strongly in something. I have a faith that there's someone above me, but I want to learn this on my own. You appreciate something a lot more when you can say that "I did this myself" and not that I had help. I can feel religion slowly coming back into me as the time goes on. All it takes is some time.

VI. How would you like to be different or to change? Or, how did you get that way?

I don't really want to change except maybe to be able to express my emotional feelings in words in an easier manner. My parents helped me very much in the way I grew up. I am usually permitted to do what I feel is best for myself and in this way I learn at the same time.

The Image of Self: Gwen

I. Describe your physical self.

I am a small person, petite as some would call it. I suppose my shape is what can be expected for as small as I am (five feet, one-half inch). I have small features. Attractiveness—well, I feel there is room for improvement (a big one), but my boyfriend says there isn't, that I'm perfect, so "what to do?" Other people have told me I'm attractive. My one good aspect is my hair, which is usually clean and shines.

II. Describe your mental self.

According to the I.Q. test I took, I'm supposed to be pretty good, but my grades indicate otherwise. My thinking is often incoherent. I have the ability, the potential to learn, but I never developed proper study habits and I don't really know how to study. My parents think of me as very capable of learning and I know sometimes I disappoint them. Subjects like music (especially), art, P.E., I pick up easily, but others like psychology, literature, history are my downfall. I daydream constantly.

III. Describe your emotional self.

Emotionally I am immature and very confused. My disposition is changeable, but generally very good. My moods come fast and furious. I can be a completely different person from one day to the next. I can get angry very easily, especially in the past six months since I've had problems with my boyfrined and our families. His mother has told me a couple of times that I'm immature.

I am usually happy and love to be with people, especially children.

IV. Describe your social self.

In one word—shy! My social self is probably my poorest aspect. I'm very hard to get to know and sometimes I get the feeling that people are uncomfortable around me. I feel more comfortable in a small group than in face-to-face relationships. I'm much more comfortable with people of my own sex. With the opposite sex I am usually quiet and at a loss for words. I wish I could change and be more outgoing, but I don't know how.

V. Describe your moral or spiritual self.

Morally—wow! I need help but who do I go to? I have good morals; never dreamed of premarital intercourse. But my boyfriend and I have been separated (by *force*) for five months and often I wonder: "Maybe if I have his baby they'll see we love each other." I have high standards, otherwise good morals and values.

I believe in God, attend church every week, and lately have found myself praying—something I rarely do.

VI. How would you like to be different or change?

How do I say it—I'd like to be a little better built and get my face cleared up. I'm tired of looking like a boy. I would like to grow up emotionally and most of all, I'd like to have my boyfriend back. I'm a much more stable person when I'm allowed to see him.

The Image of Self: Sandy

I. Describe your physical self.

I'm tall and thin. Sometimes I think I'm too slender. However, I can wear almost any style of clothing, which is one advantage. I wear my hair fairly short because it's easy to take care of and because shorter hair frames my face better. My glasses bother me. I think I'm more attractive without them and hope to wear contacts as soon as I have the money to buy them. Some people tell me I look pretty without glasses—especially my boyfriend. I can see well enough without them and usually don't wear them on dates. I wish I could gain ten or fifteen pounds because I'm sure others see me as "skinny."

II. Describe your mental self.

I don't mind studying. I feel an accomplishment in learning. I especially enjoy my Spanish courses and my education courses. There's so much I don't know. I'll learn as much as I can so I can become a good teacher. I'm fairly intelligent and through good study habits manage to make very good grades. However, others see me as more intelligent than I really am. I feel as though I don't know enough to teach school. But my friends and classmates usually ask me for help with homework or other problems.

III. Describe your emotional self.

As far as my moods are concerned, I am fairly neutral. I seldom lose my temper, but neither am I usually overjoyous. I get along with everyone as a result. Lately, I have been generally depressed because of a broken engagement. I shouldn't be because I broke it. After a year of being engaged and really in love, I realized that no matter how much I loved John, I couldn't live happily with him. He was bossy and possessive of *everyone*. He didn't listen to his parents or me when he got a notion in his head.

IV. Describe your social self.

I'm much more at ease in a small group than in a large group. If I'm with people I know, it's easy to talk to members of either sex. But if I don't know anyone in the group, I'd rather talk to a member of my sex. I'm at ease with older or younger people. Everyone fascinates me whether a child, a young adult, or a middle-aged person. At first encounter, I feel that people see me as uninteresting. But after a conversation or over a period of time, they seem to like me more. I especially make good impressions with older people.

V. Describe your moral or spiritual self.

I was raised in a religious home. My parents were fairly strict in their discipline. I went to a few parties, but certainly not beer parties. My parents are very concerned about who I date. They controlled almost every aspect of my life until I came to college. My moral values have changed somewhat since then. I can tolerate being around booze and have even enjoyed drinking wine. However, I have never let myself go to the point of getting drunk. After being engaged for a year my ideas about sex have changed completely. I don't feel that a couple has to wait till marriage for intercourse. However, they must be very careful! My parents are shocked by this view!

VI. How would you like to be different or to change?

I would like to weigh more and be able to express my emotions in stronger actions.

The Image of Self: Karen

I. Describe your physical self.

I have always been tall and "thin," though I've been filling out in the waist since coming to college. My figure is pretty good—tinier girls in my hall call me "Super Bod(y)" when I wear my sexy slip. I'm fairly plain but cute (freckles still!), and active. My clothes vary from mini to conservative to maxi, and my wardrobe is neither extensive nor expensive. I'm now considering changing my appearance by a different hairstyle (cut shorter).

II. Describe your mental self.

I realize from the grades I've received all through school that I am an above average student. I don't find college so very different or even much harder subject and workwise than high school. Rarely do I miss a night of studying during the week, and I usually make up on Sunday night what I neglect Friday and Saturday nights. I copy over neatly into notebooks what notes I sloppily take in class—this takes a lot of extra work and time, but I find I learn the material better that way. I usually study most the night before a test.

III. Describe your emotional self.

I know that recently I've become quieter around others. My interests are limited to working, studying, art, Frank, and home. I just can't see getting "worked up" over little things. I'm usually happy but often nasty and not very nice when I'm neglected or "picked at." I do a lot of "mental planning" and get kind of upset when things don't turn out.

IV. Describe your social self.

I like large groups better than small ones because I'm not "stuck" with dull or irritating people. There is less need to talk to and to include *everyone* in a large group and there's more freedom of thought and talk. Girls are always willing to talk and listen, but when the same old subjects are hashed over, I'd leave. Guys are okay but don't usually want to sit and gab for a

4/THE SELF-CONCEPT: HOW TO CHANGE IT

long time about hundreds of different things. Frank says I'm *too* friendly.

V. Describe your moral or spiritual self.

I believe in myself, mostly. I talked with a girl we call "Judy Bible" and her thoughts are that prayer is the best thing of all—does wonders. Bull! I got what I have mostly through my own work or through my parents. There may be a God (I don't know) and if there is, fine. But I can't see what all the fuss is about. I do what's best or most pleasurable at the time, hoping that I've learned what's right and wrong.

VI. How would you like to be different or to change? Or, how did you get that way?

I got this way definitely through my entire home setting—the way the house is built, our land, our location, my brothers (no sister), my *Dad* especially, and the silent guidance of my Mom. Dad is still the director of activities, but Mom is the provider and takes care of the little, needed things. I really am happy I've grown up who and what I *have* grown up to be.

Case Study Questions

1. In many of the descriptive statements concerning the girls' different aspects of the "self," there seems to be a strong influence from other people as to how they view themselves. In what ways is this apparent?
2. Some researchers have suggested that individuals in the age group between eighteen and twenty-two tend to become independent of their families and strive for self-sufficiency. In what ways are the girls' descriptions related to this suggestion?
3. How could the descriptive statements be made more functional in keeping with the requirements suggested in the text with respect to the descriptive stage of a self-analysis?

SELF-TEST

Multiple Choice

1. Larry the "social incompetent" refrains from attending parties and other social gatherings because:
    a. books mean more to him than interpersonal relationships
    b. parties are not very stimulating
    c. his professor told him not to go
    d. they make him uncomfortable
2. The circular relationship that exists between expectations and outcome can be broken by:
    a. a complete revision of the self-concept
    b. a revision of the expectations
    c. an adjustment in self-concept
    d. faith and support
3. The step of writing down your self-description is crucial in the analysis of the self-concept because:
    a. writing is usually therapeutic in itself
    b. it helps to focus your thinking
    c. individuals with negative self-concepts are usually dishonest
    d. individuals with negative self-concepts have poor memories
4. Which of the following is not true of our self-labels?
    a. the labels tend to be come more generalized
    b. we tend to view them as separate units
    c. the labels tend to be vague
    d. all of the above
5. Description is the first stage of self-analysis and involves two steps:
    a. isolation of the problem and situational description
    b. functional analysis and isolation of the problem
    c. situational description and self-report
    d. self-monitoring and functional analysis
6. Which of the following is true about the self-concept?
    a. It is affected by external variables.
    b. It is affected by internal variables.
    c. It is affected by both internal and external variables.
    d. It is affected by neither internal nor external variables.
7. According to social learning theory, "person variables" refer to:
    a. idiopathic behavioral patterns
    b. idiosyncratic behavioral patterns
    c. the influence of "significant" others
    d. individual styles of thinking
8. Mistaken and painful emotional conclusions result from which step of the A-B-C process?
    a. A—the activating event
    b. B—the individual's belief system
    c. C—the emotional consequence
    d. a combination of A and C
9. According to Albert Ellis, which of the following would *not* be considered as one of the functional components of the A-B-C process?
    a. beliefs
    b. consequent emotions
    c. activating events
    d. anticipated behaviors

10. Negative self-labeling is maintained, as are all types of behaviors. Which of the following is considered to be the maintaining factor?
    a. self-talk
    b. consequent emotions
    c. activating behaviors
    d. anticipated behaviors
11. A likely consequence of having a self-concept with only a few categories is:
    a. a strong self-concept
    b. a weak self-concept
    c. negative self-labeling
    d. positive self-labeling
12. The negative self-label is defined as being a statement to yourself that you have failed to live up to:
    a. your parental ideas
    b. your own standards
    c. your negative self-image
    d. your positive self-image
13. The "perfectionist" has standards that can result in which of the following?
    a. self-denial
    b. self-praise
    c. self-contempt
    d. self-confidence
14. Of the following, which should be considered true of the ideal self?
    a. it should be directive, and, as a result, control behavior
    b. it should dominate the individual's self-concept
    c. it should foster fantasy experiences
    d. all of the above
15. Many psychologists feel that a major cause of emotional maladjustment is:
    a. the constant craving for disapproval that goes unfulfilled
    b. the constant craving for disapproval that is fulfilled from time to time
    c. the constant craving for approval that is fulfilled from time to time
    d. the constant craving for approval that goes unfulfilled
16. Sociologist David Riesman (1950) suggests that a person becomes "other-directed" because of:
    a. a lack of firm expectations
    b. shifts in social values
    c. the need of other persons to provide direction
    d. all of the above
17. Which of the following statements concerning social standards is *false*?
    a. Often they contribute to negative self-labels.
    b. They are relative to time and place.
    c. They are static.
    d. We must decide for ourselves which to adhere to and which to ignore.
18. The final description of a person's ideal self should be:
    a. realistic
    b. goal-directed
    c. consistent with self-standards
    d. all of the above
19. Which of the following would not be engaged in when manipulating self-talk?
    a. talking back
    b. acting on back-talk
    c. preventing self-talk
    d. listening to self-talk
20. Successful cognitive restructuring will probably cause the individual to:
    a. progress toward goals
    b. become oriented to reality and reason
    c. become more "free"
    d. all of the above

True-False

1. Problematic self-labels, unlike problematic behaviors, exist only in our minds.
2. When making a self-analysis, it is important never to disclose your "real life story" to anyone, especially close friends.
3. It is fairly accurate to think that our self-concept is, to some extent, the mirror of external circumstances.
4. According to Ellis and Harper (1976), people tend to filter their perceptions through their belief systems and to come out with emotions.
5. In most cases, negative self-labeling is based on irrational beliefs.
6. A major problem with negative self-labeling is that the label tends to cover all aspects of behavior indiscriminately.
7. Human behavior can be best viewed in black and white terms.
8. Individuals who are always in complete control of themselves and of the situation tend to be emotionally vulnerable.
9. In order for the ideal self to be helpful, it should not be tyrannical and inflexible.
10. According to Fritz Perls, mistakes are not sins, they are creative ways of doing something new.
11. An important thing to remember about self-label is that any revisions should always conform to the social standards.

4/THE SELF-CONCEPT: HOW TO CHANGE IT

12. Negative self-labels are often caused by the "tyranny of the shoulds."
13. The self-concept is usually an objective, factual self-report.
14. It is important that a program of change in the self-concept include a description of the ideal self that is free of perfectionism.
15. The best place to break the circular relationship between perceptions, actions, and self-concept is between perceptions and self-concept.

Completion

1. The self-concept, since it provides its own nourishment, is considered to be _____.
2. The variables that can be seen, touched, and the like, are referred to as _____ variables.
3. Our private interpretations of the environment are referred to as our _____ processes.
4. Highly individual styles of thinking about what happens to us refers to _____ variables.
5. In most cases of negative self-labeling, the variable that needs to be changed is the person's _____.
6. Individuals with a positive self-concept are characterized as having _____ self-image.
7. Perfectionism is one way of worshipping false gods; _____ is another.
8. Social standards are relative to _____ and _____.
9. According to sociologist David Riesman, a person becomes _____ _____ because of shifting social values.
10. The self-concept is not an objective factual report of the self. Rather, it is considered to be a _____ vision of the self.
11. When searching for possible constructive feedback, the information you should pay closest attention to is that which makes you feel _____.
12. The procedure for modifying your self-talk is called _____ _____.
13. _____ is a collection of sentences that we have internalized in the course of our past experiences.
14. The key to a successful modification of your negative self-labeling is to replace the old vicious cycle with a _____ one.
15. It is an accurate assumption that the successful manipulation of negative self-talk will result in the reward of _____.

Essay Questions

1. Discuss the purpose of functional analysis in changing the self-concept. (pp. 90–91)
2. Discuss the "A-B-C" process and its relation to "person variables" and negative self-labeling. (pp. 91–93)
3. Discuss the relationship between "perfectionism," "conventionality," and negative self-labeling. (pp. 97–100)
4. Some individuals in our society have been characterized as becoming "other-directed." What factors seem to be responsible for this type of behavior? (pp. 100–102)
5. Define cognitive restructuring and describe its role in changing negative self-labeling. (pp. 104–106)

SELF-TEST ANSWERS

Multiple Choice

1. d (p. 88)
2. c (p. 88)
3. b (p. 88)
4. b (p. 88)
5. a (pp. 88–90)
6. c (pp. 90–91)
7. d (p. 91)
8. b (p. 91)
9. d (p. 91)
10. a (p. 91)
11. c (p. 96)
12. b (p. 97)
13. c (p. 99)
14. c (p. 99)
15. d (p. 101)
16. d (p. 101)
17. c (pp. 100–101)
18. d (pp. 102–103)
19. c (p. 105)
20. d (p. 106)

True-False

1. true (p. 88)
2. false (p. 89)
3. true (p. 90)
4. true (p. 91)
5. true (pp. 92–93)
6. true (p. 96)
7. false (p. 97)
8. false (p. 99)
9. true (p. 99)
10. true (p. 100)
11. false (p. 100)
12. true (p. 102)
13. false (p. 102)
14. true (p. 102)
15. false (p. 105)

Completion

1. self-perpetuating (p. 88)
2. external (p. 90)
3. cognitive (p. 90)
4. person (p. 91)
5. self-talk (pp. 92–93)
6. broad (p. 96)
7. conventionality (p. 100)
8. time, place (p. 100)
9. other-directed (p. 101)
10. subjective (p. 102)
11. uncomfortable (p. 104)
12. cognitive restructuring (p. 104)
13. Self-talk (pp. 104–105)
14. benign (p. 106)
15. freedom (p. 106)

5
Self-Control: What It Is and How It Develops

CHAPTER OUTLINE

WHAT IS SELF-CONTROL
Self-Control and External Control
Self-Control and Freedom
Perceived Locus of Control

THE DEVELOPMENT OF SELF-CONTROL: PROCESSES
Respondent Conditioning
Operant Conditioning
Reinforcement
   Extinction
Generalization and Discrimination
Shaping
Modeling
Avoidance Learning
Intermittent Reinforcement

THE DEVELOPMENT OF SELF-CONTROL: RESULTS
Bodily Control
Control over Impulsive Behaviors
Reactions to the Self
Problems in Self-Control

READING

Their Own Worst Enemies

RICHARD DRISCOLL

In my practice I have come to know a great many inveterate self-critics, given to asserting their failings in as much detail as the listener seems willing to endure. The species is not all that rare and includes a variety of breeds. Self-critics may be boorish whiners or charmingly droll, but these are only surface characteristics. The common denominator is the habit of putting themselves down.

While most people criticize themselves occassionally, the habitual self-critic does so with unusual frequency and severity. So heavy is his investment in always talking about his own inadequacies that if he is contradicted—if he is assured that his self-assessment is mistaken in whole or in part—he may only become angry and more entrenched in his beliefs about himself.

What most significantly distinguishes one self-critic from another is motive, and the possible motives of the self-critic are many and can combine like molecules. Usually we think of such people as lacking in confidence, or feeling inferior, or believing themselves wrong about something. While there is truth in these explanations, they overlook the personal and social functions of self-criticism. People make their "I'm no good" statements not just because they sincerely believe them to be so, but also in order to accomplish something. People can criticize themselves as a way of sending a message to others, as a means of, say, expressing hostility or anger, or of establishing social status or position. The adolescent who announces that he can't do anything right, that he is always messing up, may be seeking to avoid responsibility. The woman who keeps insisting to her husband that she is dull and stupid and a poor mother may be trying to frustrate and annoy him because he is insensitive to her real concerns. The motive for putting oneself down can be as self-sacrificing as a misguided effort to keep a family together or as self-serving as an attempt to

43

be seen as someone who lives up to extraordinarily high standards.

Whatever the motive, the self-critical person causes himself discomfort and even pain, and may have little awareness that he is the perpetrator of his own distress. He also does not see that his excessive self-criticism is an understandable response to the circumstances of his life. But failing to grasp the reason behind his self-criticism, he is in a poor position to do much about it.

In analyzing the types of self-criticism, we must look at what the person is actually doing: what he intends, what he achieves, and what satisfaction he may gain. From my own practice of psychotherapy as well as the experiences of other clinicians, I have tried to sort out the various motives for self-criticism, constructive and destructive, and to assess its social as well as individual functions.

Mobilizing Pressure to Improve

Some people criticize themselves in an effort to get a better understanding of their actions or to force themselves to do better next time.

The line between sensible and unreasonable self-criticism is sometimes thin. A person who is critical of his own math ability may reasonably decide, for example, that he is poor at algebra and ought to avoid the course. And a young girl may question whether she is experienced enough or popular enough to date an older boy in her school. Is she right? Or merely afraid? Or both?

Self-criticism also mobilizes discomfort and brings pressure on people to do better. To get a job done, they "put the screws" to themselves. Especially when they have little interest in the job, they castigate themselves for lack of enthusiasm or energy and exhort themselves to try harder. Being really tough on themselves does increase motivation, at least temporarily, and often long enough to do the job. But if they fail, as occassionally happens, the result may be a cycle of disappointment and anger that leads to even harsher self-criticism.

This pateron of self-criticism has been identified in Gestalt therapy's image of the Top Dog/Under Dog content, in which Top Dog tries to force improvement and Under Dog resents the effort and resists it.

We can see the process begin in the early relationship between such people and their parents. Often the parents criticized the children in order to get them to see their mistakes and to improve their conduct. When children of such parents grow up, they may see themselves as incompetent or lazy, and believe that they cannot accomplish anything without constant self-pressure. In some instances, they have been pressuring themselves for so long that they have failed to develop any interests, any intrinsic involvements, any sense of what they genuinely want to do, as opposed to what they have merely assumed that they should do.

People who criticize themselves as a way to self-improvement should ask themselves, "Is it working? Is more pressure going to work any better?" These questions should help them to realize that their self-criticism is a form of victimization, not a technique by which they continuously do better. For if their excessive self-criticism were indeed effective, they would be near perfect!

A Check on Ambition

Self-criticism may be a way of restraining oneself from trying to do something that may be dangerous or unethical. When a person crticizes his own abilities or status, he reminds—or convinces—himself that overly ambitious attempts to change that position may be doomed to failure. Consider the analysis of black families by William Grier and Price Cobbs, published in 1968. Grier and Cobbs found that black mothers who were usually loving could also be harshly critical and demeaning toward their children—especially the boys, thus undermining their confidence and masculinity. While the criticism appeared hostile, the authors concluded that its real aim was to teach the boys their "place" in order to promote their safety.

Through self-criticism, people may similarly talk themselves out of buying an expensive car, seeking a promotion at work, or having a love affair. One patient, an attractive married woman, felt that her husband was not meeting her needs and had treated her badly. It would serve him right if she had an affair, she said, and she planned to do so. But she also felt that having an affair would be immoral and might be discovered. What to do? She became preoccupied with what she considered her unattractive features. This obsession with own physical flaws hurt her self-confidence and, in effect, restrained her from having an affair.

Just such reasoning helps to explain why many teenagers are almost compulsively concerned about their appearance. According to the social expectations of their own group, teenagers should not only meet and date members of the opposite sex, they must also enjoy and be adept at such relationships. For some teenagers, these expectations are frightening threats to their self-esteem. They would rather criticize their own looks and limit their social activity than be publicly embarrassed.

Playing It Safe

People who have modest expectations, who play it safe, may be surprised by good news, but they will not be startled by failure or disappointment. They expect that. Issues of control are important in this case of self-criticism. People who put themselves down do not allow circumstances—or other people—to do it for them.

Obviously, self-criticism can also be a strategy to ward off attacks by others. People who present themselves as being insecure, frightened, or barely able to manage, tend to prevent other people from criticizing them. After all, one would have to be a hard-hearted person to attack anyone who is such a mess!

Because our culture considers modesty a virtue, anyone who appears immodest may be asking for trouble. Consider a mother who announces to a group of adults that she is a good parent and that her children are turning out well. If other parents are present who are having difficulties with their children, they are not likely to try to learn from her, but may attempt to undermine the woman with comments like: "Ah, just wait till the kid gets to be a teenager—then you'll be in a for a big shock" or "That's what I thought too, until I learned better."

People who play it safe tend to feel that attacks on them are justified. They need to understand that the attacks are frequently motivated by competitiveness and jealousy—and that one doesn't have to accept them helplessly but can fight back.

Humility and Superiority

When a person acknowledges wrongdoing by saying "I was wrong" or "I was mean and selfish," he may be doing penance in the traditional sense. He is also showing good faith to others by saying, in effect, that the transgressed standards do count; in the process he affirms himself as a defender of what is right.

Let us see what else may be involved. By acknowledging guilt, people often set a precedent that invites others to acknowledge their own parts in a conflict. In many situations, admitting one's guilt becomes a way of getting others to admit theirs. As a result, the guilt is diffused, and one gains in moral stature by having been the first to say, "Yes, it was my fault."

There is a second twist to coming clean. At times, it can convey an individual's high moral standards. The image of the "hanging judge" is appropriate here. The hanging judge, angry and vindictive, seeks the destruction of the criminal. Similarly, the vindictiveness of people who excoriate themselves for a wrongdoing, sometimes for a rather ordinary lapse, says that they believe that "doing right" is of supreme importance. Deploring their sins is a way of insisting that they want to be beyond reproach, that their standards are never relaxed. In their hands, self-criticism becomes a device for gaining moral points.

Self-criticism can also be a device for asserting one's general superiority. Take the reviewer who rarely finds anything good to say about a movie, book, or play. Such a super-critic says that his standards are so fine and so high that not much can satisfy him. In similar fashion, people establish the superiority of their standards by constantly renouncing their less than perfect performances. Their self-criticism, harsh and continual, announces that they are above making mistakes and that their imperfect behavior is not a reflection of their true selves.

Consider the graduate who cannot decide on any dissertation topic and stick to it. One topic is not interesting enough, another not important enough, and so on. The student wants to write something exceptional, but he has no guarantees that anything he starts will be outstanding. He renounces his attempts not because he feels inferior but to uphold his self-image as a person who expects great accomplishments from himself.

Statements to Others

Self-criticism can also be a statement to other people not to make any demands. The adolescent who insists on his lack of responsibility is an example. By declaring that he is irresponsible, he tells people that they should not expect anything of him. He is saying, in the formulation of transactional analysis, "Don't expect too much from me because, you see, I've got this wooden leg."

People sometimes pick up the wooden-leg strategy as children from parents who use it to obligate them. As adults, they use it to get even and outmanipulate other people. It is not unusual to see friends or family members actually competing to be seen as the most miserable person in the group.

Yet another form of self-criticism aims at evoking sympathy. By being overly tough on themselves, people who feel lonely and unloved invite their friends and acquaintances to reassure them of their worth. These friends often will share in the misery, saddened by what they hear, and frustrated by an inability to do anything about it other than offer words of comfort. To the extent that misery loves company, self-critics of this type often get what they love. To the extent that they do, they gain an added advantage—avoiding an unfavorable comparison between their own unhappiness and the happier situation of their friends.

Sympathy-seeking self-critics tend to be hard on their friends. In the first place, these self-critics don't want the sympathy to stop. As long as friends keep attending to them, they need not do anything to change their situation. But after a time, friends tend to be weary of a constant stream of self-depreciation. Often they will drift away, leaving the lonely sympathy-seeking self-critic even more lonely, more in need of sympathy, more self-critical, searching for new sympathetic listeners. It is a cycle that can be broken only when the self-critic moves beyond egocentric unhappiness and learns to talk with people about something other than his or her problems.

Hidden Motives

Some forms of self-criticism are not so much requests for a response as they are vehicles for expressing feelings that are difficult to express more directly.

Consider an incident in which a wife has spent hours making a special meal. The husband comes home late, eats mostly in silence, but comments that the duck is dry, perhaps overcooked. The wife states angrily that she is an awful cook, that absolutely nothing that she does is ever right. Dumping the dry duck in the garbage, platter and all, she runs from the room. The wife is ostensibly putting herself down, but by indirection, she lets her husband know that he has hurt her, and she tries to make him squirm.

Hostile self-critics do not always know that they are being hostile. If one of the wife's friends said that she would have been angry too, the woman might respond, "But I wasn't angry, I was just terribly hurt and upset." But if the friend said, "Your husband's comment was unfair and was enough to make you angry," such a remark would legitimize the anger and allow the woman to accept it.

Hostile self-critics have reservations about speaking up for themselves. They feel that it is selfish and wrong to put their own interests ahead of others'. They choose instead to camouflage their hostility by apparently turning it against themselves, and they strike out through self-criticism.

Another use of self-criticism is to give assurance that one is a dutiful and loving child. This seemingly odd use of self-criticism has grim beginnings. A child who grows up under the whip of strong parental criticism often comes to believe that he retains his place in the family only by accepting the criticism of his parents. The result is self-criticism. As an adult, the person is likely to continue berating himself in order to maintain his emotional place beside his parents, especially if he does not have a family of his own.

Understandably, such adults often have strongly conflicting feelings about their parents. They feel wronged by the harsh treatment that they have received, but they are unable to oppose parental authority and set themselves on an independent course. As long as they believe that they have no other place where they belong, they will continue to upbraid themselves, despite the sometimes intense discomfort that accompanies their self-disparagement.

Self-criticism can also express angry opposition to the reassurance of others. In medicine, the term "iatrogenic effects" refers to the negative side effects of an attempt to heal or cure a patient. When friends reassure a self-critical person and tell him that he is being too hard on himself, the self-critic—quite unlike the sympathy seeker—may regard such comments as an explicit contradiction of his own views. Nobody likes to be contradicted, so the person reacts by insisting on his inadequacies. He may snap back with: "I am not exaggerating. I really am stupid [or ugly, or irresponsible, or whatever] and you will not convince me otherwise!"

What is going on here is that the self-critical person is divided: critic and victim in one. When friends offer comfort, they address the victim, but without knowing it, they oppose the critic. Their comfort simultaneously conveys the message that the person's self-appraisal is wrong and of no real consequence. The friends' unintended opposition is a challenge to the self-critic's last vestige of esteem and status. Self-critics fight back tenaciously to maintain their right to make their own self-appraisals, however negative.

Breaking the Pattern

A women who kept telling her husband and friends that she was stupid and a poor mother shows how several motives for self-criticism may appear in combination. When the woman, a schoolteacher, criticized herself, her husband and friends reassured her continually—but to no avail. What they failed to understand was the reason for her self-condemnation. The reassurance gave her the sympathy she was seeking, thus providing the license for further self-criticism, and it also contradicted her, thus provoking her to defend her claims of being stupid and incompetent. Her husband and friends should have forgone the reassurance and said, neutrally, "Sounds like you are being very tough on yourself." Such a statement would have told the woman that they understood that she was upset and unhappy—without feeding her self-criticism.

There were other sources of her self-criticism. The woman had a competitive and controlling mother who criticized her for the way she was raising her own children. By repeatedly citing her own faults, the woman in effect agreed with her mother, so as to stop further criticism and avoid confrontations that might have jeopardized their relationship.

There are less self-destructive ways of disarming criticism. For example, the woman might have said: "Mother, you sound as if you feel it is your place to tell me how to raise my children." Or she might have used some sort of paradoxical challenge, such as: "Mother, I realize that I'm fallible, but perhaps with your continuing criticism, I may learn to be as good with my children as you wish me to be." The mother might not have liked such a comeback, but would undoubtedly have found it hard to argue with.

This client, who came to me depressed and unhappy in her marriage, had decided that it was better to gain sympathy for being too tough on herself than to be attacked by her mother for showing confidence. The pain she felt brought her to me, for like most self-critics, she failed to see that she was the perpetrator of her own harsh treatment.

Self-critical people experience condemnation, degradation, and humiliation as if they had originated in someone else. Given the distress generated by extreme self-criticism—for no one enjoys believing that he or she is incompetent, unloved, ugly, or irresponsible—it is no surprise that self-critics are often unable to attribute their plan to their own choices and actions. But this leaves them in a poor position to think through these choices and actions.

People need to see that they do not condemn themselves merely because they believe that they are stupid or incompetent, but always to accomplish something: to pressure themselves to improve, to gain sympathy, to avoid responsibility, or any of the other reasons that we have discussed. Understanding the reasons for being self-critical is the first step in altering those reasons and breaking the pattern.

The various schools of psychotherapy each contribute something to understanding the different motives for self-criticism. We noted the applicability of Top Dog/Under Dog analysis when people are constantly self-critical in order to pressure themselves to improve; Top Dog is attempting to correct, while Under Dog is resisting. When people criticize themselves as a way of doing penance, the Freudian idea of the strict superego applies. When people use self-criticism as a disguised expression of hostility, transactional analysts note the satisfaction gained from the turnabout and called it "playing a game."

But no single theory deals adequately with the range of self-critic's subtle maneuvers. A pragmatic, eclectic approach to understanding such people is thus essential. People who use self-criticism to evoke sympathy must be treated differently from those who use it to express anger. Both may need different advice than those who denounce themselves to stonewall further attacks. Finally, some people may be unduly self-critical for any combination of the reasons we have discussed, and thus pose more complex problems.

In every instance, however, self-critics need to understand that they are doing the criticizing. Once it dawns on them that they are acting on intelligible reasons and are in charge that *they* are perpetuating their own unhappiness, they may find a way to silence the harsh critics inside themselves.

Reading Questions

1. Briefly summarize what Richard Driscoll means by a severe self-critic.
2. Describe two or three of the motives behind self-criticism.
3. Explain how Driscoll helps the critic to be less self-critical.

RESEARCH STUDY

Investigator:	Laura Humphrey.
Source, date:	"Children's Self-Control in Relation to Perceived Social Environment," *Journal of Personality and Social Psychology*, 1984, *46*, 178-188.
Location:	University of Wisconsin Hospital and Clinic, Madison, Wisconsin.
Subjects:	755 children from 36 fourth and fifth grade classes.
Materials:	Classroom environment scale, Primary Grade Class Environment Form, Children's Perceived Self-Control Scale, Teacher's self-control rating scale.

While research has attended to the characteristics of children who do or do not exercise self-control, little attention has been given to the characteristics of social environments (e.g., school classrooms) in influencing self-control in the children in those environments. In this study, it was anticipated that in classrooms where there were clear organizational structures and codes of conduct, students would display higher levels of self-control than in classrooms where they were less clear organizational structure and fewer codes of conduct.

To test this hypothesis, the research gave 755 children and their teachers from 36 fourth and fifth grade classrooms questionnaires to assess their perception of their classroom social environment, noting in particular the degree of structure and existence of codes of conduct in the classroom. In addition, each child's level of self-control was measured by the child him/herself, the teacher, and an observer using a brief rating scale.

The results of the study indicated that the degree of self-control displayed by the students was related to the degree of organizational structure and presence of codes of conduct in the classroom. Interestingly, the students' perception of these social environmental factors was most related to their level of self-control. Where they perceived greatest structure and the most direction, they exercised greatest self-control. Teacher perceptions of classroom structure did not relate to student self-control.

Research Study Questions

1. What aspects of the social environment of the classroom were expected to be related to student self-control?
2. What was measured in this study and by whom?
3. What was found to be related and unrelated to student self-control?

CASE STUDY

On the back of an envelope found among his effects after his death in a plane crash, former Atomic Energy Commission chairman Gordon Dean had scribbled:

Lessons Learned

1. Never lose your capacity for enthusiasm.
2. Never lose your capacity for indignation.
3. Never judge people, don't type them too quickly; but in a pinch never first assume that a man is bad; first assume always that he is good and that at worst he is in the gray area between bad and good.
4. Never be impressed by wealth alone or thrown by poverty.
5. If you can't be generous when it's hard to be, you won't be when it's easy.
6. The greatest builder of confidence is the ability to do something—almost anything—well.
7. When that confidence comes, then strive for humility; you aren't as good as all that.
8. And the way to become truly useful is to seek the best that other brains have to offer. Use them to supplement your own, and be prepared to give credit to them when they have helped.
9. The greatest tragedies in world and personal events stem from misunderstandings.
Answer: communicate.

So, meet a communicator. And his wife, the inventor of a communications systems that might have baffled or discouraged Samuel F.B. Morse, Alexander Graham Bell, Guglielmo Marconi and Aleksandr Popov. They are Corbin and Kay Allerdice, parents of three sons. Allerdice was one of the bright young men of the Atomic Energy Commission and, later, the World Bank. He couldn't miss in that league of intellectuals.

Then, a strange thing. One afternoon while at work at the World Bank headquarters in Washington, Allerdice detected what he easily identified as a common sniffly cold coming on. He told his secretary that he was going to knock off work early, go home, take a couple of aspirins, go to bed . . . and he'd be in early the next morning.

He couldn't wake up the next morning. Kay called their doctor, their doctor called a neurologist. The neurologist determined that Allerdice had been stricken by a massive virus attack on his central nervous system.

For weeks, the animated young officer lay flat on his back, eyes closed, unable to speak, fed intravenously. He was a faintly breathing dead man, a quadraplegic.

One day he opened his eyes. The smallest muscles in his body, those that activate the eyelids, had somehow been reborn. Kay, who had kept the lonely vigils, bounded from her chair at the side of his bed and stood at its foot, the better to watch the face of her husband. She looked into his opened eyes, twin pools of doubt, wonder, even dispair.

"Hello, Corb," she said. There was no response, no reaction. He looked at her unblinkingly.

A miraculous thought came to her in her terrible anxiety to get through to him. "Corb," she said, "I want to see if you know me. If you know me, tell me by blinking your eyes. Blink your eyes, Corb. Now."

Allerdice blinked his eyes and, overcome with gratitude that his brain still lived, the good wife set out to devise means of utilizing that simple action of his eyes to establish a rapport with the mute and graven man.

She found it.

"Tell you what," she said one day. "I know there must be a lot of things you want to say to me. So let's try this: I'm going to recite the alphabet, over and over and over. You keep your eyes open while I'm doing it. When I get a letter which is part of a word you want me to know, you blink your eyes and I'll write it down. And sooner or later, I'll know what you're saying to me."

By that excruciatingly tedious method the Allerdices found communion once more. In time, after her countless recitations of the alphabet, he communicated the news that some sense of feeling had returned to a couple of his fingers on his right hand. He had a request or two. He wanted his typewriter wheeled to the side of his bed, a pulley built to support his hand over the keyboard, and to be rolled on his side so that he could see the keys. That took days, probably weeks.

But when all was attended to, Allerdice was able to touch, not really depress, the letters of the words he wanted to transmit, while Kay looked over his shoulder. It speeded up their communication a hundredfold.

Later, two engineer friends designed a novel system that mated an electric typewriter with a clear screen which fit over his bed like a combination of a dinner tray and windshield. When Allerdice touched a key the letter would light up on the screen, backward for the man in bed, frontward for those visitors who sat or stood at the bottom of his bed.

Now he could address himself to groups, not just the faithful wife counting and recording the blinking of his eyes. He could carry on not only modest "conversations" but participate in debates. To save him the trouble of spelling out his dissent, if the one-sided talk concerned a political issue, say, Corbin`s wizard friends wired up a rasping disapproval button.

Allerdice went the distance at Dr. Howard Rusk's remarkable rehabilitation center at Bellevue Hospital in New York City, where a host of stricken celebrities, including Joseph P. Kennedy, Sr., sire of the remarkable and ill-starred clan, Roy Campanella, one of the great baseball catchers of his time, and Jim Hagerty, President Eisenhower's press secretary, fought to rise above it.

For the past few years, Allerdice has been confined to the Newton D. Baker Veterans Hospital, Martinsburg, West Virginia. He has kept himself busy by writing a history of the Atomic Energy Commission and the remarkable personnel which produced the first A-bomb. Praeger Publishers have recently distributed it to college libraries as one of a series on government departments and agencies. Corb was helped and encouraged in his efforts by his friend Edward R. Trapnell, with whom he worked at AEC.

"We worked on the book over a period of five years, but Corb kept plugging away despite the fact that I sometimes couldn't work on it with him for weeks at a time because of job pressures and a heart attack I had in 1971. Corb is still brave and bright, his mind sharp. He punches an electric typewriter (using a roll of paper) at a rate of about five to seven punches a minute. . . ."

That is not going to break the late Billy Rose's record for speed-typing, but Allerdice has achieved a miracle Rose and a zillion other better-known inhabitants of this globe stumbled over, for one reason and another.

Corbin Allerdice has communicated.

So can you.

Case Study Questions

1. In what way could Corbin Allerdice's sudden medical condition relate to Martin Seligman's notion of helplessness and "unexpected" death?
2. If loss of control and feelings of helplessness and hopelessness can push a person closer to death, what role did his wife's inventiveness play in keeping Corbin Allerdice alive?
3. Gordon Dean's last act in life was to communicate. How does communication affect the concept of helplessness and survival?

SELF-TEST

Multiple Choice

1. Langer and Rodin's experiment with nursing home residents showed that:
    a. increasing the amount of control that the residents had over their lives made little difference in how they felt about themselves
    b. most elderly people desire less, not more, control over their lives

c. the more control we have over our lives, the happier and more productive we are
d. it is nearly impossible to increase the amount of self-control in an institutionalized population

2. The general meaning of the term self-control refers to a person's influence over and regulation of all the following *except*:
   a. his physical processes
   b. his social processes
   c. his psychological processes
   d. his behavioral processes

3. In our society, the practice of punishing people for violating the law presupposes which of the following?
   a. that people are instinctively evil
   b. that people have no choice but to break the law
   c. that people make the free choice to violate the law
   d. that people are not capable of free choice

4. According to Freud, the moral standards and self-ideals of a person develop as a result of:
   a. identification with the opposite-sex parent
   b. fearing the opposite-sex parent
   c. identifcation with the same-sex parent
   d. fearing the same-sex parent

5. In the respondent conditioning experiment with the salivation of dogs, at what point was the sound of the bell presented?
   a. the exact moment the food was presented
   b. about 1/2 second after the food was presented
   c. about 1/2 second before the food was presented
   d. about 1 second before the food was presented

6. The psychologist best associated with respondent conditioning is:
   a. Pavlov
   b. Thorndike
   c. Skinner
   d. Freud

7. The process of learning which actions are strengthened or weakened by their consequences is called:
   a. classical conditioning
   b. respondent conditioning
   c. operant conditioning
   d. associative conditioning

8. Removing what set of stimuli tends to strengthen the behavior that precedes it?
   a. aversive stimuli
   b. primary reinforcers
   c. conditioned reinforcers
   d. positive stimuli

9. Which one of the following stimuli tends to weaken a behavior upon its removal?
   a. negative stimuli
   b. conditioned negative reinforcers
   c. aversive stimuli
   d. positive stimuli

10. In order to discourage a child's temper tantrums, psychologists suggest:
    a. the use of positive reinforcement
    b. the use of negative reinforcement
    c. the use of punishment
    d. the use of operant extinction

11. Through the process of discrimination, we are able to:
    a. identify those stimuli that signal appropriate and rewarding situations
    b. channel our needs and desires toward appropriate outlets
    c. learn which behaviors are appropriate for which situations
    d. all of the above

12. Which of the following refers to the learning of a response through the positive reinforcement of successive approximations of that response?
    a. the process of operant conditioning
    b. the process of operant shaping
    c. the process of respondent shaping
    d. the process of respondent conditioning

13. The learning process that is capable of molding our responses without the use of direct reinforcement is called:
    a. modeling
    b. operant extinction
    c. operant shaping
    d. operant conditioning

14. Avoidance behaviors are considered to be difficult to unlearn because:
    a. the avoidance behavior is repeatedly rewarded by positive reinforcement
    b. the avoidance behavior is not susceptible to extinction effects
    c. the avoidance behavior is very generalized
    d. all of the above

15. Human behavior is typically maintained in the "real" world by which of the following?
    a. each response is usually accompanied by reinforcement
    b. every second response is reinforced
    c. after an interval time, reinforcement is given regardless of the response
    d. after a number of responses have been made, reinforcement is given

5/SELF-CONTROL: WHAT IT IS AND HOW IT DEVELOPS

16. Humans learn more about self-control than they will ever learn for the rest of their lives during which period in their development?
    a. between birth and age one
    b. between age one and age two
    c. between age two and age three
    d. between age three and age five
17. Which of the following is *not* considered a "naturally" emerging skill?
    a. walking
    b. talking
    c. laughing
    d. toilet training
18. Which of the following crucial factors affect the postponement of rewards?
    a. trust, self-confidence, maturation
    b. goal-orientation, trust, self-confidence
    c. self-confidence, goal-orientation, maturation
    d. maturation, trust, goal-orientation
19. Experiments have shown which of the following to be quickly learned through the process of modeling?
    a. patterns of concrete external reinforcement
    b. patterns of concrete self-reinforcement
    c. patterns of intangible external reinforcement
    d. patterns of intangible self-reinforcement
20. Behavior theory suggests that faulty self-control is developed through:
    a. absent learning
    b. inappropriate learning
    c. lack of feedback
    d. all of the above

True-False

1. In self-control, the individual sets his or her own standards for performance and is rewarded by others for meeting those standards.
2. One reason that psychologists lean toward determinism is that none of us are able to control all the environmental factors that influence us.
3. People who believe they control what happens to them appear to have greater success in controlling their lives.
4. McDonald's hopes that, through the process of operant conditioning, our mouths will water and our stomachs will growl when we see the golden arches.
5. In respondent conditioning, the pleasant stimulus follows the response, whereas in operant conditioning, the pleasant stimulus precedes the response.
6. In our highly mechanized society, parents are still the only ones to supply the consequences that teach us self-control.
7. The presentation of a pleasant stimulus will usually have a strengthening effect on undesirable and desirable behavior.
8. Extinction usually involves the removal of the stimulus that has maintained a conditioned response.
9. The process of discrimination means learning to distinguish among similar stimuli and to tailor one's responses accordingly.
10. Operant response shaping is the process responsible for the learning of many complex skills, such as cooking or driving a car.
11. In most cases, the power of modeling to avoid the "do as I say, not as I do" approach to child-rearing is very apparent.
12. The process of learning to avoid typically requires the influence of both operant and respondent conditioning.
13. Responses built up through intermittent reinforcement are much more permanent than those that have been reinforced continuously.
14. Responses that have been reinforced in an intermittent manner tend to be highly resistant to extinction effects.
15. Toilet training, unlike talking and walking, is not a naturally emerging skill.

Completion

1. _____ refers to a person's influence over and regulation of the set of processes that constitute the self.
2. While many psychologists personally support the notion of free choice, as scientists they lean toward _____.
3. The recent psychological term of _____ _____ _____ _____ refers to our notions of who or what controls our lives.
4. According to Freud, the superego develops in the child as a final outcome of the famous _____ _____.
5. The type of learning whereby a neutral stimulus is paired with a pleasant stimulus until the organism learns to respond to the neutral stimulus as it would to the pleasant stimulus is called _____ _____.
6. Thorndike formulated what he called the _____ _____ _____ ,

which states that responses leading to satisfying consequences are strengthened and are likely to be repeated.
7. It is characteristic of respondent conditioning that the pleasant or unpleasant stimulus _____ the response.
8. Through the mechanism of _____ _____ we learn to control and direct our behavior in order to obtain rewards and avoid punishments.
9. The set of stimuli that strengthen the behaviors they follow are called _____.
10. Stimuli that have been associated with primary reinforcers, and thus have the same effects on behavior, are called _____ _____.
11. _____ refers to the process whereby a conditioned response expands to include not only the original stimulus but similar stimuli as well.
12. Through the procedure of trying out the same response in different situations, we learn to identify those _____ stimuli that signal the situations in which that response is appropriate.
13. The learning of a response through the reinforcement of successive approximations of that response is called _____.
14. The method of learning through the imitation of others is called _____.
15. Human behavior is generally maintained by _____ reinforcement.

Essay Questions

1. How does Sigmund Freud account for the capacity of humans to develop self-control? (p. 120)
2. Define and provide an example of each of the following terms: (1) reinforcers (2) primary reinforcer, (3) conditioned reinforcer, (4) positive reinforcement, (5) negative reinforcement, (6) punishment, and (7) extinction. (p. 125)
3. Define the terms "shaping" and "modeling." Provide an example of how each can be utilized alone or together in the learning of either cooking, dressing, or walking. (pp. 127–129)
4. In the "real" world, human behavior is maintained not by continuous reinforcement but by intermittent reinforcement. What is the difference between these two types of reinforcement? Why is intermittent reinforcement more enduring? (pp. 130–131)
5. Discuss the mechanisms of how human beings learn the following three skills: controlling their bodies, controlling impulses, and how to react to themselves. (pp. 131–134)

5/SELF-CONTROL: WHAT IT IS AND HOW IT DEVELOPS

SELF-TEST ANSWERS

Multiple Choice
1. c (pp. 115–116)
2. b (p. 116)
3. c (p. 118)
4. c (p. 120)
5. b (p. 120)
6. a (p. 120)
7. c (p. 122)
8. a (p. 125)
9. d (pp. 125–126)
10. d (p. 126)
11. d (pp. 126–127)
12. b (p. 127)
13. a (pp. 127–128)
14. b (p. 130)
15. d (p. 130)
16. a (p. 131)
17. d (p. 131)
18. b (p. 133)
19. b (p. 133)
20. d (p. 134)

True-False
1. false (p. 117)
2. true (p. 118)
3. true (p. 119)
4. false (p. 121)
5. false (p. 123)
6. false (pp. 123–124)
7. true (p. 125)
8. true (pp. 125–126)
9. true (p. 126)
10. true (p. 127)
11. true (p. 129)
12. true (pp. 129–130)
13. true (pp. 130–131)
14. true (p. 131)
15. true (p. 131)

Completion
1. Self-control (p. 116)
2. determinism (p. 118)
3. perceived locus of control (p. 119)
4. Oedipus complex (p. 120)
5. respondent conditioning (p. 120)
6. law of effect (p. 122)
7. precedes (pp. 122–123)
8. operant conditioning (p. 123)
9. reinforcers (p. 125)
10. conditioned reinforcers (p. 125)
11. Generalization (p. 126)
12. discriminative (p. 126)
13. shaping (p. 127)
14. modeling (p. 127)
15. intermittent (p. 130)

6
Self-Control: How to Change It

CHAPTER OUTLINE

ANALYZING YOUR SELF-CONTROL
Description
Functional Analysis

IMPROVING SELF-CONTROL
Manipulating Antecedent Stimuli
    Environmental planning
    Redirecting attention
    Relabeling and organizing
Meddling with Responses
    Chaining
    Incompatible behaviors
    Shaping
Manipulating Consequences
    Utilizing feedback
    Providing self-reward
    Using the Premack Principle
    Administering punishment
Three Don'ts

READING

Mind Games Procrastinators Play

JANE B. BURKA AND LENORA M. YUEN

Procrastinators are given to moralizing, at least when they try to explain why they habitually put things off. They are lazy, they say, and undisciplined, and they just don't know how to organize their time.

Their view of themselves sounds reasonable enough, and it is widely accepted. In fact, one conventional way of helping procrastinators is to teach them some time-management techniques.

But the problem is more complicated than that. We have worked with many procrastinators—students who come to the Counseling Center of the University of California at Berkeley and people from the San Francisco Bay area whom we see in private practice—and we believe that chronic postponing is a complex psychological problem that rarely yields to simple remedies.

Procrastination is not just a bad habit but a way of expressing internal conflict and protecting a vulnerable sense of self-esteem. In our experience, few people can give up procrastinating until they understand the function procrastination serves in their own lives. They also need to know why their self-esteem is low and how putting things off acts as a buffer for their shaky sense of self-worth. It is not that insight alone can cure, but that understanding the hidden roots of procrastination often seems to weaken them.

Over the last three years, we have developed what we believe to be a unique treatment approach that integrates strategies from the behavioral, cognitive, and psychodynamic schools of psychological thought. We offer students at Berkeley participation in a time-limited group that continues through one academic term, that is, for eight or nine weeks. For the general public, we have developed a two-day workshop, with a two-week break between sessions. Our treatment plan includes teaching time-organizing strategies as a first step. However, procrastinators usually come to realize that these strategies are not effective, at least not by themselves. That realization often motivates them to look deeper into themselves in order to discover the particular function of habitual postponing in their own lives.

To illustrate our approach, we will introduce several typical, if imaginary, procrastinators, composites of real clients we have seen.

David is a lawyer with a large corporate firm. He was an academic star in college and was accepted into a competitive law school. There he struggled with procrastination, sometimes staying up all night to write his briefs or study for exams, but always managing to do well. With great pride he joined a prestigious law firm, hoping to become an outstanding lawyer, to impress his colleagues, and eventually to be named a partner in the firm.

As he began working, however, David began to procrastinate. Although he thought a lot about a case, he put off doing the necessary background research. He wanted to prepare a defense that was unassailable. When he worked, all he could think of was the inadequacy of his arguments; it was easier to put off the work than to think of being criticized. Although David managed to look busy, he knew he wasn't accomplishing much, and he was plagued by a feeling of fraudulence. As the court date drew near, he began to panic because he hadn't allowed enough time to write an adequate brief.

"Being a good lawyer means everything to me," David said. "But I seem to spend all my time worrying about being great and very little time actually working at it." Gradually he began to recognize that procrastination helps him avoid facing an important issue: can he be as competent a lawyer as his student record promised? By waiting too long to begin writing up his research, David has avoided a test of his true potential. In other words, he is afraid of failing to meet his own high standards, which demand an outstanding performance every time. With this standard, it is not surprising that David couldn't face writing. Ironically, procrastination was the mechanism that allowed him to write at all. By waiting until there was too little time to write a "great" brief, he could finally let himself off the hook with the thought "It's too late to make it brilliant; just get the damn thing done!"

David's work will not be a reflection of his true ability, but of his skill at brinkmanship; it demonstrates how well he is able to produce under last-minute pressure. Procrastination has made a realistic appraisal of his ability impossible. No one will ever know how good a job David *could* have done if he had allowed enough time. If David's performance doesn't live up to his or others' expectations, he can always say, "I could have done a lot better if I'd just had another week." And if he does well in spite of his last-minute effort, he can congratulate himself for having pulled it off in a pinch. Thus, procrastination serves to maintain the illusion of brilliance, but the illusion is never tested.

When Joanne went to work for a real-estate company, she surprised herself by providing to be more effective at selling than she had expected. Although she had always wanted a career, she had dropped out of college, married, and had two children. Several years later, recognizing how much a career meant to her, she took evening courses, got her real-estate license, and found a job.

Joanne was organized, communicated well with clients, and worked hard. But after initial success, her progress slowed. She put off calling interested buyers and lost several deals. Casual errands and family projects seemed to take on new importance to her, and she began to feel that she just didn't have enough energy to cover all the territory that the real-estate firm had assigned to her. As her sales figures dropped, Joanne began to question whether she was really able to handle real-estate work—or any career at all. Joanne mentioned that her older sister Helen, who worked as a sales clerk, had seemed depressed ever since Joanne began her real-estate job. She realized that she felt guilty about leaving Helen behind. To avoid success, which might mean hurting and abandoning her sister, she hurt herself; she became a procrastinator. Whereas David learned in the course of treatment that he was afraid of not doing well enough, Joanne found out that she was afraid of doing too well. She was frightened of her success, and instead of making an all-out effort to move ahead, she procrastinated.

Dick is a salesman for a growing computer company. He plays soccer and leads a busy social life. Although he procrastinates, his outgoing personality helps cover up his lack of preparation, so that his sales figures remain high. Dick said that although he generally confides freely in his friends, he never tells them about his good sales record because he expects them to make fun of him for being a workaholic. Although he received a letter of commendation for his outstanding work, he refused to let it appear in the company newsletter. He feared that other salesmen would be jealous and would shun him, leaving him isolated and lonely. Eventually he came to see that procrastinating enables him to reduce his sales volume so that he won't stand out too much. Whenever he makes a lucrative deal despite his delaying tactics, he attributes his success to last-minute luck rather than to ability. In short, Dick, too, fears success.

Henry, a 50-year-old, accountant, never finishes his work on schedule. He delays paying bills and returning telephone calls, and puts off doing things that other people expect of him. "I just can't seem to do what I'm supposed to do," he lamented. "If they say have it ready by Tuesday, I know I won't have it until Thursday. It's as if they say, 'Do it now,' and I say, 'I'll do it when I damn well please.'" He has lost two previous jobs because of his tardiness and now is in danger of losing another.

Henry did not realize that procrastination is his way of rebelling against a feeling of being controlled or dominated. For him, any expectation, schedule, or rule represents a battle to be won or lost. Adhering to someone else's time schedule means losing. Procrastination becomes a means of retaining a sense of power and control, even though the only power he has is to say "No!" Although Henry's procrastination is ultimately self-defeating, his achievement lies in defeating someone else.

Carol, a graduate student in English literature, is another person who rebels by procrastinating. She thrives on attention from her professors and often attempts to form a special relationship with them. Her professor of modern drama was disappointing to her because his lectures were confusing and poorly prepared. Carol interpreted his disorganization to mean that he wasn't interested either in the course material or in the students. Of her failure to turn in a paper, she said angrily, "If he doesn't care about the course, why should I care about the paper?" In her disappointment, she was using procrastination as a means of revenge.

Our procrastination groups, which have eight to 12 members, evolve through three phases, each characterized by a predominant mood. Optimism is the mood of the first two or three sessions. The next three meetings tend to be marked by pessimism, which gives way to realism in the two final sessions. A typical group goes something like this:

Optimism: During the first stage, humor and hopefulness prevail about a habit that has previously been a source of shame, humiliation, and despair. Participants express surprise at finding others who share their predicament, and they are relieved to exchange their procrastination "war stories." Henry had a particularly horrendous one to tell. He described a time when he waited so long to begin a complex audit that in order to get an extra week's time, he told his client that his wife was ill in the hospital. The client, anxious about the audit, called Henry at home, where his wife answered. Unaware of Henry's fabrication, she responded to the client's concern for her health with great surprise. The stunned client reported the discrepancy to Henry's supervisor, who fired him.

At the first session, we ask the groups to take a close look at the thinking patterns that have fostered their procrastination by making it seem to them logical and justified. One specific thing we ask the group to do is draw up a list of the excuses they use. One of David's favorites is, "I'll wait until I'm inspired to start working." Joanne convinces herself with "I've been working so hard I deserve a break." When the list has grown long, we suggest that participants monitor their thoughts and pay attention to their own excuses as they occur.

In the beginning, the group members are less interested in why they put things off than in learning ways to stop. They hope that just being in the group will eliminate procrastination effortlessly, instantaneously, and forever. Taking their desire for quick results into account, we devote part of the first three sessions to outlining behavioral techniques that can be used to help get work done. For instance, we ask each participant to set one personal goal to be achieved before the sessions end. The resolve must be defined behaviorally: "ending procrastination" is a noble goal, but "turning in a history paper on February 8" is a behavioral one. The goal has to be specific, observable, and divided into the component steps necessary for completion. Such specificity is always a challenge for procrastinators, who are used to thinking about work in global terms.

At this point we also introduce time-management techniques. Most procrastinators believe that unless they have a large block of time available, there is no point in getting started. We discuss the "Swiss cheese" method of time management that Alan Lakein, a management consultant, proposed in 1973. He advised "poking holes" in an overwhelming project by taking just a few minutes to accomplish one small piece of it. In accordance with this idea, we suggest that even a half-hour of work is an accomplishment. Using what our colleague Neil Fiore, a psychologist, calls the "un-schedule," we ask the participants to determine how much time they already commit to regular activities and responsibilities; the time remaining can be thought of as the maximum time available for studying, preparing law cases, contacting real-estate clients, or the like. Each half-hour of work is noted on the schedule after it has been accomplished. We encourage participants to reward themselves for any progress along the road to completion. Most procrastinators value only the finished product; we want to help them see that intermediate steps are also accomplishments.

Pessimism: By the fourth session, stage two is usually under way. Most participants feel disappointed in the group and in themselves, because learning specific time-management techniques has not solved their problems. Their fantasy of a magical cure has been shattered, and pessimism is pronounced. When it comes to putting their new techniques into practice, most members behave predictably; they procrastinate in this as in everything else. Although a majority of the group has made some progress by now, they still are not satisfied. Ignoring what they have accomplished, they focus on how much is left to do.

Occasionally, progress provokes anxiety rather than relief. Henry had always defined himself as a procrastinator, and as he began to change, he grew concerned about his identity. "If I'm not a procrastinator anymore," he worried, "what am I?"

But there is a bright side to all this. As experiences of procrastination inevitably occur, we help clients redefine them as opportunities for further learning rather than as new failures. Moreover, once it becomes clear that techniques alone do not cure, clients become more willing to examine underlying psychological issues. Together, group members begin to discuss the perfectionism and the low self-esteem that characterize most of them. They begin to see that family expectations have often played a part in their difficulties. They also begin to find out that some of them fear either failure or success, and that others have a strong need to rebel.

In almost every case, we see the same all-or-nothing thinking that David Burns observed among perfectionists ("The Perfectionist's Script for Self-Defeat," *Psychology Today*, November 1980). We try to help procrastinators recognize this kind of thinking in themselves. They become aware that they set high standards and expect to achieve them easily. They also begin to see that as long as things go well, they make progress, while as soon as the first obstacle is encountered, they feel defeated and stop working. The very fact of having to work hard, they come to understand, makes them feel inadequate or dumb.

Without lecturing, we introduce group members to a theory that helps explain the high standards held by procrastinators. The theory, proposed by another of our colleagues, Richard Beery, a psychologist, suggests that people who fear failure have accepted an equation with three parts. They believe that their performance is a reflection of their ability, and that ability is a reflection of self-worth. In other words, "My worth as a person is defined by my ability, and my ability is defined by what I produce." (Self-worth equals Ability equals Performance.) Since each product is an indicator of self-worth, the only way to feel worthy or important is to produce something great, time after time. One imperfect product is enough to upset the procrastinator's shaky sense of self-worth. Procrastination, however, breaks this equation. No longer does performance reflect true ability. Instead, it reflects how well you are able to pull things together at the last minute. The test of ability, and therefore the test of self-worth, is prevented by procrastination. (Self-worth equals Ability but does not equal Performance.)

We have observed that most procrastinators accept the self-worth equation without question. As David said, "I'm afraid of what I will produce because it feels worse to put out something bad than to procrastinate. It's a fear of judgment, of being laughed at. Better to show them nothing than to show them something stupid."

By this time, most members of the group begin to see that they are not lazy but afraid of doing poorly, of doing too well, or of expressing resentment in direct ways instead of indirectly through procrastination. We ask them what they think might happen if they did indeed stop procrastinating. For Dick, success meant taking a stand, making himself visible to the world, and exposing himself to insatiable demands for continued top-notch performance. "I'm afraid of being publicly visible and getting shot down," he said. "Maybe I won't be strong enough to fight back. Besides, if I became really successful, I'd have to live up to that success all the time." Both Henry and Carol feared that if they stopped procrastinating, they would lose the special, albeit sometimes unpleasant, relationships they developed with authority figures. "If I stop procrastinating," Carol said, "I might find out I'm just mediocre, and no one would be interested in me."

Group members begin to understand that their fears stem from low self-esteem. Diminished self-worth therefore becomes a principal topic of discussion: how did they acquire it and how can they get rid of it?

Participants begin to talk about the families they grew up in. We have observed two predominant family patterns. Some group members, including David and Carol, came from families in which there was much pressure to succeed. This pressure was sometimes overt, as in the case of David. His mother often looked over his report cards, which usually had all A's except for a single B, and asked, "Why did you get this B?" In other cases, the pressure was communicated more subtly. Carol's father often said to her, "Of course you did well! We know you can do anything you set your mind to." On the surface such a comment sounds supportive, but it conveys an implicit expectation that the child should never fail. David summed up his experience of family pressure by saying: "It seemed that they loved me for what I did, not for who I was." If performance was the basis for love, he risked losing that love if he couldn't measure up.

The other typical family pattern we have observed is the family that doubted the ability of the child to succeed. Bright students who were guided away from college-preparatory classes or children who were held back because of early reading problems are examples of those who might not have learned to trust their intelligence or their ability. Joanne recalled how her family had discouraged her from pursuing an education and a career. "What makes you think you're so smart?" her sister had demanded. Similarly, Henry, upon passing his CPA exam, heard from his father, "Isn't is a surprise that you've come all this way? I never would have expected it." These kinds of messages may create feelings of conflict and confusion about success.

A different kind of family situation had contributed to Dick's lifelong procrastination. He had a tense relationship with his father, who was a highly successful engineer. Although ambitious, Dick had difficulty doing work that would help him win recognition and promotion. He worried that his father would resent his success and would retaliate, perhaps by giving bad advice, or by being cold or critical. In effect, his family lived by implicit rules stating that only one family member could be successful.

Realism: By the time this third phase begins, most group members have gained some insight into the psychological roots of procrastination in their lives and are in a better position to understand why their habit is so persistent. This in turn stimulates examination of the unrealistic expectations they had originally held for the group. Participants begin to realize that slow progress is progress nonetheless. They also begin to find some middle ground between "I must be perfect" and "I am nothing."

The behavioral goals they had set for themselves remain a focus of discussion, and progress (or lack of it) continues to be reviewed at each session. During the last two meetings, participants exchange feedback with each other and with us. In doing so, they tend to be realistic about each other's limits, and yet they accept and care for each other.

How useful is psychological insight in dealing with habitual procrastination? One way of judging is to look at the effectiveness of our procrastination treatment, which stresses the value of insight supplemented by behavioral measures. While formal research has yet to be completed, we have examined the anonymous self-report evaluations that are requested of all students who use Counseling Center services. Over the three years that the procrastination groups have been offered, approximately 150 students have participated. Eighty-six percent of the students who responded reported that their overall experience was "satisfactory" or "very satisfactory." Ninety-one percent rated the group as "very helpful" or "extremely helpful" in accomplishing their goals. Increased self-acceptance was reported by 91 percent of the respondents and increased self-understanding by 89 percent. Seventy-four percent claimed an improved ability to study and 71 percent reported an increase in their ability to handle academic stress. Improvement in handling general stress was indicated by 69 percent, and finally, 60 percent reported greater motivation in school.

Our clinical impression has been that most students seem to benefit from the group. Academically, there may be improvement in the student's grades or in the timeliness of work. On a more personal level, the process of self-examination may help a group member to clarify his or her priorities. Some participants invest more importance in their education. Others discover that procrastination has obscured the fact that they actually prefer not to be in school at this time. A few may even decide to take a leave of absence; for them, such a decision represents success.

Some people, however, do not find the groups very helpful. Those for whom rebellion is the major issue continue to rebel in the group, where their resistance takes the form of failure to make use of what the group offers. Other clients are so easily discouraged that they give up after one or two sessions.

A group counseling program specifically for procrastinators offers several advantages. First, participants publicly acknowledge that procrastination is interfering with their lives and that they need help. Second, each member contracts with the group to accomplish one goal; this accountability helps motivate them to work toward their goals. Third, procrastinators can see in others what they cannot see in themselves. Becoming aware of others' unrealistic expectations and perfectionist standards helps them see these same patterns in their own behavior. Finally, in the group, procrastinators have the opportunity to be helpful to others and to be valued for personal qualities independent of their accomplishments.

So far, few groups like ours are offered elsewhere in the country, as far as we know, but conventional psychological counseling can help hard-core procrastinators understand and change their behavior. People who want to do something about their problem on their own can try to apply time-management techniques, but they might also consider the possibility that the unrealistically high standards they have set for themselves are actually self-defeating.

Reading Questions

1. Describe some of the functions served by procrastination.
2. Briefly summarize the three stages of treating procrastination.
3. Comment on the importance of treating procrastination by using groups.

RESEARCH STUDY

Investigators: Elizabeth Johnston-O'Connor and Daniel Kirshenbaum.
Source, date: "Something Succeeds Like Success: Positive Self-Monitoring for Unskilled Golfers," *Cognitive Therapy and Research*, 1986, 123–126.
Location: Rochester, New York.
Subjects: 109 unskilled volunteers (non-golfers).
Materials: Videotape, *Golf My Way* (1974) by Jack Nicklaus, wiffle golf balls.

A distinction has been made regarding the self-monitoring of positive (successful) behaviors and the self-monitoring of negative (unsuccessful) behaviors. This study set out to determine if the self-monitoring of positive behaviors, those that lead to the successful swinging of a golf club, would result in better performance than the self-monitoring of all behaviors, whether they lead to a successful swing or not. In addition, the researchers also checked to see if providing videotaped feedback was better than receiving no feedback.

To examine these questions, the researchers had 109 unskilled (non-golf playing) volunteers try to hit a golf ball that was being videotaped. They were then divided into six groups with one group watching the videotape while focusing on the proper elements of swing as provided in instructions given them, one group watching the videotape while attending in general to their efforts, and one group just watching the videotape with no instruction. The other three groups were told to think about what they had just done, with one group focusing on the proper elements of style, one group thinking about their efforts, and one group just thinking. Subsequently all subjects were given a follow-up test of their performance.

The results demonstrated that focusing on the successful aspects of the golf swing resulted in the best postexperimental performance. In addition, those viewing the videotape did better than those just thinking about their performance. Thus the authors concluded that focusing on the positive aspects of functioning in self-monitoring leads to better performance.

Research Study Questions

1. What did the researchers hope to determine in their study of self-monitoring of golf swings?
2. What were the different groups told to attend to while watching the videotape of their golf swing?
3. What were the results of the study regarding self-monitoring of a golf swing?

CASE STUDY

Frank's Prison

STEPHEN M. JOHNSON

Frank was thirty-four when he finally decided to seek help with his problems. He had been married four times and was currently in a monogamous and unhappy relationship with a much younger woman. According to Frank, his current relationship was much like what he had experienced in his marriages. He had met Cheryl only a week after his separation from his fourth wife. They went out together a few times and seemed to enjoy each other's company. She told him later what other women had told him in the past, that she was impressed and pleased by his gentlemanliness and the fact that he never "pushed her" sexually. In our therapy sessions, he indicated that he had always been successful with this type of shy and inhibited woman, and, as he saw it, the secret of his success was his polite reticence concerning sex. As with the other women before her, he waited for Cheryl to make a sexual advances to him. But once Frank slept with a woman, he felt obligated to her and responsible for her. According to him, it was not love that had prompted commitment and marriage in the past, but rather a sense of duty to those who had become dependent upon him. In each of his four marriages, the idea of legal union had come from the woman, and Frank had just gone along, thinking he was doing the right thing.

His current relationship was becoming repetitive and boring, just like all the others. Cheryl would come to his apartment every night at about six o'clock; she would cook dinner for the two of them, and they would then watch television until eleven, when she would go home; she still lived with her parents. Frank would then stay up late watching more television, get up late the next morning, and often arrive late for work. Sometimes, when Cheryl initiated it, they would have sex together, but that too was becoming boring for him, and as often as not he was unable to get or maintain an erection. This appeared to puzzle and distress Cheryl, but they never really talked about it. Frank said that this rigid and boring pattern was rarely broken up by other activities, but that he now wanted to become involved in other things, such as engaging in an evening sports activity and seeing other women. But he was afraid that, if he tried to be more independent, he might lose Cheryl. So he continued to settle, as he had so often before, for a dull, constricted relationship. There was only one difference, this fifth time around: he had begun to suspect that something was basically wrong.

At first it wasn't clear what had perpetuated this series of compromising relationships. Frank was a relatively attractive and intelligent man who presumably had the skills for developing and maintaining relationships far more rewarding than the ones he had had. Certainly, there was more going on here than a simple case of an exaggerated sense of obligation. What was in this for Frank? From patient and detailed history taking, his therapist learned that Frank had never really lived on his own as an adult. The pattern he described as typical had begun almost immediately after he left high school and had continued until the day he sought professional assistance. He had never learned to cook, keep house, attend to his clothes, or do a myriad of other things that his mother, and then other women, had seen to for him.

Moreover, he had a recurring ulcer condition that would act up from time to time, particularly when he did not take proper care of himself. If he drank, failed to get enough rest, or became overly stressed, his ulcer symptoms would flare up and he would be ill for several days. And, a you might expect, he was not very good at disciplining his diet or other living patterns. During those brief times on his own, his health would deteriorate markedly. In his current relationship, his sleeping habits were worse because Cheryl had to sleep at home.

Finally, he had learned to be a good boy; and he had learned that there were certain expectations in life that you had to live up to. If another took care of you and expected you to stay home, be faithful, and live locked into a tedious relationship, that was what you did—up to a point. In each of his four marriages, Frank had finally broken out. In each marriage, he had resented the mothering, the restriction, the boredom, and—perhaps most of all—his own weakness. When all these things became intolerable, he would slowly and painfully leave the relationship, first through his impotence and then through other forms of polite but deadly withdrawal. Some men and women settle for this kind of infantile and depressing life until they die. Frank was a little bit ahead of these people for he would settle, then rebel, then resettle and rebel. Although he was only dimly aware of it at the time, his coming for assistance marked the beginning of his breaking away from this pattern that was so destructive to him and to the women who played out the other half of his script.

The solution for Frank was a difficult one . . . Frank has had to learn a greater level of self-discipline in controlling his diet, sleep and work habits. He has had to learn self-care skills in order to get by without his exaggerated sense of obligation, to learn to say no when he wants to, and to say yes to his own desires. In short, he has had to fill in the gaps in himself in order to live well alone or to hope for a mature and fulfilling relationship with another.

Case Study Questions

1. Describe the pattern of relationships that Frank had gotten into in his four marriages.
2. How was the relationship he was currently in with Cheryl similar to his past relationships?
3. What did Frank need to do in order to get out of his habitual self-defeating pattern?

SELF-TEST

Multiple Choice

1. Most behavioral psychologists feel that the act of self-control is made possible by manipulating:
   a. only internal variables
   b. only external variables
   c. both internal and external variables
   d. either internal or external variables
2. The three basic factors involved in self-control include all the following *except*:
   a. deliberate choice
   b. elimination of a negatively valued behavior by means of extinction
   c. choosing between two conflicting behaviors

d. the manipulation of stimuli to make one behavior more probable
3. Many psychologists feel that the individual who is truly free is:
   a. in intimate contact with his environment
   b. in intimate contact with himself
   c. an active personal scientist
   d. all of the above
4. The analysis of self-control requires that the description of the problem involve all the following rules *except*:
   a. simplicity
   b. parsimony
   c. specificity
   d. objectivity
5. Record keeping serves all the following functions in self-monitoring behavior *except*:
   a. records provide a convenient pretreatment standard for comparison
   b. records may reveal inaccuracies in descriptions
   c. records tend to make the description more specific
   d. records provide a simplified graphic picture of the behavior
6. Which of the following variables correlate with a particular behavior?
   a. internal stimuli which precede the behavior in question
   b. external stimuli which precede the behavior in question
   c. internal stimuli which follow the behavior in question
   d. all of the above
7. The techniques for experimenting with your own behavior have been categorized into groups of threes involving the manipulation of:
   a. subsequent responses, consequent events, and person variables
   b. consequent events, person variables, and antecedent stimuli
   c. antecedent stimuli, subsequent responses, and consequent events
   d. person variables, subsequent responses, and antecedent stimuli
8. Depending on whether you are trying to increase or decrease a behavior, environmental planning would involve:
   a. avoiding certain stimuli
   b. the manipulation of associations
   c. the manipulation of delays
   d. all of the above
9. Those strategies that effectively delay bad habits typically:
   a. facilitate automatic behavior
   b. prevent impulsive behavior
   c. force us to make unconscious choices
   d. all of the above
10. According to Freud, delay tactics usually prevent which of the following psychic structures from working?
    a. the id
    b. the ego
    c. the superego
    d. the libido
11. Increasing a particular behavior would involve which of the following techniques?
    a. separating the behavior from its environmental cues
    b. limiting the number of stimuli paired with a certain behavior
    c. limiting the number of behaviors paired with a certain stimulus
    d. all of the above
12. Which of the following is not a means of manipulating internal antecedent stimuli?
    a. redirecting attention
    b. organizing
    c. chaining
    d. relabelling
13. The modification of complex behaviors (changing a sequence of mini-behaviors) would involve:
    a. interrupting the chain
    b. lengthening the chain
    c. scrambling the chain
    d. all of the above
14. The rules to follow when shaping a behavior would include all the following *except*:
    a. reinforcing each step in the progression
    b. progressing in small units
    c. being perfectly comfortable with each preceding step
    d. gradual increases or decreases in the behavior that is changed
15. Which reinforcing consequences is the most important in a self-control program?
    a. money
    b. sex
    c. feedback
    d. food
16. Once your self-control program is well under way, which of the following would be most effective in making behaviors permanent?
    a. large rewards immediately following a self-control requirement
    b. large rewards immediately after every other instance of a self-control requirement

    c. small rewards immediately following a self-control requirement
    d. small rewards immediately after the fifth instance of a self-control requirement

17. New Year's resolutions tend to be such notorious failures because they are:
    a. much too specific
    b. much too vague
    c. usually said in jest
    d. situation specific

18. According to most psychologists, punishment is much less effective than reward as a self-control technique because:
    a. punishment tends to lose its potency
    b. punishment tends to generate "bad" feelings
    c. punishment only indicates "wrong" behaviors
    d. all of the above

19. Which of the following would best exemplify negative self-punishment?
    a. giving a dollar to charity when you fail to meet your self-control requirements
    b. standing in a cold shower when you fail to meet your self-control requirements
    c. indulging yourself for not meeting your self-control requirements
    d. buying only one ice cream soda for not meeting your self-control requirements

20. The "three don'ts" of a self-control program contain all the following *except*:
    a. don't give up
    b. don't reinforce every successful step
    c. don't expect either immediate results or continuous results
    d. don't create unrealistic goals or requirements

True-False

1. In Homer's epic poem, *The Odyssey*, the hero, Odysseus, has himself tied to the ship's mast as an act of self-control.
2. According to the definition of self-control, a person who successfully gave up smoking five years ago is not exercising self-control.
3. To many psychologists, the amount of freedom we have is dependent on our ability to manipulate the factors controlling our behavior.
4. The initial phase of a functional analysis involves looking for variables that seem to correlate with the behavior in question.
5. If an unwanted behavior is being triggered by an antecedent stimulus, it is best to confront that stimulus as often as possible so that extinction will occur.
6. The individual engaged in a self-control program is advised not to tackle more than one problem behavior at a time.
7. The class of stimuli known as "setting events" are usually too subtle to be modified.
8. Building in delays tends to force us to make conscious choices.
9. Removal of delays can serve to increase a particular behavior.
10. Stimulus-narrowing involves engaging in a behavior in one specific situation.
11. Research has shown that attending to the hazardous aspects of cigarette smoking has the effect of increasing cigarette smoking.
12. Although the behavior of smoking may seem to be a long chain of responses, it is actually a rather elementary response.
13. One rule for shaping a particular behavior is to proceed in a gradual manner without expecting too much too soon.
14. Perhaps the most important reinforcing consequence in a self-control program is to keep yourself informed as to how you are doing.
15. The effects of punishment seem to be a function of its ability to teach new behaviors.

Completion

1. According to most behaviorists, the act of self-control is made possible by manipulating the _____ or _____ variables that influence the behavior in question.
2. When conducting a self-analysis, a problem should be described according to the three rules of simplicity, _____, and _____.
3. If in your functional analysis you discover that a particular variable is maintaining a particular behavior, then by definition that variable is a _____.
4. A pretreatment standard of comparison is called a _____.
5. The first step in the functional analysis of a problem behavior is to look for the internal and external stimuli that _____ the behavior.
6. Conditioned stimuli capable of acting as triggers of behavior are called _____ _____.
7. The process of arranging the stimuli in your environment so that they trigger the desired behaviors, and not the undesirable behaviors, is referred to as _____ _____.

6/SELF-CONTROL: HOW TO CHANGE IT

8. For the most part, the practice in the Middle Ages of outfitting a wife with a chastity belt succeeded in creating _____.
9. Stimulus-narrowing has been defined as an enforced program of _____ learning.
10. The process of redirecting attention involves the manipulation of _____ antecedent stimuli.
11. A _____ behavior is actually a sequence of mini-behaviors, each of which constitutes the trigger for the next.
12. The gradual creation of a target behavior that starts with a current behavior and progresses toward the target in small, manageable steps is referred to as _____.
13. The class of stimuli, defined by their effects, that are capable of controlling behavior whether or not we manipulate them are called _____.
14. Perhaps the most important positive consequence you can provide for yourself in a self-control program is _____.
15. The _____ _____ states that high frequency behaviors can modify low frequency behaviors if the performance of the high frequency behaviors is made contingent upon the occurrence of the low frequency behaviors.

Essay Questions

1. What is the strict behavioral definition of self-control? Why is the person who successfully gave up smoking five years ago and still refrains from smoking not exercising self-control? (pp. 141–142)
2. Discuss the function of "environmental planning" in the modification of both desirable and undesirable behaviors. (pp. 148–150)
3. Define the term "chaining" and provide at least three examples of it. How can the knowledge of a chained behavior aid in the increase and decrease of that behavior? (pp. 154–155)
4. Discuss how "shaping" can achieve the behaviors of consuming fewer calories and of jogging longer distances. Include in your answer the reasons for following the three important rules of shaping. (p. 156)
5. Providing yourself with feedback is an important reinforcing consequence in a self-control program. What are some possible sources of this feedback? Which is the most important and why (hint: reactive)? (pp. 157–158)

SELF-TEST ANSWERS

Multiple Choice
1. d (p. 142)
2. b (p. 142)
3. d (p. 143)
4. b (pp. 143–144)
5. d (p. 146)
6. d (p. 147)
7. c (p. 147)
8. d (p. 148)
9. b (p. 149)
10. a (p. 149)
11. c (p. 150)
12. c (pp. 151–152)
13. d (pp. 154–155)
14. a (p. 156)
15. c (p. 157)
16. d (p. 158)
17. b (p. 159)
18. d (p. 161)
19. b (p. 161)
20. b (pp. 161–162)

True-False
1. true (p. 142)
2. true (p. 142)
3. true (p. 143)
4. true (pp. 146–147)
5. false (p. 147)
6. true (p. 147)
7. false (p. 148)
8. true (p. 148)
9. true (p. 148)
10. true (p. 149)
11. true (pp. 151–152)
12. false (p. 154)
13. true (p. 156)
14. true (p. 157)
15. false (p. 161)

Completion
1. internal, external (p. 142)
2. objectivity, specificity (p. 143)
3. reinforcer (p. 144)
4. baseline (p. 146)
5. precede (p. 147)
6. setting events (or cues) (p. 148)
7. environmental planning (p. 148)
8. delays (p. 148)
9. discrimination (p. 149)
10. internal (p. 152)
11. chained (p. 154)
12. shaping (p. 156)
13. reinforcers (p. 157)
14. feedback (p. 157)
15. Premack Principle (p. 159)

7
Three Self-Control Problems: Diet and Exercise, Study Habits, and Anxiety

CHAPTER OUTLINE

DIET AND EXERCISE
Analyzing Your Eating Habits
   What exactly do you eat?
      External antecedents
      Internal antecedents
      Eating behavior: The frenetic fork
Changing Your Eating Behavior
   Stimulus-narrowing and redirecting attention
   Delaying and chaining
   Mental image
Changing Your Exercise Pattern
STUDY HABITS
Analyzing Your Study Behavior
   How much time do you spend studying?
   How is the time distributed?
   When do you study?
   Where do you study?
   How well do you concentrate?
   What is your attitude?
   What is your method of study?
Managing Your Study Time
   Environmental planning
   Scheduling
   Getting full use of your study time: the SQ3R method
ANXIETY
Analyzing Your Anxiety
Managing Anxiety
   Environmental planning
   Relabeling and self-talk
   Desensitization
Stress and Physical Exercise

READING

Don't Sell Habit-Breakers Short

STANLEY SCHACHTER

It is generally accepted that smoking and overeating are extraordinarily difficult conditions to correct. Psychiatrist Albert Stunkard has concluded that "most obese people will not stay in treatment of obesity. Of those who stay in treatment, most will not lose weight, and of those who do lose weight, most will regain it."

This depressing overview is based on Stunkard's survey of numerous studies of the treatment of obesity, as well as on his own analysis of the weight histories of 100 obese patients of the Nutrition Clinic of New York Hospital. After two years, only two people had managed to maintain a weight loss of 20 pounds. This state of affairs appears still to be the case 20 years after Stunkard's review. Those who have reviewed the literature on the treatment of cigarette smoking report similarly pessimistic results. Howard Leventhal, a psychologist, and Paul Cleary, a sociologist, have summarized the situation in smoking therapy: "That so many people who are motivated to seek therapy drop out of treatment, and that so many people eventually return to the habit after initially curtailing their smoking, underscores the scope of the task that one is faced with in dealing with the smoking problem."

Psychologists William Hunt and Joseph Matarazzo draw the same somber conclusions, and on the basis of an analysis of 87 studies, they note the startling resemblance of studies of smoking to studies of heroin addiction and alcoholism. In all three conditions, roughly 65 percent of the successfully treated patients relapse within three months after concluding therapy; within one year, 80 percent of the former patients have become recidivists.

Obviously, there is much basis for pessimism, and there is probably overwhelming professional consensus that addictive-appetitive behavior is markedly resistant to long-term modification. Yet despite this general consensus, something is curiously awry. Though therapists may find smoking notoriously difficult to cure, surveys show that literally millions of Americans have dropped the habit. The cachet of scientifically collected evidence seems unnecessary; virtually everyone knows people who have quit smoking.

Evidence exists that even narcotic addiction may not be the intractable condition that it has long been considered. In a study of returned Vietnam veteran drug-users, Lee Robins noted "a surprisingly high remission rate for heroin addiction" without benefit of continuing treatment

For both nicotine and heroin addiction, then, there are indications that a successful cure may be far more common than heretofore thought. Though one can devise more exotic hypotheses, explanations for the discrepancy between professional opinion and apparent fact may be embarrassingly simple. First, people who cure themselves do not go to therapists. Our view of the intractability of the addictive states may have been molded largely by a group of people who, unable or unwilling to help themselves, go to therapists for help, thereby becoming the only easily available subjects for studies of recidivism and addiction.

Second, the inferences drawn from studies of therapeutic effectiveness are based on single attempts to cure some addictive state. In fact, people try to quit repeatedly, and it may be that success rates with multiple attempts are greater than with single attempts, with or without the benefit of professional help.

Though I know of no related evidence on obesity, common sense suggests that the same interpretive problems may well hold for this conditions. People who cure themselves without help do not become part of the data, and as a result, obesity's reputation for intractability may also have been grossly exaggerated.

To investigate the possible discrepancy between professional opinion and apparent fact, I interviewed 161 people in 1979-80 for full descriptions of their smoking and weight histories. I sought to interview the entire membership of two carefully selected groups, rather than a randomly selected population. Given the rationale for the study, it seemed crucial to minimize the effects of people's varying willingness to be interviewed. It seemed possible that those who had tried and failed to lose weight or quit smoking might be less willing to talk about their experiences, or might be the sort of people who don't care for interviews.

The first group I studied was the Psychology Department of Columbia University, which consisted of 84 people, 83 of whom agreed to be interviewed. There were 28 faculty members, 43 graduate students and postdoctoral fellows, and 12 secretaries and technicians. There were 46 men and 37 women, ranging in age from 21 to 64.

The second group was a substantial portion of the entrepreneurial and working population of Amagansett, New York, a small town in eastern Long Island, where I have spent my summers for 20 years. Amagansett is a seaside resort community with a permanent population estimated by the local power company to be about 1,500, and an additional summer population estimated by the town historian to be between 1,500 and 2,000.

I gathered my samples from two areas in the town. In midtown Amagansett, I interviewed people working in shops and enterprises on a 750-foot stretch of the busiest portion of the main street. I wanted my sample to consist largely of longtime year-round residents of the area, so I attempted to interview the people working in all of those enterprises that remained open throughout the year and that had been in business for at least a year. Of the 48 people who worked in the 14 enterprises that satisfied the criteria, 47 agreed to be interviewed during the late spring of 1980.

Success Rate for Smokers Who Tried to Quit

	Number who tried to quit smoking	Percent who succeeded
Amagansett	39	61.5
Columbia	38	65.8
Total	77	63.6

An additional group of subjects came from two "open all year" enterprises on the outskirts of town: the 26 employees of a supermarket and the five employees of an automobile agency. All told, 78 of a possible 79 people in this small-town sample agreed to be interviewed. There were 44 men and 34 women, ranging from 16 to 79 years old.

These groups, then, were quite different. The Columbia group was largely academic, completely urban, and ethnically diverse, with large numbers of Jews and Hispanics as well as a considerable sprinkling of "Americans" from all over the country. The Amagansett group was largely entrepreneurial and blue-collar, mostly small-town born and bred. To the extent that their smoking and weight histories were similar or different, we can begin to make guesses about whether one can generalize the findings.

After obtaining each subject's estimates of his weight and height, I asked whether he had ever been a smoker. If so, the interview continued. "Now I'd like to go from the time of your first cigarette to the present. As well as you're able, I'd like you to tell me your smoking history. From the time of your first serious cigarette to now, I'd like to know roughly how much you smoked per day and what brand. If at any point along the way you stopped smoking or cut down, I'd like to know about that." During the subject's narrative, I probed constantly to make sure that I was obtaining a complete history of his smoking habits, including detailed descriptions of any attempts to quit. Once the smoking history was completed, I used the same approach to learn the individual's lifetime weight history.

In general, there were no problems in getting my subjects to talk about these matters; in fact, most people seemed eager to talk about their struggles with cigarettes and diets. The only real problem was that the memories of older people tended to be somewhat vague. Otherwise, people were reasonably confident in their reports of how much they smoked and weighed at various ages.

The findings strongly supported my suspicions: The rates of successful self-cure of cigarette smoking and of obesity are considerably higher than any yet reported in the literature on curing these problems through various therapy programs.

There were 94 people in the two populations with histories of cigarette smoking. Of these, 77 had at some time attempted to quit. Overall 63.6 percent of those who attempted to quit smoking had succeeded at the time of their interview. (See box on page 72.) Although a few of them admitted to taking an occasional puff at a party or some such occasion, they nonetheless described themselves as successful quitters, and the large majority were complete abstainers. On the average, the successful quitters had cut out smoking for 7.4 years. Some 87.8 percent of these quitters had been nonsmokers for a year or more and 98 percent for three or more months.

Comparing the figures with the roughly 10 percent to 25 percent of the therapeutic population who remain quitters one year after therapy, it is clear that in both populations those who attempted to quit on their own were at least two to three times more successful than were people in other studies who went for professional help. The fact that the successful quitting rate is similar in two very different populations—one urban and academic, the other small-town and largely entrepreneurial and working-class—indicates that a high rate of successful quitting is not a characteristic that belongs to one particular kind of group.

As for losing weight, of the 161 people in these two groups, 46 (27 men and 19 women) had a history of obesity—meaning that currently or in the past, they were 15 percent or more overweight as calculated from the table of average weight published by the Society of Actuaries. Forty of the 46 had actively tried to lose weight, and six (all of them men) insisted that they didn't give a damn and had never dieted or exercised in order to lose weight.

As the box below shows, 62.5 percent of those who attempted to lose weight can be considered successful cures, according to the following criteria:
1. They had at some time in their lives been obese.
2. Their present weight was a least 10 percent less than it had been immediately before undertaking their weight-loss regimen.
3. They were no longer fat—that is, they were now less than 10 percent overweight.

Success Rate for Obese People Who Tried to Lose Weight

	Number who tried to lose weight	Percent who succeeded
Columbia	18	72.0
Amagansett	22	54.4
Total	40	62.5

These are very tough criteria. Successful cures were really complete cures. They had all lost substantial—in some cases huge—amounts of weight. From their weight histories, it is calculated that they had lost an average of 34.7 pounds and roughly maintained this weight loss for an average of 11.2 years.

The Columbia Psychology Department was somewhat more successful than the Amagansett group, but the success rates of both groups were so much greater than anything in the therapeutic literature that it seems pointless to dwell on possible reasons for the relatively trivial differences between these urban and small-town populations.

Compare the weight loss in the two populations with the results of a 1979 review of 10 major studies employing behavior-modification techniques, by far the most effective of all nonsurgical treatments for weight loss. In a one-year follow-up of patients in these studies, the average weight loss was 10.9 pounds. The three studies that had two-year or longer follow-up periods reported weight loss averaging 10.4 pounds. By contrast, formerly obese men in the Amagansett and the Columbia samples (excluding, of course, the six indifferent obese men) had kept off an average of 26.8 pounds in the mean 9.7 years since starting their weight-loss procedures. The women reported having kept off an average of 24.8 pounds in 7.5 years. It seems clear that the obese members of these populations were markedly better able to lose and to keep off weight than were the obese patients in the studies that examined therapeutic effectiveness.

The differences in success rates could conceivably be explained by the fact that the patients in the therapeutic studies tended to be heavier than the obese of Amagansett or the Columbia Psychology Department. Therefore, I did a separate analysis of the heaviest members of these two groups—those who were more than 30 percent overweight. Of this group, 63.6 percent were classified as successful cures. They had lost an average of 46.7 pounds and had been within a few pounds of their present weight for an average of 8.6 years.

It is the case, then, that in nontherapeutic populations the rates of successful self-cure of cigarette smoking and of obesity are considerably higher than anything reported in the therapeutic literature—a conclusion based on a study of virtually everyone in two quite different groups. The fact that the rates of self-cure are so similar in the two groups is evidence that these findings are generalizable beyond any single demographic group.

Obviously, these rates of cure are at best gross estimates of national trends. For cigarette smoking, at least, they are probably somewhat high. In both groups, the well educated are overrepresented, laborers underrepresented, and farmers not represented at all. Since it is known that for smoking, "quit rates" tend to be relatively high for the educated and low for the working classes, it seems likely that the rate of 63.6 percent successful quitters in this study is on the high side.

Evidence for this can be found in the results of a recent questionnaire study of a national probability sample of approximatley 12,000 people, conducted by the Public Health Service. Of this group, 54 percent were present or former cigarette smokers. Some 74.8 percent of them had actively tried to quit smoking, and of those who tried, 50.4 percent had succeeded—a figure lower than that obtained in the Amagansett and Columbia populations but still markedly higher than almost anything in the therapeutic literature. In the Public Health study, those who quit had been off cigarettes for an average, roughly estimated, of seven years, a figure closely in line with the 7.4 years of the Amagansett and Columbia populations.

It appears that the generally accepted professional and public impression that nicotine addiction and obesity are almost hopelessly difficult conditions to correct is flatly wrong. People can and do cure themselves of smoking and obesity. They do so in large numbers and for long periods of time, and in many cases, apparently, they're able to do so permanently.

The reputation for intractability that these disorders possess is undoubtedly the product of the huge number of studies that have demonstrated the ineffectiveness of therapy. How can one explain the fact that the rates of therapeutic success are generally so pitiable when compared to the rates of self-cure in a nonself-selected populations? Certainly the most obvious explanation must be in terms of self-selection. Only those people who are unwilling or unable to help themselves go to others; those people who cure themselves do not go to therapists.

Though this was my original hypothesis, I now suspect that there is considerably more involved than one more embarrassing demonstration that grossly distorted samples lead to grossly distorted conclusions. The inferences that have been drawn from studies of therapeutic effectiveness are curiously misleading. They correctly describe the results of a *single* attempt to quit smoking or lose weight or what have you, but from such results nothing should be inferred about the probable success of a *lifetime* of effort to quit smoking or lose weight. Yet these are precisely the inferences that have been drawn again and again. Because literally hundreds of studies of single attempts to cure some addictive disorder have reported pathetic rates of success, it has been assumed that addictive behavior is an unyielding, almost hopeless disorder.

The logical difficulties involved in such a conclusion become evident when one considers the information gathered in the retrospective self-reports of the Amagansett and Columbia groups. Each of these statements described a lifetime of effort to control weight or to stop smoking—a lifetime that may have involved one or many attempts to quit.

If it is assumed that the proportion of successful quitters cumulatively increases with successive attempts, it becomes clear why generalizations based on the results of single therapeutic attempts to cure are probably unwarranted. For example, let us assume that for any single attempt to quit, 10 percent of those who try succeed permanently—a figure in line with cure rates reported in most therapeutic studies. Let us further assume that at some later time all of those who failed try again. Again, 10 percent succeed. Cumulatively, then 19 percent of those who have tried once or twice will have succeeded. A third attempt will have succeeded. A third attempt to quit, again assuming a 10 percent success rate, would yield a cumulative rate of 27 percent. And so on. This general line of reasoning makes it seem highly likely that retrospective interviews with people who have at some time sought help will yield higher cure rates than those reported in studies of one-shot therapeutic intervention.

Unfortunately, there were too few people in the Amagansett and Columbia populations to permit any firm conclusions, but for these few subjects, the data indicate that this is indeed the case. There were 14 people who at some time in their lives had sought help in their attempts to lose weight or quit smoking, two for smoking and 12 for obesity. Their "helpers" included psychotherapists, physicians, hypnotists, and groups such as Weight Watchers. Six of these 14 people—42.9 percent—were categorized as successful cures—a rate considerably greater than almost anything reported in the therapeutic literature. To me, at least, this shows that the reputation of these conditions for hopeless intractability may, in part, be an unfortunate byproduct of the fact that almost all tests of the matter had involved evaluation of a single attempt to quit.

Encouraging though these cure rates are, they still do not match the rates for those in the Amagansett-Columbia populations who had never sought help. Of these, 69.2 percent of the 26 fat people were classified as cured, and 65.3 percent of the 75 smokers were regarded as successful quitters. Obviously, there are still far too few cases to permit solidly based conclusions, but the fact that the cure rates for those who have never had help are higher than for those who have does suggest that there is a residual—that there remain differences still to be explained.

If, in future research, such differences persist, it seems to me that the explanation must lie either in the perversity of those who seek help, or in the perversity of the therapeutic process—an intriguing guess, certainly, for if correct it opens up the exciting possibility that clinical psychology and psychiatry are even now as capable of inadvertent mischief as are the proven medical specialities.

Reading Questions

1. Indicate the "professional" findings concerning smoking cessation and weight reduction.
2. Describe Schachter's findings concerning smoking cessation and weight reductions.
3. Comment on what Schachter concludes could be the reasons for the differences between his findings and those of the "professionals."

RESEARCH STUDY

Investigators: Mark Dean, Richard Malott, and Barbara Fulton.
Source, date: "The Effects of Self-Management and Training on Academic Performance," *Teaching of Psychology*, 1983, *10*, 78–81.
Location: Western Michigan University.
Subjects: 15 college students enrolled in undergraduate psychology courses.
Materials: Self-management and calendar, undergraduate psychology courses.

The purpose of the study was to determine if academic performance could be improved through the development of improved study skills provided by training in self-management techniques. In particular, two self-management techniques were targeted for training: self-monitoring and self-recording of study time and self-reinforcement.

In a series of experiments, students enrolled in undergraduate psychology courses received self-management training on a one-on-one basis for six sessions with the researchers. During these sessions, the students were taught to monitor and record their study behavior, organize their time, plan their environments for studying, and arrange for reinforcements for their studying.

The effectiveness of the training was determined by comparing the students' academic performance and study time before the training with that during and after the training. The data indicated a significant increase in study time and an improvement in grades by an average of one letter grade. The researchers concluded that self-management training was an effective method for improving academic performance.

Research Study Questions

1. What did the researchers hope to determine in their study of the effects of self-management training on academic performance?
2. What were the students taught in their self-management training?
3. What did the researchers find from this study on the effects of self-management training on academic performance?

CASE STUDY

The Effects of a Self-Control Weight Loss Program on an Obese Woman

JOHN E. MARTIN AND DAVID A. SACHS

Ann was an intelligent, active, 55 year-old housewife. She had sustained a major heart attack (minimal damage) 3 years before, and had been warned by three physicians during the past year that she was in danger of another due to her overweight condition. Numerous attempts had been made to get her to lose weight, all unsuccessful. She was 5 ft. 5 in. tall and, at the initiation of the study, weighed 180 lbs. She reported that her weight ranged around 180 lbs. for at least 4 years before the initiation of the study, with a maximum weight during this 4-year period reported to be 186 lbs.

Procedure

After having cleared the weight loss program with her physician, she and one of us met for the first of two 1-hour sessions.

In *Session One* two main points were discussed. The first point stressed eating as an immediately reinforcing activity (good taste, full stomach), whereas the punishment for overeating is delayed (health, appearance, and subsequent negative emotional state). The second point had to do with eating behavior often being unrelated to hunger states, a "habit" due to its association with certain or many stimulus situations (i.e., watching television and eating or reading and eating). The following nine recommendations were made:

1. After each meal or snack, write down what you ate and how much, the time of day, and what you were doing and how you felt just before eating.
2. Weigh yourself every morning, record and chart the weight.
3. Always eat sitting down, in one or two designated places.
4. Always put food on a plate or in a dish and use the proper utensils.
5. Never watch television, read a book, listen to the radio etc. when your are eating.
6. Avoid walking through or working in the kitchen as much as possible.
7. Eat between meal snacks only at specified times, and in the designated place.
8. When tempted to eat, other than at meal times, write down all the reasons why you should not eat (health, appearance etc.) or use any other means you find effective in keeping you from eating (e.g., viewing pictures of a fat you).
9. Reward yourself for resisting food, and for weight loss—both overtly (watch your favorite T.V. program, read in your favorite book etc.) and covertly (congratulate yourself). Be sure to set up with your husband or other 3rd party a major reward for losing and keeping off the amount of weight you originally wanted to lose (i.e., golf weekend, new wardrobe, vacation somewhere).

Ann was told that the above procedures would help bring compulsive eating under appropriate stimulus control, and that for best results she should start with (1) and (2) and not add (3) until (1) and (2) were being followed without difficulty. She was told not to add (4) until (3) was being successfully followed, and so on. She was also told that weight loss should not exceed 2 lbs. per week, for health reasons. It was explained that the program was aimed at changing eating habits rather than food intake and that, initially, weight loss was not the important factor for overall success.

At the completion of Session One, Ann signed a contract* pledging to follow the program, and was given copies of the procedures and the contract to post in a prominent place.

During Session One, Ann decided that she wanted to lose 25 lbs. A contract was set up with her husband, who promised her a new wardrobe and a golf weekend if 25 lbs. were lost and kept off.

Ann was instructed to contact one of us if any difficulties arose, or if she had any pertinent questions

---

*I do hereby pledge to stick to the rules and suggestions of the weight loss program. I am serious enough about losing weight to use these techniques to actually lose weight, and keep it off. I understand that I will be changing many well-learned habits and it will not be quick or easy.

Throughout the study one of us made phone contact twice weekly.

After approximately 1 1/2 weeks, *Session Two* was conducted. The criterion for the occurrence of the second session was the successful application of 1–9. Five more recommendations were made during this session, and a copy given to the subject for posting:

10. Chew food slowly and carefully, with great care and attention to taste and texture.
11. Swallow food completely before putting next amount of food on your fork—try to have at least a 5-sec. interval between bites.
12. Practice taking short breaks of not eating during meals (i.e., getting up from the table and walking around, doing something else, or just sitting).
13. Leave a bite or two of food on your plate.
14. Whenever possible eat low-calorie foods and beverages.

Ann was instructed to add 10–14 one at a time, in order, only after the previous suggestion was comfortably a part of her behavioral repertoire. It was explained that eating is a complex chain of behaviors which has to be altered gradually and with no adversive side-effects. Therefore, it was suggested that procedure 10–12 should be started only at or near the end of the meal when she was not as hungry.

Results

Ann's weight was reduced a total of 15 lbs. in 31 days. On the 31st day, she reported that she felt more physically and mentally healthy and was able to "do more and more each day." She also reported that she was playing much more golf, and had greatly diminished her alcohol consumption.

Without permission, Ann did not eat on the 30th and 31st day in her desire to obtain a 15 lb. loss. She celebrated reaching this goal with approximately 5 oz. of alcohol. That evening, she used a mild depressant to induce sleep. According to her physician, these immediate preceding events, in combination with low blood sugar, required a brief period of hospitalization. There was a small observed change in her E.K.G. over the previous month, and there were some evidences, according to her physician, of physical and mental fatigue. Recovery was "complete" in 7 days, at which time Ann returned home. She voluntarily terminated the formal program after her hospitalization. However, a follow-up 14 months later indicated that her weight was 162 lbs.

References

Bandura, A. (1969) *Principles of Behavior Modification*, Holt, Rinehart & Winston, New York.

Bruch, H. (1957) *The Importance of Overweight*, Norton, New York.

Cautela, J. R. (1969) Behavior therapy and self-control: Techniques and implications, *Behavior Therapy: Appraisal and Status* (Edited by Franks, C.), McGraw-Hill, New York.

Erickson, M. A. (1960) The utilization of patient behavior in the hypnotherapy of obesity: Three case reports, *Am. J. clin. Hyph.*, **3**, 112-116.

Ferster, C. D., Nurnberger, J. L., and Levitt, E. G. (1962) The control of eating, *J. Math.* **1**. 87-109.

Harmon, A. R., Purkonen, R. A., and Rasmussen, L. P. (1958) Obesity: A physical and emotional problem, *Nursing Outlook*, **6**, 452-456.

Harris, M. B. (1969) Self-directed program for weight control: A pilot study, *J. abnorm. Psych.*, **74**, 263-270.

Homme, L. E. (1965) Perspectives in psychology: **XXIV**, control of coverants, the operants of the mind, *Psychol. Rec.* **15**, 501-511.

Jeffrey, D., Christenson, E., and Pappas, J. (1972) *A case study report of a behavioral modification weight reduction group: Treatment and follow-up*. Paper read before Rocky Mountain Psychological Association, May 12.

Mann, R. A. (1971) *The use of contingency contracting to control obesity in adult subjects*. Paper presented at the Western Psychological Association, San Francisco, California, April.

Schachter, S. (1967) *Obesity as a cognitive error*. Speech presented at Stanford Medical School, February 14.

Silverstone, J. T. and Soloman, T. (1965) The long-term management of obesity in general practice, *Br. J. Clin. Prac.* **19**, 395-398.

Stollak, G. E. (1966) *Weight loss obtained under various experimental procedures*. Paper presented at the meeting of the Midwestern Psychological Association, Chicago, May.

Stuart, R. B. (1967) Behavioral control of overeating, *Behav. Res. & Therapy*, **5**, 357-365.

Stuart, R. B. (1971) A three dimensional program for the treatment of obesity, *Behav. Res. & Therapy*, **9**, 177-186.

Stuart, R. B. and Davis, B. (1972) *Slim Chance in a Fat World: Behavioral Control of Obesity*, Research Press, Champaign, Ill.

Stunkard, A. J. (1958) The management of obesity, *N. Y. State J. Med.* **58**, 79-87.

Stunkard, A. J. and Koch, C. (1964) The interpretation of gastric motility. I. Apparent bias in the reports of hunger of obese persons, *Archs Gen. Psychiat.* **11**, 74-82.

Thorpe, J. G., Schmidt, E., Brown, P. T., and Castell, D. (1964) Aversion relief therapy: A new method for general application, *Behav. Res. & Therapy*, **2**, 71-82.

Wolpe, J. (1958) *Psychotherapy by Reciprocal Inhibition*, Stanford University Press, Stanford.

Young, C. M., Moore, N. S., Berresford, K., Einset, B. McK., and Waldner, B. G. (1955) The problem of the obese patient, *J. Am. Diet. Assoc.*, **31**, 1111-1115.

Case Study Questions

1. Overeating is said to have both positive and negative consequences. How are these consequences related to the treatment of Ann's problem?
2. What are some of the procedures that can be followed in order to bring compulsive eating under approximate stimulus control? Why is this a necessary part of the treatment?
3. Eating is a complex chain of behaviors rather than a discrete act. How can this knowledge aid in the treatment of obesity?

SELF-TEST

Multiple Choice

1. The three most common self-control problems included all the following *except*:
   a. anxiety
   b. diet and exercise
   c. study habits
   d. alcoholism
2. Which of the following statements best describes the overweight person?
   a. He tends to regulate his eating behavior according to some internal clock.
   b. He tends to regulate his eating behavior according to some external clock.
   c. He does not seem to be able to regulate his eating behavior.
   d. He regulates his eating behavior in the same way as nonoverweight persons.
3. An important part of any weight control program is a complete record of relevant antecedent stimuli. This record should include all the following *except*:
   a. the specific quantity of food consumed at each meal
   b. the exact times you engage in eating behaviors
   c. those places where your eat
   d. all distractions present at each eating occasion
4. The problem of having several stimulus events functioning as triggers for eating behavior can be most effectively dealt with by instituting:
   a. a specific operant shaping program
   b. a backward chaining program
   c. a systematic desensitization program
   d. a stimulus-narrowing program
5. The ultimate in eating control is to make a rule that states:
   a. chew each bite at least thirty-two times
   b. leave at least one bite of food on your plate when you finish eating
   c. delay each bit by a three-minute period of time
   d. eat your food with a "baby" fork
6. One example of the use of antecedents in controlling one's behavior is:
   a. avoiding all thoughts of food
   b. a negative mental image followed by a positive mental image
   c. exercising before eating meals
   d. none of the above
7. Permanent weight loss can be achieved through the creation of:
   a. strict short-term diet programs
   b. cognitive techniques
   c. new habits
   d. all of the above
8. Which of the following is generally accepted as the more efficient means of information retention and subsequent recall?
   a. lexical synthesis
   b. massed practice
   c. distributed practice
   d. rapid practice
9. To manipulate the antecedents for studying and inattention, environmental planning should include:
   a. tuning out distractions rather than avoiding them
   b. selecting no more than three study locations
   c. admitting only study-related behaviors in a study location
   d. all of the above
10. A reasonable solution to the study problem of procrastination is the technique of:
    a. parataxic distribution

b. functional recitation
   c. cognitive and behavioral organization
   d. higher order scheduling
11. In order for a study schedule to be optimally effective, it should include:
    a. those times allotted for set activities, such as meals, class time, and so on
    b. those times allotted for reinforcements and breaks
    c. those times allotted for the study of specific topics
    d. all of the above
12. The SQ3R study method involves which of the following tasks?
    a. survey, question, read, recapitulate, review
    b. survey, question, read, recapitulate, recite
    c. survey, question, read, re-read, review
    d. survey, question, read, recite, review
13. In the SQR3 study method, at what point should you close your book, formulate questions, and try to answer the questions from memory?
    a. after you have finished reading the entire chapter
    b. after you have finished reading each subheading
    c. after you have finished reading at least two subheadings
    d. none of the above
14. The question phase of the SQ3R study method generally involves formulating:
    a. no more than seven questions per chapter
    b. as many questions per chapter as possible
    c. as many questions per chapter as there are headings and subheadings
    d. at least three questions for each subheading
15. Sigmund Freud theorized that unrealistic anxiety is due to:
    a. unconscious aggressive impulses
    b. repressed desires
    c. regressive ego functioning
    d. all of the above
16. Regardless of its etiology, a strong anxiety reaction has which of the following components:
    a. behavioral, emotional, cognitive
    b. physiological, behavioral, emotional
    c. cognitive, physiological, behavioral
    d. emotional, cognitive, physiological
17. The cognitive process of anxiety-producing self-talk can be effectively reversed by which characteristic:
    a. optimism
    b. pessimism
    c. realism
    d. negativism
18. According to psychologist Joseph Wolpe, desensitization is based on the principal of:
    a. breaking the anxiety-response chain
    b. providing an alternative response to anxiety
    c. providing a coping response to anxiety
    d. utilizing an incompatible response as an inhibition of anxiety
19. The individual in a relaxed state who confronts a graded series of anxiety-provoking cues through imaginal presentation is:
    a. attempting to reduce anxiety by *in vivo* desensitization
    b. attempting to reduce anxiety by covert self-talk
    c. attempting to reduce anxiety by armchair desensitization
    d. attempting to reduce anxiety by covert modeling
20. *In vivo* desensitization depends upon the effectiveness of a cue word to produce almost immediate substantial relaxation. This cue word generally gains its effectiveness through:
    a. operant conditioning processes
    b. instrumental conditioning processes
    c. respondent conditioning processes
    d. backward conditioning processes

True-False

1. According to a 1984 market research firm, only 10 percent of women and 5 percent of men were on diets.
2. Recent research has established that overweight people tend to be rapid and intense eaters.
3. Typically, the eating chain is much longer than is the smoking chain.
4. Antecedents usually involve a negative and a positive mental image.
5. Constant dieting may make a mild weight problem become more serious.
6. It is a generally accepted fact that studying for five hours a day practically guarantees academic success.
7. A number of psychologists have pointed out that the textbook reading methods used by most students are far too passive.
8. One limitation of the SQ3R method is that it is designed for textbooks with headings and summaries.
9. According to behavioral theory, unrealistic anxieties are the result of operant conditioning.
10. Generally speaking, moderate levels of anxiety are often normal but are always unhealthy.

11. It has been frequently demonstrated that anxiety tends to enhance problem-solving abilities.
12. Many of the internal triggers of anxiety are composed of negative self-talk and irrational beliefs.
13. According to Joseph Wolpe, a response that is incompatible with anxiety can weaken the bond between anxiety-provoking stimuli and the anxiety.
14. The graded series of anxiety-provoking cues used in desensitization is called the "anxiety list."
15. The success of *in vivo* desensitization depends upon conditioning yourself to associate some cue word with the state of deep muscle relaxation.

Completion

1. When initiating a weight reduction program, photographing yourself functions as visual _____.
2. In an exercise program, the most indispensable reward is _____.
3. Factors that aid in permanent weight loss are _____, good nutrition, and exercise.
4. One can use _____ and _____ to break up or stretch out the eating chain.
5. _____ is the input, processing, and storage of information that can be retrieved at some later time.
6. The type of learning where big chunks of material are studied after long periods of no studying is called _____ _____.
7. Perhaps the deadliest enemy of studying is _____.
8. When adding a system of daily rewards to your study schedule, you should mind the _____ principle.
9. A number of psychologists have noted that the reading method of most students is far too _____.
10. Anxiety depends not only on "person variables" but also on the _____ stimulus in question.
11. The temporary relief gained from retreating from an anxiety-provoking situation constitutes _____ reinforcement.
12. Desensitization is a technique used to reduce _____.
13. Wolpe used deep muscular relaxation as the _____ response for weakening the associations between anxiety and the stimuli that produced anxiety.
14. In a desensitization procedure, a graded series of anxiety-provoking cues serves as a _____ _____.
15. The success of *in vivo* desensitization depends upon conditioning yourself to associate some _____ word with the state of deep muscle relaxation.

Essay Questions

1. Discuss some of the reasons that behavior change should proceed in a gradual manner rather than immediately or abruptly. What are the disadvantages of proceeding abruptly? (p. 181)
2. Discuss the steps involved in the SQ3R study method. (pp. 186–188)
3. Describe the three components of a strong anxiety reaction. How do these components indicate that a person is "getting better" at dealing with anxiety? (p. 189)
4. Discuss the steps involved in analyzing an anxiety reaction and its subsequent management. (pp. 190–194)
5. Discuss the similarities and differences between the counterconditioning methods of armchair desensitization and *in vivo* desensitization. (pp. 194–198)

SELF-TEST ANSWERS

Multiple Choice

1. d (p. 171)
2. b (p. 174)
3. a (pp. 174–176)
4. d (p. 178)
5. b (p. 179)
6. b (p. 180)
7. c (p. 181)
8. c (p. 182)
9. c (pp. 183–184)
10. c (p. 185)
11. d (pp. 185–186)
12. d (p. 187)
13. b (p. 187)
14. c (p. 187)
15. a (p. 189)
16. d (p. 189)
17. c (p. 193)
18. d (p. 193)
19. c (p. 194)
20. c (pp. 196–198)

True-False

1. false (p. 172)
2. true (p. 176)
3. true (p. 179)
4. true (p. 180)
5. true (p. 172)
6. false (p. 182)
7. true (p. 186)
8. false (p. 188)
9. false (p. 189)
10. false (pp. 189–190)
11. false (p. 191)
12. true (p. 193)
13. true (p. 193)
14. false (p. 194)
15. true (p. 197)

Completion

1. baseline (p. 173)
2. feedback (p. 180)
3. gradualness (p. 173)
4. delaying, chaining (p. 179)
5. Learning (p. 181)
6. massed practice (p. 182)
7. inattention (pp. 182–183)
8. Premack (p. 186)
9. passive (p. 186)
10. anxiety-provoking (p. 190)
11. negative (p. 191)
12. anxiety (p. 193)
13. incompatible (p. 193)
14. fear hierarchy (p. 194)
15. cue (p. 197)

8
The Social Self: How We Interact

CHAPTER OUTLINE

OUR SOCIAL LIVES
The Need for Others
The Socially Created Self
   Monkeys reared in isolation
   Isolated and institutionalized children

STUDYING SOCIAL INTERACTION
The Complexity of Social Interaction
Theories of Social Psychology
   Attribution theory
   Role theory
   Communication theory
   Social exchange theory
Applying the Theories of Social Psychology to Adjustment

READING

Loneliness

JEFF MEER

Bill is a graduate student in architecture at a major university in the Northeast. He is shy, and when he speaks, he does so softly, with a slight Alabama drawl. Bill spends Monday through Friday going to class, chatting with friends and doing course work. Weekends, he is alone. Sarah is a mid-level executive in a *Fortune* 500 company. She is a bright, take-charge person who on any given day is as likely to be in Dallas as in New York. She has dozens of acquaintances, friends in five cities and never a moment to herself. At age 40, she wonders if it is possible for her to have a fulfilling relationship with another person.

Bill and Sarah are composites rather than specific individuals, but their real-life counterparts share a common bond. They are lonely, as many Americans are these days. Based on a survey of a cross section of the American population in 1972, University of Massachusetts sociologist Robert Weiss estimates that between 50 million and 60 million Americans, as much as a quarter of the population, feel extremely lonely at some time during any given month. The problem is so pervasive that a billion-dollar "loneliness industry," including videodating clubs, health spas and self-help books, has sprung up to meet the desire of so many people to do something about their loneliness.

Psychologists and other social scientists looking for the causes of loneliness have been hampered by its subjective nature and varied manifestations. Although the feeling is common, people experience it in many different ways, under many different conditions.

Psychologist Jeffrey Young of Columbia University describes three kinds of loneliness: transient, situational and chronic. "Transient loneliness lasts between a few minutes and a few hours," he says, "and because the symptoms are not severe, not much attention has been devoted to it." Situational loneliness results from an important event—a divorce, a death in the family or a geographic move. The effects can be both physical and mental—headaches, sleep problems, anxiety, depression—and can last up to a year.

For some lonely people, however, temporary circumstances aren't the basic problem. They have difficulty making social contact and achieving intimacy even when conditions are favorable. Young classifies individuals who feel lonely for more than two years at a time when no traumatic event has taken place as chronically lonely. "When people are lonely for that length of time, typically they blame themselves and their personality traits rather than circumstances," he says. "Chronically lonely people can become convinced that there is little or nothing they can do to improve their condition."

Young admits that the distinction between situational and chronic loneliness is often blurry. "There may be a prolonged adjustment period to something like divorce or college, and we don`t know at exactly what point it becomes a life pattern or problem," he says, "but in general, we're talking about two very different animals."

In his 1977 book, *The Broken Heart,* psychologist James Lynch wrote persuasively about the thousands of people who live alone and are more likely to suffer from physical problems such as heart disease and cirrhosis of the liver.

His most recent book, *The Language of the Heart*, further explains the vicious cycle of loneliness, high blood pressure and heart disease. Lynch reports extensive evidence that blood pressure increases during conversation. Since lonely people have few conversations, that would seem to be a plus for them. Unfortunately, the inner turmoil from unexpressed emotional problems can also cause chronic high blood pressure. Thus, many chronically lonely people seem caught between undesirable options: They can avoid conversations and suffer silently with hypertension, or they can seek out conversations to avoid isolation but which raise blood pressure. Lynch advocates a six-month program in which hypertensive and lonely patients learn to talk about their emotions while keeping their blood pressure at safe levels. Of course, not all lonely people are hypertensive. But Lynch's ideas may apply to many of them, particularly those who are middle-aged or older.

Researchers agree that the number of social contacts someone has is only one factor in loneliness. Psychologist Cecilia Solano of Wake Forest University points out, for example, that loneliness is partly a matter of expectations—how many contacts people expect or think is normal—as well as how many they actually have. Circumstances that make one person lonely may make another person feel overburdened with attention. In other instances it is timing that makes someone feel lonely. Staying home alone on a Saturday night can seem catastrophic to a young person, but staying home alone on a Tuesday night may be a welcome respite.

"Lonely people don't necessarily have fewer total contacts than anyone else," says University of Iowa psychologist Carolyn Cutrona, "but, more importantly, the quality of their contacts may be poorer." An especially insidious problem with the chronically lonely, she notes, is that even when they have the chance of fulfilling social contact, they don't take advantage of it because they don't seem to recognize that the chance is there.

University of California at Los Angeles psychologist Letitia Anne Peplau, who helped develop the UCLA Loneliness Scale, believes that the feeling develops when desires or needs for intimacy and attachment don't match up with the quality or quantity of social contacts one has or thinks one has.

Peplau, who coedited a National Institute of Mental Health report, *Preventing the Harmful Consequences of Severe and Persistent Loneliness*, believes that the distinction between desires and needs is crucial to an understanding of loneliness. "There may be some universal social needs that are wired into our makeup," Peplau says, "but these are tempered by the views about relationships and the meaning of the good life that different cultures develop."

The same distinction affects the difference between actual and perceived social contacts—how we view the relationships we do have. "Experience about relationships is filtered through our individual evaluation process," Peplau says. "The amount of time spent with another person, the degree to which two lives are intertwined and the desirability of the arrangement are all in the eye of the beholder."

There are different sources for social contact, and we gain different kinds of benefits from each. Weiss, often called the father of loneliness research, points out that we count on our families whenever the chips are down, no matter what the problem. We look to parents and teachers for guidance and trustworthy advice, and we look primarily to friends to share common interests and recreation. We gain strength from knowing that children and others depend upon us, and our co-workers and family reassure us about our competence and ability. Finally, we look to spouses or romantic partners for the attachment from which we derive safety and security.

Things can begin going wrong for chronically lonely people as early as childhood and adolescence. Psychologist Nicholas Zill reports that 9 percent of 2,279 children between the ages of 7 and 11 that he interviewed said they often felt "lonely and wished they had more friends." By the time the same children had reached the ages of 12 to 16, 10 percent reported being lonely "a lot." Zill believes that the loneliness he measured is "fairly stable over time" and so might qualify as chronic loneliness.

One pattern of behavior puts children at risk for being lonely, reports educational psychologist Steven Asher of the University of Illinois. "Aggressive, domineering kids are likely to be rejected by their peers," he says, "and we have found that these children are particularly likely to be lonely." Other research indicates that shy, introverted children may be at risk, too.

A few studies have shown that, as expected, cold parents are likely to have children who are lonely. Rejection probably also plays a role in the unusually high level of loneliness reported by kids whose parents are divorced. "It may be that children of divorced parents keep trying to bring about a reconciliation between their parent which is doomed to failure," psychologist Phillip Shaver says. He notes that the younger the children are when the divorce takes place, the more likely they are to report loneliness later. Children between the ages of 3 and 6 don't have the cognitive equipment to understand why their parents have split up, he says, and they tent to blame themselves for a failure to reunite their parents.

Shaver and psychologist Carin Rubinstein did not find similar loneliness in children whose parents had died. "Children at age 3 don't understand death," Shaver says, "but they do accept the fact that it is forever and, unlike divorce, there is nothing they can do to reverse it."

Economic factors can also come into play. Psychologist Tim Brennan of Boulder, Colorado, conducted a national survey of 1,800 teenagers from 11 to 17 years old and reports that the lower the socioeconomic group, the more likely a child is to report being lonely. "At least among this group of kids," he says, "high loneliness has a lot to do with feelings of being discriminated against and being rejected."

Loneliness increases during times of change and turmoil. Nowhere is that more evident than during adolescence and early adulthood, when loneliness, especially the situational kind, hits hardest. A 1978 survey by Rubinstein and Shaver of 27,000 people older than 18 found the highest rate of loneliness in those between 18 and 25 years old. Other researchers agree that loneliness soars rapidly during the teenage years. Some researchers believe that the mounting rates of suicide among teenagers may be a grim reminder of the intensity of the feeling among some adolescents.

Cutrona, Peplau and psychologist Dan Russell of the University of Iowa asked 162 college freshmen about loneliness and found that about 52 percent were situationally lonely; they reported being lonely at the beginning of the year but had adjusted by the middle of the spring semester. Another 13.5 percent, though, were chronically lonely; they still felt left out up to seven months after beginning classes. These students blamed their loneliness on shyness, fear of rejection and lack of knowledge about social skills.

The situationally lonely said that they gradually made friends to overcome their loneliness, but the chronically lonely felt that, although they may have made friends, the only thing that could halt their lonely feelings was finding a romantic partner, something they didn't seem to be able to do. "It could be that the chronically lonely college students have overlooked friendship as one way out of the bind they're in," Cutrona says, "but on the other hand, their insistence might indicate that they need intimate attachment more than other people do."

Loneliness can and does continue for many, but Rubinstein and Shaver found the frequency of loneliness dropped steadily with age until it reached a minimum in those 70 or more years old. "Older people become more self-sufficient and their lives are simpler," comments psychologist Ann Gerson. "They have a better idea than younger people do of what to expect from relationships."

Gerson, who practices in Salt Lake City, Utah, notes that there is a danger in removing some older people from the social networks that have been sustaining them. In a sample of 158 older people in Winnipeg, Gerson and colleague Daniel Perlman found that friendships meant more than their relationships with family. "A family that moves grandma across state lines to be closer to them might well consider that they could be causing her to be lonelier than she would have been around her friends," Gerson says.

Many people believe that older people and others who live alone are automatically lonely. But even though being single and being lonely are sometimes linked in prople's minds, behavioral scientists who have studied the subject think that the connection is mistaken.

As psychologist Judy Rollins at Kansas State University notes, "Being single has always been associated with being alone which, in turn, was thought of as a lonely and negative state, but this is not accurate," Three quarters of the 99 people she questioned said they would be satisfied if they never married or remarried.

Sociologist Peter Stein of William Paterson College in New Jersey, who interviewed 60 single men and women who were all relatively happy with their lot, believes that, "The things that push people away from being single, such as not being isolated, are not the same things that pull people toward marriage."

Researchers originally thought that women were more prone to loneliness than men were. But that idea is being qualified by recent research. Psychologists Harry Reis and Ladd Wheeler at the University of Rochester found, in a study of 53 women and 43 men, that a reliable way to predict whether people were lonely was to find out if they could communicate intimately with a woman.

Reis explains that women are better at communicating on the one-to-one level than men are because they have been socialized that way. This leads, he believes, to disproportionate numbers of men who are lonely because they think they don't get along with other individuals.

Reis also believes that men have been taught not to admit to being lonely, and he thinks that this bias could help account for past studies that found more lonely women than men. "It really depends on how directly you ask the questions and which questions you ask," he says.

Writer Louise Bernikow interviewed more than 150 men and women for a forthcoming book on loneliness. She believes that many men, and increasing numbers of women, are compensating for loneliness by becoming workaholics. "Men in this country have always been encouraged to value satisfying working lives over satisfying personal lives," she says, "and now women are making that same choice." But there are pitfalls associated with workaholism. "The exchange is never really complete," Bernikow says. Some wealthy and powerful men and women are surrounded by people all the time, but they "are still unhappy and wonder to themselves, 'Is this all there is?'" she says.

Not all chronically lonely people are depressed and not all depressed people are lonely, but quite a few are both. Young has coined the term "lonely depression" to describe a spiraling pattern of mental disturbance he sees frequently in his practice. "Patients often do not complain of loneliness right away, but their depression can best be understood in terms of loneliness," he says. Since many lonely people also are introverted, their depression can feed upon itself and cause the spiral of negative feelings about themselves to deepen.

The lonely people afraid of initiating any contact with others can be classified as social phobics, Young says. But the majority do not avoid social contact but find themselves unable, for whatever reason, to perform up to their own expectations in more intimate situations. If their unfulfilling behavior goes on long enough, he argues, lonely people begin to avoid deepening any of their relationships and end up feeling completely isolated.

University of Tulsa psychologist Warren Jones compared how lonely and nonlonely students dealt with new acquaintances during a 15-minute conversation. He found that the lonely students did not get to know the new people as well as did the students who were not lonely. The lonely students also believed that their new acquaintances didn`t like them. The new acquaintances told Jones that they didn't feel this way, but that, in fact, the lonely students did not seem to like themselves very much.

Part of their difficulty, Jones reports, is that lonely people often don't realize or can't understand the impression that they create in other people. The lonely students were more negative, in general, and lonely men reported "not liking" their new acquaintances much more frequently than the men who were not lonely did.

Loneliness normally motivates people to get out and meet others, but it doesn't work that way for the chronically lonely who are afraid of most social contact. Instead, they simply ignore suggestions about places they might go or things they might do to relieve their loneliness.

Psychologist Karen Rook, of the University of California at Irvine, believes that cognitive behavior therapy may be useful for some chronically lonely people who don't have the energy to undertake their own battle. The aim of this kind of therapy, she says, is to isolate the sources of distorted self-images and help lonely people monitor their behavior. "We can get people to stop seeing themselves as 'incurable,' and start them toward challenging and eradicating these thoughts," Rook says. Other approaches, such as client-centered or psychodynamic therapy, use the therapist-patient realtionship to explore how the patient relates to the outside world. These approaches may prove helpful for those who find that they have difficulty developing more intimate attachments.

There are times, however, when loneliness is not a problem in need of a solution but a perfectly normal response to certain circumstances. Many changes in personal or environmental circumstances can trigger a person's feelings of inadequacy about social contacts. Leaving for college, breaking off a romantic relationship, changing marital status and moving to a new location are only a few of the common events that lead to situational loneliness. Some good can come out of these bad feelings. Albert Cain, professor of psychology at the University of Michigan, believes that loneliness and solitude can be fruitful, at times. "One should not assume that loneliness is automatically and intrinsically pathological and damaging," he says, "since it can also be used as a time of redress, resilience and turning toward and strengthening of internal resources."

For others, we are learning better ways of minimizing loneliness. Rook says that social-skills groups can teach lonely people how to open conversations and to handle conflict or disappointment when they develop. "In social-skills training groups, we often find it useful to teach people how to match the level of disclosure of their conversational partner," Rook expalins. "If lonely people disclose too much of themselves, they may make their partner uncomfortable, but if they disclose too little, they may never reach the level of intimacy they are looking for," she says. Rook also emphasizes learning how to invite people to join in activities.

But we have to be careful in trying to eliminate the loneliness that psychologist Jones calls "the common cold of psychopathology." As Peplau notes, "loneliness is like physical pain. It's a useful warning signal. It warns you that some important need is going unfulfilled."

Reading Questions

1. Psychologist Jeffrey Young describes three kinds of loneliness. Name and describe each.
2. According to this article, what effect does age have on loneliness?
3. According to recent research studies, men are more prone to loneliness than women. Why?

RESEARCH STUDY

Investigator:	Patricia Noller.
Source, date:	"Misunderstandings in Marital Communication: A Study of Couples' Nonverbal Communication," *Journal of Personality and Social Behavior*, 1980, *39*, 1135-1148.
Location:	University of Queensland.
Subjects:	48 married couples.
Materials:	Marital Adjustment Test, Marital Communication Scale, cards with description of situations, and videotape machine.

Communication within the marital relationship is particularly critical for the sucess of the relationship. Unfortunately, communication is the source of many problems in marriage due to the intensity of the relationship and the large number and variety of communications. Nonverbal communications are an additional source of difficulty because they are not governed by explicit rules, and thus it can be harder to send and receive them accurately.

Studies have shown that problems arise at the point of sending a message, in encoding, or at the point of receiving a message, in decoding. Encoding involves the skill of sending a message clearly so it can be understood by a receiver. Decoding involves the skill of accurately recognizing cues provided in the message.

The present study was created to study the relationship between marital adjustment and accuracy in communication. In particular, this study investigated the role of the skills of encoding and decoding nonverbal communication in marital adjustment. In addition, it considered the relative encoding and decoding skills of men and women.

Couples were differentiated according to their level of adjustment as indicated by the Marital Adjustment Test. Next, one couple at a time, each couple was put in the experimental room alone and given sets of messages on cards. Taking turns, each husband and wife sent (encoded) and received (decoded) nonverbal messages. The sender had a choice of three intentions (positive, negative, and neutral) to convey in the message. The receiver had to determine which intention was being communicated. The sessions were videotaped and evaluated. Communication was seen as accurate if the intention of the sender matched the intention perceived by the receiver.

The results indicated that couples whose marital adjustment was high were able to communicate more accurately and effectively than were couples whose marital adjustment was low. Further, females were found to be more skillful encoders (senders) of nonverbal messages than were males. This was particularly true for messages with positive intention. Finally, when decoding errors were made, females more often made them in a positive direction and males more often made them in a negative direction.

For marital counseling, one implication of these results is that greater attention may need to be given to developing husbands' skills in sending positive messages and in interpreting the nonverbal messages of their wives.

Research Study Questions

1. What aspect of communication did this study investigate?
2. How was the relationship between marital adjustment and communication studied?
3. What were the results of the study, and what implication was suggested for marital counseling?

CASE STUDY

An Open Relationship

GEORGE KALUGER AND MERIEM FAIR KALUGER

Donna and I had been engaged for about half a year when we decided to live together for a week. We left for college a week early during the summer before my senior year.

We realized life together would be different from our dating and engaged relations but just how much different we didn't know. Two couples whom we knew and whose marriages were "on the rocks" advised us to live together for a while before marriage to be more certain that we could be happy with each other twenty-four hours a day. It's true that seven days might not be enough to tell anything about our relationship, but I must say, after our experience we both felt that we had gained a great deal of insight about each other and our relationship in general.

We moved into my apartment on a Saturday morning, so we actually had nine days until classes started. The first day was set aside to get everything in some sort of order and to do general cleaning. Our thoughts seemed to be centered on the idea of how wonderful it would be if we were married and this was our first apartment together.

The freedom we had enjoyed the three previous years at college seemed so much sweeter after a summer of being at home under "parental guidance." We were filled with the excitement of returning to this freedom, and especially so because we returned with each other.

During our stay together, we realized how much we didn't know about each other—spiritually, emotionally, physically and socially. For example, we quickly learned that each other's early morning grumpiness was short-lived and, in a way, humorous. I began to understand why a girl has to start getting ready for a date an hour before her date. Donna in turn was amazed at how I could get ready in the span of five minutes.

Helping each other with everyday routine such as vacuuming and cooking was so much more enjoyable than ever before. Washing the car and shopping also took on added meaning since it was for and by us.

We had a lot of time alone together. We talked about our feelings on different topics to a greater extent than we ever had before. Through these in-depth talks we learned a great deal about each other. Inner feelings we had been reluctant to disclose before now seemed much easier to express. I'm basically quiet and don't talk very much. I often don't express my feelings, but with Donna I felt an urge to let her know what my feelings were because I felt she was sincerely interested. She also became more open and we grew much closer as a result of our open expression of our feelings.

One area which caused some friction was the pace of each of our lives. I'm very active and have to be doing something or going somewhere. I hate to let anything go until tomorrow and feel that the more I get done today, the more things I can get done tomorrow. I am also impatient in many situations. Donna, on the other hand, is almost my opposite in that she hates to rush or to be hurried. She enjoys taking her time and can`t see any sense in hurrying through anything. Trying to find a happy medium where both of us are happy is difficult and we still have some trouble with it occasionally. We both respect each other's position as we try to become more compatible.

We found our ideas on sex, and the human body in general, to be different. We both felt sex was an expression of love and should be given and received as such. This view had not been Donna's original outlook, but through sincere talks and my openness she gradually took on my viewpoint. I come from an extremely uninhibited family. My parents had literature for us children on birth and conception and would answer any of our questions honestly. We were taught that there was nothing sinful about the human body. It was not an uncommon event to see one another nude while dressing or going to or from the bathroom. We would often skinny-dip in the pool before going to bed.

Donna's background was very inhibited, and her sexual knowledge came entirely from a sex education class and her peers. Her parents viewed sex as dirty and sinful and they never talked to her about it.

Our first sexual relations were enjoyable even though she was scared. She thought it was wonderful because we viewed sex as a shared expression of love. We now feel that the best and only way to deal with sex is openly and honestly.

Through our experiences we learned many things, but perhaps the most important thing was that love is sharing—total sharing of mind, body and soul into a beautiful relationship.

Case Study Questions

1. What is an open and honest relationship? Why is it important in dyadic interaction?
2. Do you feel that the "experimental week" was an adequate length of time to establish an open relationship?
3. What effect would feelings that a listener is sincerely interested in what you are saying have on a relationship?

SELF-TEST

Multiple Choice

1. Adjustment refers to the continuous interaction with which of the following factors?
   a. ourselves
   b. others
   c. our world
   d. all of the above
2. Which of the following would *not* be considered as a concrete particular of our relationship with others?
   a. a birthday card
   b. a handshake
   c. a feeling of anger
   d. sarcastic tone of voice
3. The term "social" is best applied to which of the following?
   a. work-oriented interactions with others
   b. conflict-oriented interactions with others
   c. recreational interactions with others
   d. all interactions involving two or more people
4. The dependent variable in Harry Harlow's experiment with infant monkeys was:
   a. the length of time in isolation
   b. the type of surrogate mother
   c. the amount of time spent with a surrogate mother
   d. the extent of cooperative play
5. The experiment by Harry Harlow suggests that:
   a. infant monkeys prefer food over water
   b. surrogate mothers are more efficient than "real" mothers
   c. the need for contact with others depends on the need for food
   d. the need for contact with others is independent of the need for food
6. The behavioral position describing how the human need for contact with others emerges is that parents act as:

a. a releaser stimulus
   b. a holding stimulus
   c. a pairing stimulus
   d. a conditioned stimulus
7. For the most part, the data about our need for others come from what kind of research?
   a. research with lower economic families
   b. research with college students
   c. research with animals
   d. none of the above
8. Several psychology experiments have shown that persons who are under the stress of fear are highly motivated to:
   a. isolate themselves from others
   b. seek others out for sexual gratification
   c. seek others out for comfort
   d. seek others out for protection
9. Monkeys reared in isolation did all of the following *except*:
   a. exhibited fear of other monkeys
   b. had trouble mating
   c. ignored their infants until it was life-threatening to the infants
   d. showed appropriate "play" behaviors
10. Anna, the child discussed in the text, became that way because:
    a. she was raised by animals
    b. she was locked in the bathroom
    c. she was possessed by demons
    d. she was kept in the attic
11. The occurrence of feral children provides striking evidence of:
    a. the power of negative reinforcement
    b. the adaptability of the human child
    c. the power of human contact
    d. language development in the human child
12. The concept that distrubed interactions in childhood can create a disturbed adult is most closely associated with:
    a. Karen Horney
    b. Erich Fromm
    c. Alfred Adler
    d. Sigmund Freud
13. The cluster of stimuli presented to you by your dyadic partner is usually:
    a. always changing
    b. very stable
    c. grossly simplified
    d. none of the above
14. Fritz Heider, the originator of attribution theory, suggests that a person tries to guess what is causing another person's behavior because:
    a. people are inherently paranoid
    b. people are inherently inquisitive
    c. people are inherently motivated to control others
    d. people are motivated to make sense out of behavior
15. Which of the following would *not* be one of Harold Kelley's criteria for interpreting other people's behavior?
    a. consistency
    b. intention
    c. likelihood
    d. external pressures
16. A marriage in which the male partner expects his wife to have a career, while the female partner wants to keep house and have her husband support her is an example of:
    a. role conflict
    b. role dissensus
    c. role failure
    d. role consensus
17. Communication theorists hold that the *usual* culprit of disturbed relationships, and particularly disturbed marriages, is a pattern of:
    a. unclear communications
    b. demanding communications
    c. complementary communications
    d. aggressive communications
18. Social exchange theory claims that relationships are based on:
    a. unselfish love
    b. mutual profit
    c. similar background
    d. similar personality types
19. Social exchange theory is said to be based on both economics and behavioral psychology. From which behavioral principles do we learn how to pursue rewards?
    a. the principles of existential yield
    b. the principles of cognitive-behavioral organization
    c. the principles of response cost
    d. the principles of operant and respondent conditioning
20. What can absorb minor injustics in a marriage?
    a. love
    b. negotiation
    c. aggression
    d. freedom

True-False

1. According to Harry Stack Sullivan, people are the most complex but easiest things we have to deal with.

2. A sarcastic tone or a gentle greeting can serve as a concrete aspect of a relationship.
3. The term "social" is applicable to any interaction involving two or more persons.
4. The independent variable in Harry Harlow's experiment was the type of isolation used.
5. According to behavioral theory, the parent can function as a releaser stimulus that reinforces the infant's behaviors.
6. Stimulus deprivation has consequences ranging from boredom to severely disturbed thought processes.
7. Monkeys reared in isolation showed no disturbance when returned to other monkeys.
8. Family therapy, marriage counseling and group therapy are all based on the belief that it is not the person who is disturbed, but the interaction.
9. The powerful effects of social interaction guarantee healthy development in the human.
10. Body language is just as influential in an interaction as is verbal communication.
11. According to attribution theory, the central aspect of a social interaction is the perceived cause of the other person's behavior.
12. Fritz Heider, the originator of attribution theory, states that people are highly motivated to make sense out of human behavior.
13. People are usually held more responsible for actions that are internally motivated.
14. Marriage counselors often stress the need for some dishonesty about expectations and desires in a marriage.
15. According to Letha Scanzoni and John Scanzoni, "Marriage requires two legs—love and justice."

Completion

1. In the experiment conducted by Harry Harlow, the infant monkeys usually spent more time with the _____ mother.
2. One theory of how the human need for contact with others emerges is that the parents act as a _____ stimulus, eliciting instinctive social responses.
3. Research has discovered that humans deprived of _____ can eventually become seriously disturbed.
4. The notion that maladjustment is the result of _____ _____ has been accepted by every school of psychology.
5. Whereas general psychology studies the individual in isolation, the job of social psychology is to study _____ behavior.
6. While you are speaking to an attractive male who is sitting in front of you, he leans forward toward you. Most likely he is responding to you through _____ language.
7. An interaction between two people is referred to as a _____.
8. According to attribution theorist Harold Kelley, in order to feel that we have some control over our interactions we must assign _____ to behavior.
9. The sum total of the expectations for behavior in a given position in a social structure is referred to as a _____ _____.
10. The cues provided by role partners in an interaction are called role _____.
11. According to social exchange theory, relationships are determined primarily by their _____.
12. With respect to social exchange theory, Erich Fromm condemns man for having "transformed himself into a _____."
13. It is highly probable that our more intimate realtionships have both a(n) _____ and a(n) _____ view.
14. Psychologists and sociologists specializing in the study of marriage have repeatedly pointed out that satisfying marriages are based on both _____ and _____.
15. Marriage supposedly requires two legs—love and justice. Thus, when the exchange of privileges and rewards seems unjust, _____ ensues.

Essay Questions

1. Discuss the famous monkey experiment conducted by Harry Harlow in terms of the need for others. (pp. 208–209)
2. Why do human beings seek out other human beings? (p. 209)
3. Define social isolation and its relevance to abnormal development in Anna and institutionalized orphans. (pp. 210–211)
4. Define and discuss "body language." (p. 213)
5. Briefly discuss the major differences among the four theories of interaction in social psychology. (pp. 215–223)

8/THE SOCIAL SELF: HOW WE INTERACT

SELF-TEST ANSWERS

Multiple Choice
1. d (p. 205)
2. c (p. 207)
3. d (p. 207)
4. c (p. 208)
5. d (p. 208)
6. d (p. 208)
7. c (p. 208)
8. c (p. 209)
9. d (p. 210)
10. d (p. 201)
11. c (p. 201)
12. d (p. 211)
13. a (p. 214)
14. d (p. 215)
15. b (p. 215)
16. b (p. 218)
17. a (p. 221)
18. b (p. 221)
19. d (p. 222)
20. a (p. 223)

True-False
1. false (p. 205)
2. true (p. 207)
3. true (p. 207)
4. false (p. 208)
5. false (p. 208)
6. true (p. 209)
7. false (p. 210)
8. true (p. 213)
9. false (p. 210)
10. true (p. 213)
11. true (p. 215)
12. true (p. 215)
13. true (p. 216)
14. false (p. 221)
15. true (p. 223)

Completion
1. cloth (p. 208)
2. releaser (p. 208)
3. stimulation (p. 209)
4. social problems (p. 211)
5. interpersonal (p. 213)
6. body (p. 213)
7. dyad (p. 214)
8. causes (p. 215)
9. social role (pp. 217–218)
10. demands (p. 218)
11. outcomes *or* profits (p. 221)
12. commodity (p. 223)
13. idealistic, materialistic (p. 223)
14. tenderness, fairness (p. 223)
15. negotiation (p. 223)

9 Social Perception: What It Is and How It Operates

CHAPTER OUTLINE

THE DEVELOPMENT OF SOCIAL PERCEPTIONS
Infancy
Childhood
Adolescence
HOW DOES SOCIAL PERCEPTION OPERATE?
Unity
Consistency
Assumed Content
  Implicit theory of personality
Structure: What Counts Most
  Central traits
  The primacy effect
Understanding and Control

ATTRACTION
Physical Attractiveness
Competence
Proximity
Similarity
  Complementarity
Rewardingness
STEREOTYPING
Stereotypes: Accurate or Inaccurate?
The Damage Done by Stereotyping

READING

The Eye of the Beholder

THOMAS F. CASH AND LOUIS H. JANDA

Ask most people to list what makes them like someone on first meeting and they'll tell you personality, intelligence, sense of humor. But they're probably deceiving themselves. The characteristic that impresses people the most, when meeting anyone from a job applicant to a blind date, is appearance. And unfair and unenlightened as it may seem, attractive people are frequently preferred over their less attractive peers.

Research begun in the early 1970's has shown that not only do good looks influence such things as choice of friends, lovers and mates, but that they can also affect school grades, selection for jobs and even the outcome of a trial. Psychologist Ellen Berscheid of the University of Minnesota and psychologist Elaine Walster, then at the University of Wisconsin, were among the first researchers to deal with the topic of attractiveness. Their seminal 1974 paper on the subject showed that the more attractive a person, the more desirable characteristics others will attribute to him or her. Attractive people are viewed as being happier, more sensitive, more interesting, warmer, more poised, more sociable and as having better character than their less attractive counterparts. Psychologist Karen Dion of the University of Toronto has dubbed this stereotypical view as: "What is beautiful is good."

Our current work at Old Dominion University in Norfolk, Virginia, with colleagues and students focuses on the role that appearance plays in judgments made about people. Our studies have been done in a variety of settings: basic research laboratories, beauty and cosmetics industry labs, plastic and reconstructive surgery practices, psychiatric hospitals and psychotherapeutic consulting rooms.

One topic that has led to many avenues of research is how attractiveness influences sex-typing —the tendency of people to attribute certain stereotypical qualities to each sex. Besides being perceived as sensitive, kind, interesting and generally happy, attractive people tend to fit easily into sexual stereotypes, according to a study done by Barry Gillen, a social psychologist in our department.

Gillen speculated that attractive people possess two types of "goodness," one related to and the other unrelated to their sex. To test this hypothesis he showed a group of students photographs of both men and women of high, moderate and low attractiveness, as determined by the previous rankings of students according to a seven-point scale (contrary to popular belief, researchers usually don't use the Bo Derek scale of 10). The judges were asked to rate the subjects according to the masculinity, femininity and social desirability scales of the Bem Sex Role Inventory. Gillen's study found that attractive women were perceived as being more feminine, and that attractive men were viewed as being more masculine than their less attractive counterparts. This suggests a second stereotype: "What is beautiful is sex-typed."

One implication of Gillen's work that we wanted to test was whether good looks are a disadvantage for some people, especially women, in work situations that conflict with sexual stereotypes. By the late 1970's there was already a sizable body of literature documenting the problems women face because of sex-role stereotypes. We speculated that attractive women might be at a real disadvantage when they aspire to occupations in which stereotypically masculine traits—such as being strong, independent and decisive—are thought to be required for success.

To test that possibility we did a study with Gillen and Steve Burns, a student in our department, in which professional personnel consultants were hired to rate a "job applicant's" suitability for six positions. We matched the positions for the skill required, the prestige offered and the degree of supervisory independence allowed. Two jobs were stereotypically masculine (automobile salesperson and wholesale hardware shipping and receiving clerk), two feminine (telephone operator and office receptionist) and two were sex-neutral (motel desk clerk and photographic darkroom assistant).

Each of the 72 personnel consultants who participated received a résumé package for an individual that contained the typical kinds of information that a job applicant might submit: academic standing, a list of hobbies and interests, specific skills and recommendations from teachers and counselors. All of the résumés were identical with the exception of the name ("John" vs. "Janet" Williams) and the inclusion of a photograph of the applicant. Photographs showed either an extremely attractive applicant or an unattractive one, previously judged on an attractiveness scale.

The results documented the existence of both sexism and "beautyism." On the sexism front, men were given stronger endorsements by the personnel consultants for the traditionally masculine jobs, while women were rated higher for the traditionally feminine jobs. Men were also judged to have just as much chance of success on the neutral jobs as on the masculine ones, while women were perceived to be less likely to succeed on the neutral jobs than on the feminine ones.

"Beautyism" had several facets: Attractive men were favored over their less attractive male competitors for all three types of jobs. Similarly, attractiveness gave women a competitive edge against other women, but only for traditionally female or neutral jobs. When it came to jobs inappropriate to society's traditional sex roles, the attractive women were rated lower than their less attractive female competitors.

These findings gain support from a subsequent study by Madeline Heilman and Lois Saruwatari, psychologists at Yale University. They examined the effects of appearance and gender on selection for both managerial and nonmanagerial jobs. Male and female students in a business administration class received résumé packages for equally qualified candidates. Each résumé included a photograph of either an attractive or unattractive man or woman. Being attractive was always an advantage for men. Attractive men received stronger recommendations for hiring, were judged to have better qualifications and were given higher suggested starting salaries than unattractive men for both the managerial and the nonmanagerial positions.

Among women, however, those who were less attractive actually had a significant edge over their more attractive peers when seeking a place in management, a traditionally masculine occupation. Good looks were an advantage only when women were applying for the nonmanagerial positions. Attractiveness resulted in lower salary recommendations when the women were viewed as stepping into an out-of-sex-role position.

Heilman says that her findings "imply that women should strive to appear as unattractive and masculine as possible if they are to succeed in advancing their careers by moving into powerful organizational positions."

So, beauty—at least in a women—doesn't always pay in the workplace, nor does it guarantee higher marks in the classroom. Recently, we tested the notion that attractiveness can work against women attempting to cross sex-role boundaries in academic as well as work settings. We constructed a series of essays, purportedly written by college freshmen, that were equivalent in quality, but which varied in the "masculinity" or "femininity" of the topic. The essays were accompanied by photographs of attractive and unattractive "authors."

The masculine topics were "How to Hunt Safely" and "How to Buy a Used Motorcycle," and the feminine topics were "How to Make a Quilt" and "How to Give a Manicure." The essays were read and judged by 216 female college students.

Once again attractiveness proved to be an advantage for the men, regardless of the sex-typing of the essay topic. For the women, however, beauty was an advantage only when they stuck to a feminine topic. When they were presented as authors of the masculine essays, the attractive women were given a lower score relative to their less attractive peers.

It is clear that beauty can be a double-edged sword for women. Attractive women are viewed as having a host of desirable personality characteristics, except the ones needed to step out of prescribed sex roles.

What are the specific cues for gender role stereotyping? Grooming—the way people dress, use cosmetics and style their hair—appears to be a factor. The differing ideal physiques—thin for women, more muscular for men—also influence gender stereotyping, according to recent experiments by Purdue psychologists Kay Deaux and Laurie Lewis. People who are tall, strong, sturdy and broad-shouldered—regardless of gender—are viewed as more likely to have masculine personality traits, to fit the assertive, breadwinner role and to hold a traditionally masculine occupation. Meanwhile, people who are dainty, graceful and soft in voice and appearance are expected to have typically feminine traits, roles and occupations.

How does grooming affect sex-typing of attractive women, especially as it relates to their employability? This question was partially answered by a series of studies in which we asked male and female corporate personnel consultants to judge how qualified various attractive women, shown in photographs were for jobs in corporate management. In the first study, we showed 16 personnel managers photographs of women wearing various types of clothing jewelry, hairstyles and cosmetics. The results showed that the more sex-typed, or "feminized," the grooming styles, the less likely were personnel consultants to judge the women to be potential managers.

In a second study, personnel consultants judged businesswomen photographed under two different grooming conditions: one very feminine and made up, the other plainer and less sex-typed. The more feminine style included longer hair or hairstyles that concealed the face; soft sweaters, low necklines or ruffled blouses; dangling jewelry; and heavy make-up. In the other condition "candidates" wore tailored clothes with a jacket, subtle make-up and either short hair or hair swept away from the face. These criteria were chosen on the basis of descriptions given by judges in the previous study.

Once again the corporate personnel consultants made choices suggesting that the less feminine the appearance, the more competent the women, even though the candidates had been perceived by the consultants as equally attractive under both conditions. Specifically, candidates groomed in a more feminine style were perceived to be less managerial; less intrinsically interested in work; less likely to be taken seriously by others; more illogical and over-emotional in critical decision-making; less financially responsible; more helpless and dependent on the influences of others; sexier and more flirtatious in social relations; and less assertive, independent and self-confident than those groomed in less sex-typed style.

In the third phase of this project, male and female executives and managers from more than 200 corporations in major cities nationwide were shown applications containing photographs of attractive businesswomen in various grooming styles and asked how they thought they would fare in the corporate world. Once again, candidates groomed in a less sex-typed style were expected to have a better chance at reaching the management levels of the corporate structure, to be offered higher salaries and to be afforded greater social acceptance and credibility on the job than when they were groomed in a more traditionally feminine manner. These effects were especially prominent when the judges were men, often the gatekeepers of corporate management.

These studies, taken together, suggest that grooming style has a definite effect on whether women are sex-typed, and thus whether they are viewed as having good management potential. To some extent, our research has confirmed what many people always suspected: if a woman wants to succeed in a man's world, she had better not look too feminine. Several "dress for success" books have made it to the best-seller list by advising women to get ahead in business by wearing their hair short, using cosmetics sparingly and wearing conservative suits. Our research suggests, sadly, that the advice is sound.

It is interesting how deeply ingrained these attitudes are. Many people, both men and women, who are seriously concerned and offended by the sexism in our society never question this dress-for-success formula, which has different standards for men than it does for women. Men must follow certain clothing norms in the office in regard to neatness and formality, but not masculinity. No one would suggest to a man that he try not to look too masculine when he shows up at the office or expect him to comb his hair one way for the office and another way when he goes out to dinner. It is doubtful that any man has ever been advised not to look too good if he wants to be taken seriously at the next board meeting. But rules of dress for women are far more complex.

Prejudices are slow to fade away. It will be interesting to see if grooming styles for women become more flexible as they move up the corporation ladder in greater numbers and become more powerful.

Attractive women can face problems outside the boardroom as well. Everyone wants to be thought of as desirable and attractive, but a woman's beauty can invite unwanted advances and treatment as a sex object. Perhaps, then, it should come as no surprise that social psychologist Harry Reis of the University of Rochester found attractive women to be more distrustful of men than were their plainer counterparts.

Our research has also confirmed that a third stereotype exists: "What is beautiful is self-centered." We've found that many people assume that attractive people are vain and egotistical. After all, if what is beautiful is good, then the beautiful people must know how wonderful they are. Further, people of low and average attractiveness are often reluctant to choose extremely attractive mates for fear of losing them. In fact, breakups are more common among couples who are mismatched on attractiveness. So once again, thorns appear on the rose of beauty.

We have been discussing how people judge and react to the attractiveness of others. What about people's perceptions of themselves? Currently, in collaboration with Barbara Winstead, a psychologist at Old Dominion, we are examining how body images—the feelings people have about their own appearance—influence their lives. Surprisingly, how people view their own level of attractiveness has almost nothing to do with how others view them. People whom others consider beautiful may not like their looks at all. Conversely, people whom others might judge as downright unattractive or even ugly feel completely comfortable with their appearance.

Using our newly developed Winstead-Cash Body Self-Relations Questionnaire, we are beginning to accumulate evidence that body image may have as much impact on one's life as external evaluations of beauty. In a study with Steve Noles, a graduate student in the Virginia Consortium for Professional Psychology, for example, we have found a greater vulnerability to depression among people who place importance on being good-looking yet see themselves as less attractive than they really are.

Aristotle once maintained that "beauty is a greater recommendation than any letter of introduction." In many respects he was right. But then again, maybe he should have collected more data.

Reading Questions

1. For who is beauty a double-edged sword? Why?
2. What type of appearance would be more predictive of success for a female seeking a high-level managerial position?
3. Why might an employer be hesitant to hire a very feminine, attractive female for an executive-level position?

RESEARCH STUDY

Investigators:	Robert E. Kraut and Donald Poe.
Source, date:	"Behavioral Roots of Person Perception: The Deception Judgments of Customs Inspectors and Laymen," *Journal of Personality and Social Psychology*, 1980, *39*, 784-798.
Location:	Cornell University at Syracuse, New York.
Subjects:	39 customs inspectors and 49 adult residents of Syracuse, New York.
Materials:	self-monitoring scale and videotapes.

A good deal of social psychological research that has been done on how we perceive others has focused on the cognitive variables (e.g., attributions) involved in the formation of perceptions. The present study was an attempt to move away from this pattern and investigate the behavioral cues that are involved in the development of person perceptions.

An example of person perception research that involves the use of physical cues is the research on physical attractiveness. However, instead of examining physical beauty, these investigators studied the physical cues that observers use in judging truthfulness and deception. They chose trained customs inspectors and untrained laypersons as the observers, and then they compared the accuracy of the perceptions of these two groups. Finally, they attempted to determine whether persons, who differed in social sensitivity as measured by a self-monitoring scale would differ in their ability to judge deception.

First the investigators created videotapes of travelers being interrogated by customs inspectors. They used airline travelers who volunteered to participate in the study, gave some of them "contraband" to hide on themselves, and then had mock but realistic-looking inspections carried out. Videotapes were made of sixty-two interrogations with travelers, half of whom were carrying "contraband." The travelers ranged in age from 18 to 27 and had a wide variety of occupations.

The investigators showed the videotapes to 39 customs inspectors and 49 lay observers who had been recruited through a newspaper advertisement. These judges were instructed to watch the interrogations and indicate whether or not they would like to conduct a further search of the traveler.

As it turned out, the customs inspectors and laypersons were not very good at discriminating between those carrying "contraband" (i.e., those who were lying during the inspection) and those telling the truth. Further, it did not matter how the judges had scored on the self-monitoring scale; they did not differ in their ability to discriminate "smugglers" from "nonsmugglers." In fact, all judges tended to agree on what they viewed as the behavior of a liar versus the behavior of someone telling the truth.

The major cue used by the judges in deciding whether the travelers were lying or telling the truth was the travelers' comportment. Comportment that the judges considered to be indicative of a liar included hesitation in answering, brevity of answers, shift in body position, and avoidance of eye contact. In sum, if the traveler's comportment could be described as "nervous," he or she was considered a liar by the judge.

Research Study Questions

1. What aspect of person perception did this study focus on? How is this study different from other research in person perception?
2. What was the approach or method used by the investigators to study this topic?
3. Describe the results of the study.

CASE STUDY

Ken's Dating Games

STEPHEN M. JOHNSON

"I've got a woman on my hands who's driving me absolutely nuts. I've known her three weeks, and she's caused me more grief than my ex-wife did in six years." . . . "Lenore and I met only three weekends ago. Our meeting was really romantic. She had run out of gas and was standing helplessly by her car when I drove up. She's a beautiful woman, and I was terribly attracted to her from the start. I drove her to a gas station . . . we laughed a lot and seemed to hit it off immediately. We've been together a lot since then.

"The first two weeks were great, except that Lenore was pretty uptight about sleeping with me, but after a week or so we'd broken down that barrier. We planned to spend this past weekend together, from Friday to Monday morning. Well, we were going to meet Friday at my place for cocktails and dinner right after work—anyway, *I* thought it was right after work. We both get off at four-thirty, and I expected her to be at my place by five. But I was left cooling my heels in my apartment until nine-twenty, when Lenore comes waltzing in, bubbling all over and carrying a large bag of groceries. She says, 'Darling, I've got the most wonderful things for our dinner.' I could have belted her! She carries on about all the great things she's brought for dinner and how glad she is to see me, while I try to stay cool and see if she's going to have the courtesy to apologize for being four and a half hours late.

"Finally, I asked her where the hell she'd been, and why she didn't call me. She said something like, 'Well, we didn't specify a time, and I thought you were more casual about time than you apparently are. I always like to eat dinner late on weekends, and I went out after work with some marvelous friends in the office. Then I had to go home and change, and then I had to go out and buy groceries for our dinner.'"

"In the process of telling her how angry I'd been the last four and a half hours, I confessed that I called her at home and at work, where I had talked to one of her fellow workers whom I know. Now, that was a problem because she told me that she didn't want anyone at work—or her close friends, for that matter—to know about us because they gossip so much. That never made much sense to me, but I went along with it, but after three and a half hours waiting, I went ahead and called. Anyway, when I told her about that, she really flew off the handle. She accused me of totally misunderstanding her, of going back on my word, of being ungrateful for the effort she went to for dinner, and of being uptight and spying on her. And then she just stormed out. So it's me and the television set in there going crazy until about midnight, when the phone rings. She apologizes for being late and for getting so upset and running out. She told me she loved me. I accepted that apology, and I guess I apologized a little bit too, and then I asked her over. She said she'd gone to a nearby bar for a couple of drinks and was tired now and wanted to go home and go to bed. She was only five minutes away, and I couldn't really understand her, but I accepted it. She promised to come over 'first thing in the morning' and fix me a marvelous breakfast, and promised we could spend the day together. I almost asked exactly what time 'first thing in the morning' was, but I was trying to be cool, so I didn't.

"Well, I was up at seven thirty and by eight I was ready to have my marvelous breakfast. When she wasn't there by nine thirty, I started wondering the same sort of things I'd wondered about last night: Who were these marvelous friends at the office that she'd been with after work? Where did she really go after she left my place? And if she loved me so much and was so apologetic and was only five minutes away, why couldn't she come over? Why was she so concerned about her roommate and other friends not knowing about me? And who else is she seeing? You see, I had tried to find out from her what other relationships she had, but somehow I was never answered, and somehow I never have learned about that.

"Now, at eleven thirty, she finally does come by, and she really can cook a great breakfast. But, then, just as I'm about to plan the rest of our day, she says she has to drive out to her boss's house by the lake to deliver some papers. I offer to drive her and plan something out there, but she says no, her boss and some of his colleagues will be there, and it would be better if I didn't. Again, I wondered whether she's seeing her boss or someone else at the office, but I keep the wondering to myself. But at least by now I've learned to pin Lenore down on time. She promises to be back by five to fix the dinner we didn't have last night and go to a party which some of my friends were having. Well, she comes back at six (not late enough for me to say anything but late enough to bother me), and we have a really nice time and a fine dinner.

"We both were a tiny bit looped on drinks and the dinner wine, and we started to get friendly, you known, and I was just incredibly excited and wanted to make love—that woman can turn me on more than anybody I've ever known. But she didn't want to. She said it would just mess her up before the party and that we could always make love later. Well, then we go to the party, and Lenore attracts men like honey attracts flies. And she loves it. She spent about an hour out on the deck with Dick, an old friend of mine, *and* in the middle of the party she courteously excused herself and went into the bedroom to make a long telephone call. Well, I want to tell you, by the end of the party I was pissed. When we left and got into the car, I let her have it. I told her all the things she'd done wrong and all the things that I'd been wondering about since Friday. Did I get any answers? Hell, no! She just cried and asked me to take her home, which I did gladly. When I pulled away from her at the curb, I laid rubber just like I'd done in high school. God, this whole thing is just like high school, isn't it?

"Well, I had a hard time getting to sleep Saturday. I was mad at Lenore, mad at Dick, and maddest of all at myself. I finally got to sleep around three or four in the morning, and was up again at seven. When I woke up I began to have doubts about what I had done. I put myself in Lenore's position and saw that perhaps on Friday she just wanted to have some time with her friends at work and then change her clothes and pick up some things before spending the weekend with me. Even though I had planned to take us out to dinner, it was awfully nice of her to pick up all those things and to want to cook for us after working all day. And I could see how she might have misunderstood about the time. I sleep better in my own bed too, and if she were really tired, maybe it was understandable that she went home that night. And then on Saturday, well I could see why it could be important to her to keep her private life separate from her office life—she might not want me to come and meet all of her bosses. And, of course, it's not her fault if men are attracted to her, and she and Dick really do have a lot of things in common.

"So, anyway, I finally began to feel guilty for my childishness and jealousy, and I called her up and asked if we could get together and talk. So I went over to her house about noon, and we had a really nice talk, apologized to each other, and hugged and kissed, and she told me again how much she loved me and I told her the same thing. And then, about three, she said I had to leave. Of course, I asked why, and she said that someone had called and asked her out for the afternoon to sail and go for dinner. I tried to find out when that happened, and I'm not completely sure about when it did, but one thing she said to me was that she didn't know how our talk was going to go, and if it went badly she just knew she'd have to be with somebody. So, I assume that she accepted the date after we had agreed to our talk. Well, I told her that and told her I didn't understand, and she just kept repeating the same excuse. Then she said that it was really me she loved, and she promised to call me after her date was over, and if it wasn't too late, she'd come over and spend the night.

Well, now I knew I shouldn't go along with that, but, you see, I didn't want her to sleep with anybody else, and I was kind of blown away by the whole thing at that point and just said O.K. and left.

"Well, I spent another lonely evening by the TV, thinking lots of uncomfortable thoughts. She finally called at midnight and said she had just gotten home and was really tired and that she couldn't come. She said, 'I still love you.' And this time, I was just beaten. I didn't say anything because I couldn't think of anything to say. I thought about calling her back to see if she really was at home, but that would have been humiliating. I confess, too, I even thought about driving by her place to see if her car was parked outside. I'm proud to say I didn't do that either. I didn't get much sleep last night, though. I just don't known what to do with Lenore. What do you think I should do?"

Case Study Questions

1. What were the characteristics of Lenore that made her so attractive to Ken?
2. How did Ken deal with the aspects of Lenore's behavior that were inconsistent with his positive view of her?
3. What effect did Lenore's behavior have on Ken?

SELF-TEST

Multiple Choice

1. In the Eugene Gollin experiment, where a group of students was shown film clips of a woman displaying two different personality characteristics, half of the students:
   a. tried to create a unified trait of generosity
   b. reported that the woman was both generous and promiscuous
   c. ignored one of the traits and reported the other
   d. reported that the two traits displayed by the woman were incompatible
2. The one principle on which social psychologists generally agree is that the formation of a social perception:
   a. is a difficult task
   b. is a creative act
   c. is a distorted act
   d. is a fabricated act
3. Which of the following is the most accurate with regard to the human infant?
   a. She or he has a clear idea of a self.
   b. She or he has a clear idea of others.
   c. She or he has a limited awareness of others.
   d. all of the above
4. The one-year-old child who cries furiously when taken away from a parent or caretaker is probably displaying:
   a. infant anxiety
   b. stranger anxiety
   c. separation anxiety
   d. detachment anxiety
5. As the child progresses through adolescence, his or her social perceptions tend to approximate those of the adult, because of:
   a. the establishment of social roles and independence
   b. the development of speech and the establishment of complex social interactions
   c. the establishment of social roles and the development of speech
   d. the development of speech and the establishment of independence
6. As a result of the role-taking process, the child leaves behind his or her egocentric ideas and gradually learns:
   a. to take on heavier responsibilities
   b. to organize self-perceptions
   c. to identify with others' feelings
   d. all of the above
7. Solomon Asch, a social psychologist known for his studies of perception, found that from a list of seven traits, a person could:
   a. recall all seven traits following a two-day interval
   b. define each of the seven traits in a consistent fashion
   c. create a unified picture of a whole person
   d. identify which experimental confederates possessed the traits
8. The notion of "assured content" refers to which of the following?
   a. When making a social impression, we assume that our content is accurate.
   b. When making a social impression, we assume that our content is consistent.
   c. When making a social impression, we assume that unprovided content is present.
   d. When making a social impression, we assume unprovided content is irrelevant.
9. Solomon Asch notes that in the process of assigning traits to others, some traits become central while others become peripheral.

According to Asch, the two factors that influence the location of the center are:
a. the central effect and the primary trait
b. the central effect and the primacy effect
c. the central trait and the primacy effect
d. the central trait and the primary trait

10. According to recent experimental research, which of the following trait pairs has the greatest impact on social perceptions:
a. warm-cold
b. honest-dishonest
c. skinny-fat
d. young-old

11. In the experiment by Aronson, Willerman, and Floyd, subjects listened to four tape recordings of four quiz show contestants. Which contestant did the subjects like best?
a. the near-genius
b. the near-genius who spilled his coffee
c. the person showing average performance
d. the average person who spilled his coffee

12. Cherished notions about romantic love notwithstanding, it appears that, when all is said and done, the "one and only" may have a better than 50-50 chance of:
a. being a college student
b. being physically attractive
c. being competent
d. being a neighbor

13. In certain important areas, each person by fulfilling his own needs automatically:
a. fulfills the needs of another person
b. becomes the complement of another person
c. becomes sympathetic toward another person
d. comes to dominate another person

14. For the most part, we are drawn to those people who are
a. rewarding to us
b. similar to us
c. close to us
d. all of the above

15. The process of stereotyping involves all of the following perceptual processes *except*:
a. the drive for consistency
b. the phenomenon of assumed content
c. the principle of centrality
d. the Jack Stroud rule

16. Stereotyping, or the process of classifying people on the basis of their group membership, is the results of:
a. socialization
b. the Jack Stroud rule
c. cognitive drift
d. the devil effect

17. Young boys come to learn what boys and men are "supposed" to be by:
a. adopting the attitudes of those around them
b. taking behavioral or social roles
c. joining social groups
d. all of the above

18. According to most social psychologists, stereotypes are:
a. basically accurate
b. basically false
c. basically vague
d. basically informal

19. Which of the following best applies to stereotypes?
a. they exaggerate group differences
b. they ignore individual differences
c. they assume biological determination of behavior
d. all of the above

20. Which of the following stereotypes are considered learned behaviors?
a. homosexual promiscuity
b. women being more emotional than men
c. blacks being "musical"
d. all of the above

True-False

1. Psychologists have been able to assert that human infants have an extremely limited awareness of the people around them.
2. By the time a child reaches school age, ethnic and socioeconomic roles are usually well learned, while sex roles are beginning to develop.
3. The adolescent's major source of attitudes and opinions tends to be his or her peers.
4. Social psychologist Solomon Asch was able to demonstrate that a description of a whole person could be created from a list of seven adjectives.
5. According to Solomon Asch, the moment we see that two or more characteristics belong to the same person, the characteristics enter into dynamic conflict.
6. Psychologists tend to agree that the human personality is seldom as complex as our theories about it.
7. In the Asch experiment, it was found that changing a trait from "warm" to "cold" did not affect the description of the character, thus demonstrating that "warm" and "cold" are not central traits.
8. Recent experimental research has shown that the warm-cold trait pair is just one of several

trait pairs having a great impact on social impressions.
9. Asch found that subjects who were given a sequential list of six traits "tailored" the first four traits to conform to the last two traits due to what he called the recency effect.
10. Social interaction is said to have an immense impact on our lives and our personality because it molds the self-concept and forms our attitudes.
11. Although beauty may be in the eyes of the beholder, people within a given society tend to agree on what "beautiful" means.
12. Although competence is seen as a positive trait, people seem to prefer competent people who are somewhat imperfect.
13. Proximity is such a powerful factor it almost seems to guarantee attraction.
14. Among those individuals who are geographically close to us, we tend to gravitate toward those most like us.
15. Constantly disagreeing with someone you are close to is generally painful.

Completion

1. In forming our social perceptions, we are _____ , not scientists.
2. Two important facets of social perception are _____ and _____.
3. When an infant is approached or held by an unfamiliar person, the child will usually howl in protest. This response is called _____ _____.
4. Every social role carries a specific set of _____ which eventually become behavioral rules.
5. Unlike the small child, the adolescent is able to think in terms of _____.
6. The self-concept has been shown to obey what Festinger called the principle of cognitive _____.
7. The idea that people tend to supplement their social impressions by adding material not provided by the evidence is called _____ _____.
8. Because the human personality is seldom as logical as our theories claim, _____ theories of personality are a major source of mistaken impressions.
9. Asch notes that some traits become central, providing the main direction, while others become peripheral and _____.
10. In the process of bending traits to make them consistent with one another, we tend to bend other traits to conform to the _____ trait.
11. The trait pair found to have the greatest impact on social perceptions is the _____ _____ trait.
12. Psychological research suggests that _____ impressions are quite long-lasting.
13. In a second experiment, Asch found that subjects tended to use the first two out of six traits to set the direction for their impressions. He called this phenomenon the _____ _____.
14. One of the most important outcomes of social perception, which also has an effect on our likelihood of interacting with others, is _____.
15. _____ refers to another person's geographical closeness and hence his availability for interaction.

Essay Questions

1. Discuss why the formation of a social perception is considered to be a creative act. (pp. 229–230)
2. Discuss the role of "attachment" in the development of social perceptions. Include in your discussion the characteristics of stranger anxiety and separation anxiety. (pp. 230–231)
3. Discuss the study, results, and implications of the Solomon Asch experiment in which a group of people read a list of seven traits, or adjectives. (pp. 238–240)
4. Discuss the Festinger, Schachter and Beck study of the effects of proximity on attraction and social interaction. How does similarity affect the influence of proximity? (pp. 245–257)
5. The process of stereotyping can short-circuit the connection between social attraction and the factors of similarity, rewards, competence and the like. What is stereotyping, what does it involve, what is it the result of, and how does it short-circuit attraction? (pp. 250–255)

SELF-TEST ANSWERS

Multiple Choice

1. c (p. 229)
2. b (p. 230)
3. c (p. 230)
4. c (p. 231)
5. c (pp. 231–232)
6. c (p. 233)
7. c (p. 234)
8. c (p. 235)
9. c (p. 238)
10. a (pp. 238–239)
11. b (p. 245)
12. d (p. 245)
13. a (p. 248)
14. d (p. 249)
15. d (p. 250)
16. a (p. 250)
17. b (p. 250)
18. b (p. 252)
19. d (p. 252)
20. d (p. 252)

True-False

1. true (p. 230)
2. false (p. 232)
3. true (pp. 232–233)
4. true (p. 234)
5. false (p. 235)
6. false (p. 237)
7. false (p. 238)
8. false (p. 239)
9. false (p. 240)
10. true (pp. 241–242)
11. true (p. 242)
12. true (p. 244)
13. false (p. 246)
14. true (p. 247)
15. true (p. 248)

Completion

1. artists (p. 230)
2. attraction, stereotyping (p. 230)
3. stranger anxiety (p. 231)
4. expectations (p. 232)
5. concepts (p. 233)
6. consistency (p. 234)
7. assumed content (p. 235)
8. implicit (pp. 237–238)
9. dependent (p. 238)
10. central (pp. 238–239)
11. warm-cold (p. 239)
12. first (pp. 240–251)
13. primacy effect (pp. 240–241)
14. attraction (p. 241)
15. Proximity (p. 245)

10
Social Perception: How to Change It

CHAPTER OUTLINE

PROBLEM PERCEPTIONS
Wishful Thinking
Outdated Images
The Case of Julie and Steve
Solutions
   Throw him out
   Make him change
   Change the way you perceive him

ANALYZING SOCIAL PERCEPTIONS
Description
   Situational description
Functional Analysis
   External variables: The outer person
   Internal variables

REEXAMINING EXPECTATIONS
The Primacy Effect
Distorting and Screening Out
   Central traits
Inferred Qualities
Inappropriate Standards
   Be like me
   Make my dream come true
   What the neighbors think
   What you are *supposed* to do

CHANGING SOCIAL PERCEPTIONS
Gathering New Information
   Incongruous, embarrassing, or threatening information
   Feedback
Challenging Expectations Through Self-Talk
   Listening to self-talk
   Examining the expectation
   Talking back
   Acting on your back-talk
Are You Buckling Under?
   Julie and Steve: A proposal

READING

Eyewitnesses: Essential but Unreliable

ELIZABETH F. LOFTUS

The ladies and gentlemen of William Bernard Jackson's jury decided that he was guilty of rape. They made a serious mistake, and before it was discovered, Jackson had spent five years in prison. There he suffered numerous indignities and occasional attacks, until the police discovered that another man, who looked very much like Jackson, had committed the rapes.

   If you had been on the jury, you would probably have voted for conviction too. Two women had positively identified Jackson as the man who had raped them in September and October of 1977. The October victim was asked on the witness stand, "Is there any doubt in your mind as whether this man you have identified here is the man who had the sexual activity with you on October 3, 1977?" She answered "No doubt." "Could you be mistaken?" the prosecutor asked. "No, I am not mistaken," the victim stated confidently. Jackson and other defense witnesses testified that he was home when the rapes occurred. But the jury didn't believe him or them.

   This is just one of the many documented cases of mistaken eyewitness testimony that have had tragic consequences. In 1981, Steve Titus of Seattle was convicted of raping a 17-year-old woman on a secluded road; the following year he was proven to be innocent. Titus was luckier than Jackson; he never went to prison. However, Aaron Lee Owens of Oakland, California, was not as fortunate. He spent nine years in a prison for a double murder that he didn't commit. In these cases, and many others, eyewitnesses testified against the defendants, and jurors believed them.

One reason most of us, as jurors, place so much faith in eyewitness testimony is that we are unaware of how many factors influence its accuracy. To name just a few: what questions witnesses are asked by police and how the questions are phrased; the difficulty people have in distinguishing among people of other races; whether witnesses have seen photos of suspects before viewing the lineup from which they pick out the person they say committed the crime; the size, composition and type (live or photo) of the lineup itself.

I know of seven studies that assess what ordinary citizens believe about eyewitness memory. One common misconception is that police officers make better witnesses than the rest of us. As part of a larger study, my colleagues and I asked 541 registered voters in Dade County, Florida, "Do you think that the memory of law enforcement agents is better than the memory of the average citizen?" Half said yes, 38 percent said no and the rest had no opinion. When A. Daniel Yarmey of the University of Guelph asked judges, lawyers and policemen a similar question, 63 percent of the legal officials and half the police agreed that "The policeman will be superior to the civilian" in identifying robbers.

This faith in police testimony is not supported by research. Several years ago, psychologists A. H. Tinkner and E. Christopher Poulton showed a film depicting a street scene to 24 police officers and 156 civilians. The subjects were asked to watch for particular people in the film and to report instances of crimes, such as petty theft. The researchers found that the officers reported more alleged thefts than the civilians but that when it came to detecting actual crimes, the civilians did just as well.

More recently, British researcher Peter B. Ainsworth showed a 20-minute videotape to police officers and civilians. The tape depicted a number of staged criminal offenses, suspicious circumstances and traffic offenses at an urban street corner. No significant differences were found between the police and civilians in the total number of incidents reported. Apparently neither their initial training nor subsequent experience increases the ability of the police to be accurate witnesses.

Studies by others and myself have uncovered other common misconceptions about eyewitness testimony.

They include:

☐ *Witnesses remember the details of a violent crime better than those of a nonviolent one.* Research shows just the opposite: The added stress that violence creates clouds our perceptions.

☐ *Witnesses are as likely to underestimate the duration of a crime as to overestimate it.* In fact, witnesses almost invariably think a crime took longer than it did. The more violent and stressful the crime, the more witnesses overestimate its duration.

☐ *The more confident a witness seems, the more accurate the testimony is likely to be.* Research suggests that there may be little or no relationship between confidence and accuracy, especially when viewing conditions are poor.

The unreliability of confidence as a guide to accuracy has been demonstrated outside of the courtroom, too; one example is provided by accounts of an aircraft accident that killed nine people several years ago. According to *Flying* magazine, several people had seen the airplane just before impact, and one of them was certain that "it was heading right toward the ground, straight down." This witness was profoundly wrong, as shown by several photographs taken of the crash site that made it clear that the airplane hit flat and at a low enough angle to skid for almost 1,000 feet.

Despite the inaccuracies of eyewitness testimony, we can't afford to exclude it legally or ignore it as jurors. Sometimes, as in cases of rape, it is the only evidence available, and it is often correct. The question remains, what can we do to give jurors a better understanding of the uses and pitfalls of such testimony? Judges sometimes give the jury a list of instructions on the pitfalls of eyewitness testimony. But this method has not proved satisfactory, probably because as studies show, jurors either do not listen or do not understand the instructions.

Another solution, when judges permit, is to call a psychologist as an expert witness to explain how the human memory works and describe the experimental findings that apply to the case at hand. How this can affect a case is shown by a murder trial in California two years ago. On April 1, 1981, two young men were walking along Polk Street in San Francisco at about 5:30 in the evening. A car stopped near them, and the driver, a man in his 40s, motioned one of the men to get in, which he did. The car drove off. Up to this point, nothing appeared unusual. The area was known as a place where prostitutes hang out; in fact, the young man who got in the car was there hustling for "tricks." Three days later, he was found strangled in a wooded area some 75 miles south of San Francisco.

Five weeks later, the victim's friend was shown a six-person photo lineup and picked out a 47-year-old I'll call D. The quick selection of D's photograph, along with the strong emotional reaction that accompanied it (the friend became ill when he saw the photo), convinced the police that they had their man. D was tried for murder.

At his trial, the defense lawyer introduced expert testimony by a psychologist on the factors that made accurate perception and memory difficult. For example, in the late afternoon of April 1, the witness had been using marijuana, a substance likely to blur his initial perceptions and his memory of them. Furthermore, just before viewing the lineup, the witness had seen a photograph of D on a desk in the police station, an incident that could have influenced his selection. During the five weeks between April 1 and the time he saw the photographs, the witness had talked about and been questioned repeatedly about the crime, circumstances that often contaminate memory.

In the end, the jury was unable to reach a verdict. It is difficult to assess the impact of any one bit of testimony on a particular verdict. We can only speculate that the psychologist's testimony may have made the jury more cautious about accepting the eyewitness testimony. This idea is supported by recent studies showing that such expert testimony generally increases the deliberation time jurors devote to eyewitness aspects of a case.

Expert testimony on eyewitness reliability is controversial. It has its advocates and enemies in both the legal and psychological professions. For example, several judicial arguments are used routinely to exclude the testimony. One is that it "invades the province of the jury," meaning that it is the jury's job, not an expert's, to decide whether a particular witness was in a position to see, hear and remember what is being claimed in court. Another reason judges sometimes exclude such testimony is that the question of eyewitness reliability is "not beyond the knowledge and experience of a juror" and thus is not a proper subject matter for expert testimony.

In virtually all the cases in which a judge has prohibited the jury from hearing expert testimony, the higher courts have upheld the decision, and in some cases have driven home the point with negative comments about the use of psychologists. In a recent case in California, *People v. Plasencia*, Nick Plasencia Jr. was found guilty of robbery and other crimes in Los Angeles County. He had tried to introduce the testimony of a psychologist on eyewitness reliability, but the judge refused to admit it, saying that "the subject matter about which [the expert] sought to testify was too conjectural and too speculative to support any opinion he would offer." The appellate court upheld Plasencia's conviction and made known its strong feelings about the psychological testimony:

"Since our society has not reached the point where all human conduct is videotaped for later replay, resolution of disputes in our court system depends almost entirely on the testimony of witnesses who recount their observations of a myriad of events.

"These events include matters in both the criminal and civil areas of the law. The accuracy of a witness's testimony of course depends on factors which are as variable and complex as human nature itself. . . . The cornerstone of our system remains our belief in the wisdom and integrity of the jury system and the ability of 12 jurors to determine the accuracy of witnesses' testimony. The system has served us well. . . .

"It takes no expert to tell us that for various reasons, people can be mistaken about identity, or even the exact details of an observed event. Yet to present these commonly accepted and known facts in the form of an expert opinion, which opinion does nothing more than generally question the validity of one form of traditionally accepted evidence, would exaggerate the significance of that testimony and give a 'scientific aura' to a very unscientific matter.

"The fact remains, in spite of the universally recognized fallibility of human beings, persons do, on many occasions, correctly identify individuals. Evidence that under contrived test conditions, or even in real-life situations, certain persons totally unconnected with this case have been mistaken in their identification of individuals is no more relevant than evidence that in other cases, witnesses totally unconnected with this event have lied.

"It seems beyond question that the identifications in this case were correct. We find no abuse of discretion in the trial court's rejecting the proffered testimony."

Quite the opposite view was expressed by the Arizona Supreme Court in *State v. Chapple*. At the original trial, defendant Dolan Chapple had been convicted of three courts of murder and two drug-trafficking charges, chiefly on the testimony of two witnesses who identified him at the trial. Earlier they had selected him from photographs shown them by the police more than a year after the crime.

Chapple's lawyer tried to introduce expert psychological testimony on the accuracy of such identification. The judge refused to permit it on the grounds that the testimony would pertain only to matters "within the common experience" of jurors.

The high court disagreed, maintaining that expert testimony would have provided scientific data on such pertinent matters as the accuracy of delayed identification, the effect of stress on perception and the relationship between witness confidence and accuracy. "We cannot assume," the court added, "that the average juror would be aware of the variables concerning identification and memory" about which the expert would have testified. Chapple's conviction was reversed, and he has been granted a new trial.

Like lawyers and judges, psychologists disagree on whether expert testimony is a good solution to the eyewitness problem. Two of the most outspoken critics are Michael McCloskey and Howard Egeth of The Johns Hopkins University. These experimental psychologists offer four reasons why they believe that expert testimony on eyewitness reliability is a poor idea. They say that there is no evidence that such testimony is needed; that there is no evidence that it does any good or that it can provide much beyond the intuitions of ordinary experience; that the data base on which the expert must rely is not sufficiently well-developed; and that conflicting public testimony between experts would tarnish the profession's image. Given this sorry state of affairs, they argue, psychologists may do more harm than good by intruding into judicial proceedings.

Obviously, many psychologists disagree with this assessment and believe that both the law and psychology gain from mutual interaction. In the area of eyewitness testimony, information supplied by psychologists to lawyers has stimulated responses that have suggested a number of important ideas for future research.

For example, psychologists need to learn more about the ideas that the rest of us have about the operation of human perception and memory. When these ideas are wrong, psychologists need to devise ways to educate us so that the judgments we make as jurors will be more fully informed and more fair. Only through this give-and-take, and occasional biting controversy, will progress be made. It is too late to help William Jackson, or Steve Titus, or Aaron Lee Owens, but it is not yet too late for the rest of us.

Reading Questions

1. What are some common misconceptions about eyewitness testimony discussed in this article?
2. Why would a judge prohibit the testimony of a psychologist with regard to eyewitness reliability?
3. How can a psychologists's knowledge about perception and memory be used to help in the legal process?

RESEARCH STUDY

Investigators:	Roger M. Knudson, Alison A. Sommers, and Stephen L. Golding.
Source, date:	"Interpersonal Perception and Mode of Resolution in Marital Conflict," *Journal of Personality and Social Psychology*, 1980, *38*, 751-763.
Location:	University of Illinois at Urbana-Champaign.
Subjects:	young married couples.
Materials:	videotapes, videotaping equipment, and rating scales.

Conflict is an inevitable aspect of the marital relationship. How such conflict is handled may determine the course of the marriage. If conflict is handled effectively, not only are differences resolved, but the couple learn more about each other's perceptions and feelings. Knowledge of these perceptions and feelings strengthens the mutual understanding in the relationship and increases the couple's ability to handle stresses, changes, and conflict in the future.

Conflict resolution can proceed in at least two directions. When the members of a couple differ in their perceptions of a situation, the couple may seek to "resolve" conflict by simply not dealing with the issue. While such avoidance gives the impression of harmony, the two gain no greater understanding of each other's perceptions. Another alternative is for the couple to *engage* conflict by involving themselves in thrashing out the issue. Until they resolve the conflict, there may be less harmony, but once it is resolved, not only have they eliminated the conflict, they have also increased their understanding of each other.

This study was designed to investigate whether or not these different approaches to conflict resolution do indeed result in these different outcomes of understanding.

Thirty-three young married couples who volunteered to take part in the study permitted videotapes to be made of themselves while engaged in an argument about some recent issue of importance to them. Following the videotaping, each member of the couple viewed the videotape. During the replay, at particular points in the argument, each member was asked by an interviewer to indicate his or her self-perception and perception of the other person.

As expected, it was found that couples who *engaged* the issues, that is, made their own positions clear and tried to take their spouse's position into account, reached greater agreement and understanding. Couples who avoided the issues, that is, either failed to make their own positions clear or failed to take their spouse's position into account, reached less agreement and understanding. Interestingly, these "avoiding" couples thought they had increased their agreement, while in reality they had not. Indeed, they were more at variance in their perceptions, and they showed less understanding of their spouse's view of the situation.

Thus those who engaged in the conflict, working to present their own view while considering the view of the other, were more successful at conflict resolution and at increasing their mutual understanding of their perceptions of issues.

Research Study Questions

1. This study was concerned with what aspect of the marital relationship? What is the importance of this aspect?
2. How did the investigators create conditions that permitted them to study perception in marital conflict?
3. What was the relation between mode of conflict resolution and subsequent agreement and understanding?

CASE STUDY

Falling Out of Love

GEORGE KALUGER AND MERIEM FAIR KALUGER

I don't know why I chose this topic to write about. Perhaps it is because I can't seem to get away from it, and perhaps it is because I think that putting it all down in black and white will make it seem more objective and less personal. It happens to everybody, but it never happened to me before. At the age of twenty-three, it seems almost impossible that I've never been in love. Consequently, I've never felt the need to fall out of love.

He came into my life when, as the axiom states, I least expected it. I was happily going about my own business, just having a good time; then he walked into my life and took over completely. I didn't know I could be so happy. I had somebody besides my family to share with. Every day when we talked, he'd ask me how my day had gone. If I had a problem, he'd listen and advise. I seldom took his advice, but it was comforting knowing that he cared.

When Christmas came, the beautiful snow created a fairyland. He took me to meet his parents—something he does with few girls, as both he and they had assured me. We went to parties, we went dancing, we fell asleep in front of the fire. We wrestled in the snow. We got stuck in the snow. Everything we did, we did together. I baked cookies and he ate them. We weren't going to get serious, he said. We were just going to have fun.

Then on Valentine's Day, we had our first and, as a matter of fact, our only major argument. This happened on Friday. That weekend was miserable. He didn't call to break our date on Saturday; when I called him and realized that I was being "stood up," I was quite upset. I cried. My mother cried with me. She always loved Brian. "This is one boy I could gladly call 'Son,'" she'd said. Sunday was just as bad. Monday was worse! I could hardly wait to get home from the office so I could let myself "feel." I sobbed.

That night I went to a movie. Really, I only went to get out of the house. While I was gone Brian called. He called back after I got home. He'd been sick all day and hadn't gone to work. I don't remember the conversation, but I do know that he apologized and that we talked it out. He asked me how I felt and I said: "I felt like you dropped me from the third floor, watched me splatter, and laughed." He said: "I wasn't laughing." Everything, I thought, was back to normal. On Wednesday, his day off, we went out. He assured me that "all was forgiven."

From that time on, however, we saw each other less and less. I didn't go out. I still expected that he would call. When he went to the hospital for three weeks in March, I visited him every day. Since his parents don't drive, he called me for the things that he needed. I loved doing things for him, and I know he appreciated it. But when he was released from the hospital, it was the same old thing. I thought I had prepared myself not to be hurt, but when he missed calling me, I was miserable all over again.

I began to question myself and my situation. I tried to talk it out with him, but all he managed to do was to criticize me. I wanted to say: "Okay, don't bother me anymore." But I couldn't do it. I didn't want to lose him.

One time when we'd had a minor disagreement, I very coolly stated our problem as I saw it. We happened "to like each other" in spite of everything.

This should be a problem? It was for us because neither of us wanted to hurt the other—or ourselves.

Through April and May, Brian called less and less frequently. By the end of May he wasn't calling at all. How did I feel? I hurt all over. It was especially bad, too, because I'd moved into my own apartment on May 19, and I was not yet used to living alone. I felt absolutely empty. I was lonely, unsure, bereft. All I had to do with my time was to fill it with thinking. Finally he called. He made a date for the next day, and I was elated. He never came. From the heights of ecstasy to the depths of despair in twenty-four hours—that was me! There it was, all over again. All the fresh, new hurt. He called later that week and acted as if nothing at all had happened. He asked about every member of my family, about everything that I was doing. But no date!

So now I'm concentrating on falling out of love. But I find myself daydreaming about him constantly. I have long, involved, imaginary conversations with him that are filled with questions and explanations. Sometimes I quarrel with him. I remember our good times and I become depressed. When I'm shopping and I see a cute greeting card, I have to remind myself that I can't send it to him. I catch myself thinking: "I'll have to remember to tell Brian that joke . . . or this story . . . or that comment." When I buy a dress, I wonder if he will like it—then I remember that it doesn't really matter anymore. I find his name creeping into conversations that shouldn't relate to him at all. I jump when the phone rings, and I'm sad when it doesn't. Until very recently I've had no desire to see other people socially, and I've turned down more dates than I've accepted. I have so much energy that I don't know what to do with it all—and yet I have no ambition to do anything. I get violently jealous when I see couples our age having a good time with each other. I get angry with myself for feeling this way. Knowing that others have had the same experience is no consolation at all. Even the realization that I am better off without him doesn't help. Logic has absolutely nothing to do with my feelings.

So what is it like to fall out of love? It is hard. It is lonely. It is depressing. It is necessary. I keep telling myself that it gets easier every day, and most days it does. I just hope that I never have to do it again.

Case Study Questions

1. What role did first impressions and expectations play in the relationship between Brian and his "girlfriend"?
2. How was the prospect of "falling out of love" influenced by an outdated image?
3. How did Brian's "girlfriend" finally convince herself to "fall out of love"?

SELF-TEST

Multiple Choice

1. Our perception of someone we know fairly well contains three components:
    a. assumptions, evaluations, expectations
    b. expectations, knowledge, evaluations
    c. assumptions, knowledge, expectations
    d. knowledge, assumptions, evaluations
2. The three components of our perception of another are said to have:
    a. a mutually exclusive relationship
    b. a circular relationship
    c. an exhaustive relationship
    d. a systematic relationship
3. Very often, a parent's perception of his or her daughter will remain the same over the years while his or her daughter is continually growing and changing. This practice usually results in:
    a. a distorted image
    b. a repressed image
    c. an outdated image
    d. a wishful image
4. The analysis of social perceptions, like the analysis of the self-concept, requires two steps:
    a. observation and trend analysis
    b. description and factor analysis
    c. description and functional analysis
    d. observation and correlation analysis
5. In order to conduct a fairly scientific analysis of social perceptions, we must adhere to all the following principles except:
    a. objectivity
    b. simplicity
    c. observability
    d. specificity
6. An analysis of social perceptions would find which of the following statements the most useful?
    a. Joan is wasting her intelligence on that job of hers
    b. Bob is very lazy and is often selfish
    c. Carol glues herself to the TV every Saturday
    d. Bill does not treat me like he used to treat me
7. Which variables are necessary for conducting a scientific analysis of social perceptions?
    a. overt and covert variables

b. internal and external variables
   c. objective and subjective variables
   d. functional and correlational variables
8. Which of the following types of analyses will enable you to determine what is causing and maintaining your negative evaluation?
   a. trend analysis
   b. correlation analysis
   c. factor analysis
   d. functional analysis
9. The key to understanding a negative evaluation that we hold of another person, and to the negative emotions that accompany it, is:
   a. our assumptions
   b. our knowledge
   c. our evaluations
   d. our expectations
10. To get a general idea of the expectations you have of another person:
    a. look at the opposite of your complaint of the other person
    b. ask the other person what he or she expects of you
    c. consider the opposite of the other person's expectations
    d. become aware of the other person's complaint of you
11. The staying power of the first impression involves which of the following?
    a. the halo effect
    b. the primacy effect
    c. the recency effect
    d. the sliding effect
12. People tend to choose the facts that "fit" and leave behind the facts that don't fit on the basis of:
    a. implicit personality theories
    b. wishful thinking
    c. cognitive consistency
    d. all of the above
13. Most of us do not allow the awareness of current facts to influence the expectations that we hold of another person because:
    a. We tend to keep these expectations in the preconscious part of our mind.
    b. We tend to keep the expectations from being contaminated by reality.
    c. We tend to maintain these current facts in our consciousness.
    d. We tend to see these current facts as unimportant.
14. Which of the following is considered one of the most important qualities of a positive and realistic social perception?
    a. the quality of diversification
    b. the quality of specificity
    c. the quality of simplicity
    d. the quality of centrality
15. Inferences can be harmful in that:
    a. they create expectations that can't be fulfilled
    b. they almost guarantee disappointment
    c. both a and b
    d. none of the above
16. The standards that we have for the people close to us are:
    a. much lower than those that we hold for human beings in general
    b. usually higher than those that we hold for human beings in general
    c. the same as those that we hold for human beings in general
    d. much lower than those that we hold for ourselves
17. Which of the following is not one of the four common standards used to measure people close to us?
    a. ourselves
    b. our realized goals
    c. social conventions
    d. others' opinions
18. The parent who fantasizes a glorious music career for his or her child and then feels cheated when the child becomes a lawyer is an example of:
    a. judging others against social conventions
    b. judging others against other opinions
    c. judging others against ourselves
    d. judging others against unattained goals
19. Realistic perceptions tend to lead the relationship into:
    a. increased intimacy
    b. increased acceptance
    c. increased freedom
    d. all of the above
20. One of the central tenets of existential psychology is that interpersonal relationships must allow for:
    a. change
    b. fulfillment
    c. uniqueness
    d. negotiations

True-False

1. The three elements of our perception of another person seem to represent a system of interlocking circles.

2. Most people find it quite easy to revise a social impression to fit some new evidence.
3. Like the wishful image, the outdated image is a ripe source of conflict.
4. Inaccurate images may produce anger, distrust, and disappointment, but they rarely have the power to destroy a relationship altogether.
5. The analysis of social perceptions, like the analysis of self-control, requires two steps: description and factor analysis.
6. For the most part, our view of another person is complicated, subjective and vague.
7. By utilizing the method of correlation analysis, we can determine what is causing and maintaining our negative evaluation of another person.
8. The individual's interpretation of an external stimulus is represented by the letter "A" in Albert Ellis' A-B-C formula.
9. Generally speaking, the description of your main complaint about another person will closely match the opposite of your expectation.
10. The recency effect is considered to be the staying power of the first impression.
11. Often, well rounded and consistent expectations are also extremely inaccurate.
12. If we organize our perception of another person around one selected trait, then this trait is referred to as the central trait.
13. One of the most important qualities of a positive and realistic self-perception is diversification.
14. Distortions, screening-out of qualities, and inferred qualities are based on our implicit theories of personality.
15. The standards that we hold for the people close to us are usually much higher than those we hold for human beings in general.

Completion

1. Our _____ of someone we know fairly well is based on a combination of what that person could be and do with what that person should be and do.
2. The classic example of _____ _____ is the habit that parents have of nourishing fantasies about their children's future lives.
3. A(n) _____ image usually results when our perception of a person remains the same while the person continues to grow and change.
4. The analysis of social perceptions requires the two steps of _____ and _____ _____.
5. In order to have some information to work on in your analysis of social perceptions, you have to fill out your simplified statement of the problem with _____ facts and _____ details.
6. A _____ description depicts an actual situation in which another person behaves and you react to that behavior.
7. We can effectively determine what is causing and maintaining our negative evaluation of another person by utilizing the method of _____ analysis.
8. The two types of variables to consider in your analysis of social perception are _____ variables and _____ .
9. The _____ formula proposed by Albert Ellis and Robert Harper takes into account the person's interpretation of external stimuli.
10. The person-specific beliefs that a father has of his daughter are the father's _____ .
11. _____ are the key to understanding the negative emotions that accompany the negative evaluation that we hold of another person.
12. The _____ effect is considered to be the staying power of a first impression.
13. We organize our perception of another person around a _____ trait.
14. From the characteristics that we see in another person, we _____ other characteristics and add them into our set of expectations.
15. Expecting the people close to us to measure up to other people's standards places the locus of approval _____ the relationship.

Essay Questions

1. Discuss how wishful thinking and outdated images can affect social perception. (pp. 263–265)
2. In order for a description to meet the requirements of a scientific analysis, it must be simple, objective, and specific. Discuss each of these components in detail. (pp. 268–269)
3. The A-B-C formula proposed by Albert Ellis and Robert Harper takes into account a person's belief system in the analysis of psychological difficulties. How can this formula be applied to social perceptions? (pp. 271–272)
4. Discuss each of the four common standards by which we tend to measure those people close to us. (pp. 276–278)
5. What kinds of emotional signals can a person watch out for when trying to alter his or her social perception through the gathering of new information? (pp. 279–280)

SELF-TEST ANSWERS

Multiple Choice

1. b (p. 261)
2. b (p. 262)
3. c (pp. 263–265)
4. c (p. 268)
5. c (p. 268)
6. c (p. 269)
7. b (p. 270)
8. d (p. 270)
9. d (p. 271)
10. a (p. 272)
11. b (p. 272)
12. d (pp. 273–275)
13. b (pp. 273–274)
14. a (p. 275)
15. c (p. 276)
16. b (p. 276)
17. b (p. 276)
18. d (p. 277)
19. d (p. 279)
20. c (pp. 281–282)

True-False

1. true (p. 262)
2. false (p. 262)
3. true (p. 264)
4. false (pp. 264-265)
5. false (p. 268)
6. true (p. 269)
7. false (p. 270)
8. false (p. 271)
9. true (p. 272)
10. false (p. 272)
11. true (p. 274)
12. true (p. 275)
13. true (p. 275)
14. true (pp. 275-276)
15. true (p. 276)

Completion

1. expectations (p. 261)
2. wishful thinking (p. 263)
3. outdated (pp. 263-264)
4. description, functional analysis (p. 268)
5. objective, specific (p. 269)
6. situational (pp. 269-270)
7. functional (p. 270)
8. internal, external (p. 270)
9. A-B-C (p. 271)
10. expectations (p. 271)
11. Expectations (p. 271)
12. primacy (p. 272)
13. central (p. 275)
14. infer (p. 276)
15. outside (p. 278)

11
Social Influence: What It Is and How It Operates

CHAPTER OUTLINE

ATTITUDES
The Functions of Attitudes
The Origins of Attitudes: Three Sources
The Organs of Social Influence
    Parents
    Peers
    Mass media

THE PROCESSES OF INFLUENCE
Modeling
    Modeling and reinforcement
    The characteristics of the model
    Modeling and attitudes
Conformity
    The group and its norms
    The Asch study
    The causes of conformity
    The determinants of conformity
Persuasion
    The determinants of persuasion
    Propaganda

DIRECT INFLUENCE AND ADJUSTMENT
Reactance
An Active Approach to Influence

READING

The Language of Persuasion

DAVID KIPNIS AND STUART SCHMIDT

"I had all the facts and figures ready before I made my suggestions to my boss." (Manager)

"I kept insisting that we do it my way. She finally caved in." (Husband)

"I think it's about time that you stop thinking these negative things about yourself." (Psychotherapist)

"Send out more horses, skirr the country round. Hang those that talk of fear. Give me mine armour." (Macbeth, Act 5)

These diverse statements—rational, insistent, emotional—have one thing in common. They all show people trying to persuade others, a skill we all treasure. Books about power and influence are read by young executives eager for promotion, by politicians anxious to sway their constituents, by lonely people looking to win and hold a mate and by harried parents trying to make their children see the light.

Despite this interest in persuasion, most people are not really aware of how they go about it. They spend more time choosing their clothes than they do their influence styles. Even fewer are aware of how their styles affect others or themselves. Although shouts and demands may make people dance to our tune, we will probably lose their goodwill. Beyond that, our opinion of others may change for the worse when we use hard or abusive tactics.

Popular books on influencing others give contradictory advice. Some advocate assertiveness, others stealth and still others reason and logic. Could they all be right? We decided to see for ourselves what kinds of influence people actually use in personal and work situations and why they choose the tactics they do.

We conducted studies of dating couples and business managers in which the couples described how they attempted to influence their partners and the managers told how they attempted to influence their subordinates, peers and superiors at work. We then used these descriptions as the basis for separate questionnaires in which we asked other couples and managers how frequently they employed each tactic. Using factor analysis and other statistical techniques, we found that the tactics could be classified into three basic strategies—hard, soft and rational (see the "Influence Strategies" box).

These labels describe the tactics from the standpoint of the person using them. Since influencing someone is a social act, its meaning depends upon the observer's vantage point. For example, a wife might ask her husband, "I wonder what we should do about the newspapers in the garage?" The husband could consider this remark nagging to get him to clean up the garage. The wife might say her remark was simply a friendly suggestion that he consider the state of the garage. An outside observer might feel that the wife's remark was just conversation, not a real attempt to influence.

As the box illustrates, hard tactics involve demanding, shouting and assertiveness. With soft tactics, people act nice and flatter others to get their way. Rational tactics involve the use of logic and bargaining to demonstrate why compliance or compromise is the best solution.

Why do people shout and demand in one instance, flatter in a second and offer to compromise in a third? One common explanation is that the choice of tactics is based upon what "feels right" in each case. A more pragmatic answer is that the choice of tactics is based strictly on what works.

Our studies show that the reasons are more complex. When we examine how people actually use influence, we find that they use many different strategies, depending on the situation and the person being influenced. We gathered information from 195 dating and married couples, and from 360 first- and second-line managers in the United States, Australia and Great Britain. We asked which influence tactics they used, how frequently and in what conditions.

The choice of strategies varied predictably for both managers and couples. It depends on their particular objectives, relative power position and expectations about the willingness of others to do what they want. These expectations are often based on individual traits and biases rather than facts.

Objectives

One of our grandmothers always advised sweetly, "Act nice if you want a favor." We found that people

INFLUENCE STRATEGIES

STRATEGY	COUPLES	MANAGERS
Hard	I get angry and demand that he/she give in.	I simply order the person to do what I ask.
	As the first step I make him/her feel stupid and worthless.	I threaten to give an unsatisfactory performance evaluation.
	I say I'll leave him/her if my spouse does not agree.	I get higher management to back up my request.
Soft	I act warm and charming before bringing up the subject.	I act very humble while making my request.
	I am so nice that he/she cannot refuse.	I make the person feel important by saying that he/she has the brains and experience to do what I want.
Rational	I offer to compromise; I'll give up a little if she/he gives up a little.	I offer to exchange favors; You do this for me, and I'll do something for you.
	We talk, discussing our views objectively without arguments.	I explain the reason for my request.

do, indeed, vary their tactics according to what they want.

At work, for instance, managers frequently rely on soft tactics—flattery, praise, acting humble—when they want something from a boss such as time off or better assignments. However, when managers want to persuade the boss to accept ideas, such as a new work procedure, they're more likely to use reason and logic. Occasionally, they will even try hard tactics, such as going over the boss's head, if he or she can't be moved any other way.

Couples also vary their choice of tactics depending upon what they want from each other. Personal benefits such as choosing a movie or restaurant for the night call for a soft, loving approach. When they want to change a spouse's unacceptable behavior, anger, threats and other hard tactics come into play.

Power Positions

People who control resources, emotions or finances valued by others clearly have the advantage in a relationship, whether it is commercial or personal. In our research with couples, we discovered which partner was dominant by asking who made the final decision about issues such as spending money, choosing friends and other family matters. We found that people who say they control the relationship ("I have the final say") often rely on hard tactics to get their way. Those who share decision power ("We decide together") bargain rationally and often compromise. Partners who admit that they have little power ("My partner has the final say") usually favor soft tactics.

We found the same patterns among managers. The more one-sided the power relationship at work, the more likely managers are to demand, get angry and insist with people who work for them, and the more likely they are to act humble and flatter when they are persuading their bosses.

The fact that people change influence tactics depending on their power over the other person is hardly surprising. What is surprising is how universal the link is between power and tactics. Our surveys and those conducted by others have found this relationship among children trying to influence younger children or older children, and among executives dealing with executives at other companies more or less powerful than their own, as well as among spouses and business managers dealing with their own subordinates and bosses.

There seems to be an "Iron Law of Power": The greater the discrepancy in clout between the influencer and the target, the greater the likelihood that hard tactics will be used. People with power don't always use hard tactics as their first choice. At first, most simply request and explain. They turn to demands and threats (the iron fist lurking under the velvet glove of reason) only when someone seems reluctant or refuses to comply with their request.

In contrast, people with little power are likely to stop trying or immediately shift to soft tactics when they encounter resistance. They feel the costs associated with the use of hard or even rational tactics are unacceptable. They are unwilling to take the chance of angering a boss, a spouse or an older child by using anything but soft methods.

Expectations and Biases

We have found that people also vary their strategies according to how successful they expect to be in influencing their targets. When they believe that someone is likely to do what is asked, they make simple requests. When they anticipate resistance and have the power, they use hard tactics.

This anticipation may be realistic. Just as a robber knows that without a gun, a polite request for money is unlikely to persuade, a boss knows that a request for work on Saturday needs more than a smile to back it up. But less realistic personal and situational factors sometimes make us expect resistance where none exists. People who are low in self-esteem and self-confidence, for instance, have difficulty believing that others will comply with simple requests.

We found that lack of confidence and low self-esteem are characteristic of managers who bark orders and refuse to discuss the issues involved, of couples who constantly shout and scream at each other and of parents who rely on harsh discipline. These hard tactics result from the self-defeating assumption that others will not listen unless they are treated roughly.

Social situations and biases can also distort expectations of cooperation. Misunderstandings based on differences in attitudes, race or sex can lead to hard tactics. Our research, and that of others, shows that orders, shouts and threats are more likely to be used between blacks and whites or men and women. The simple perception that "these people are different than I am" leads to the idea that "they are not as reasonable as I am" and must be ordered about.

People may use influence tactics because of habit, lack of forethought or lack of social sensitivity. Most of us would be more effective persuaders if we analyzed why we act as we do. Simply writing a short description of a recent incident in which we tried to persuade someone can help us understand better our own tactics, why we use them and, perhaps, why a rational approach might be better.

People who know we have studied the matter sometimes ask, "Which tactics work best?" The answer is that they all work if they are used at the right time with the right person. But both hard and soft tactics involve costs to the user even when they succeed. Hard tactics often alienate the people being influenced and create a climate of hostility and resistance. Soft tactics—acting nice, being humble—may lessen self-respect and self-esteem. In contrast, we found that people who rely chiefly on logic, reason and compromise to get their way are the most satisfied both with their business lives and with their personal relationships.

Reading Questions

1. Explain the three types of influence strategies discussed.
2. Discuss the relationship between power and influence strategies.
3. How do a person's expectations affect his or her choice of influence strategies?

RESEARCH STUDY

Investigators: Richard T. Santee and Christina Maslach.
Source, date: "To Agree or Not to Agree: Personal Dissent amid Social Pressures to Conform," *Journal of Personality and Social Psychology*, 1982, *42*, 690-700.
Location: University of California at Berkeley.
Subjects: undergraduate students.
Materials: Texas Social Behavior Inventory, Form A, 20 brief stories of problematic social situations.

Social psychologists have paid a good deal of attention to trying to understand why people conform in social situations. The same amount of attention, however, has not been given to the reasons why people dissent in such situations.

In this study, two types of factors related to dissent in a social situation were investigated. One set of factors concerned the degree of uniformity of opinion expressed by others. Here the concern was whether or not situations in which a uniform opinion was expressed would differ from situations in which a uniform opinion was not expressed in terms of an individual's readiness to dissent. A second set of factors involved the personality characteristics of the dissenter. In particular, what, if any, aspects of a person's self-concept would lead to dissent?

In conducting the study, the investigators first assessed the self-esteem, self-monitoring, self-consciousness, shyness and social anxiety of 118 undergraduate students enrolled in an introductory psychology course. Several weeks later, the participants were each placed in a soundproof booth and over headphones were told that they would be taking part in a study on human relations. They were then presented twenty stories, each describing a particular problem. Each story ended with three alternative resolutions. The participants were to pick their preferred solution (or they could create one of their own). Half the subjects were in a condition where they heard the opinions of three other people (supposedly their peers). Some of these opinions were unanimous, some were split.

The results indicated that a person's self-concept was a powerful indicator of his or her readiness to dissent in the unanimous situations—but not in the non-unanimous situations. In particular, in unanimous situations, the degree of individuation or distractiveness (a factor composed of several self-concept variables) was positively related to dissent and the degree of social anxiety was negatively related to dissent. In addition, self-esteem and private self-consciousness were related to creative dissent (e.g., the participant created his or her own alternative resolution), since individuals who are high in these attend more to their own opinions and less to the opinions of others. No relation between self-monitoring and dissent was found. On the basis of the difference between unanimous and non-unanimous situations, the investigators suggested that individuals will be less likely to dissent in unanimous situations because such dissent requires a strong act of self-definition. Dissent in a non-unanimous situation does not require as strong an act of self-definition on the part of the individual.

Research Study Questions

1. In focusing on dissent, how did this study differ from other social psychological research on response to social pressure? What factors related to the dissent were investigated?
2. Describe the approach used by the investigators in studying dissent.
3. What were the results of the study?

CASE STUDY

Boot Camp

GEORGE KALUGER AND MERIEM FAIR KALUGER

My first trip to talk to the Coast Guard recruiter did not worry me too much because I had not signed anything or been sworn in as a member of the U.S. Coast Guard. However, I was very nervous when my parents were driving me to the recruiting office to take the oath of enlistment and leave for basic training. The whole way there, I kept wondering if I was doing the right thing. When I got out of the car and started to say good-bye to my parents, I could hardly talk. The thought of spending four years in the service had caught up to me! I actually considered turning around and going back home. But I had come this far, so I decided I'd better go through with it. the recruiter gave us one last chance to back out, but nobody did; I took the oath with several others. Immediately after taking the oath, I felt relieved; I had made my decision. However, my next step in the Coast Guard was pretty uncertain; I was far from being relaxed.

On the bus trip to Cape May, New Jersey, I was nervous and couldn't sleep. I kept wondering how bad boot camp was going to be. However tough it was going to be, I was determined to get through it with as little trouble as possible and as quickly as possible.

The bus arrived at the training center about 12:30 the following morning. I got to bed about 1:30 A.M., but I couldn't get to sleep for a long time because I worried about what tomorrow would bring.

Reveille was sounded at 4:30 A.M.; I had hardly gotten to sleep when it was time to get out of bed. The first day we did nothing but eat, get examined, and wait. I got my first look at boot camp in the daylight and I didn't particularly like what I saw—several hundred bald recruits marching around and being harassed by their Company Commanders. Since I still had my hair and civilian clothes, I stood out from the other recruits. After two days, I actually wished that they would shave my head and get it over with. The sooner I started basic training, the sooner it would be over!

After about four days of waiting around and being nervous and bored at the same time, we were finally formed into fifty-man companies. Our new Company Commander introduced himself by putting us through some pretty rough exercises, so I knew boot camp wasn't going to be fun. He didn't talk, he yelled! He didn't have to repeat anything—he just punished anyone who didn't react quickly or correctly. I never did like taking orders, and taking them from this guy was a real insult. To add injury to insult, the Company Commander gave several fellow recruits authority to order the rest of us around. This really aggravated me because these guys didn't know any more about the military than I did. But to disobey their orders was to disobey the Company Commander, and that is against military rules.

Once we were formed into companies, basic training really got underway. The first few days they didn't give us a free minute. We didn't have time to think about anything but what we were doing at that particular moment. We were always running, marching, drilling, getting lectured, eating, or cleaning. I was really ready for the few hours that we had off on Saturday and Sunday morning and evening. Even during this free time, we were not allowed to leave the barracks or even sit on our beds. We cleaned our rifles, polished our shoes and brass, and wrote letters.

One of the things that I disliked most about boot camp was the uncertainty about what would happen next. This feeling was especially true concerning physical education class, which I considered to be the worst part of basic training. Gym class consisted of two hours of exercises, harassment, and punishment. I really would have liked to have taken some physical action against our gym instructors, but I held back the urge.

I also disliked marching and drilling with our rifles. Whenever one person blundered, the whole company was punished. An M-1 (rifle) got extremely heavy when I had to hold it above my head while running around the parade grounds. I kept on going no matter how tired I was or how much it hurt because I didn't want to be the one to quit first; I wanted to show the Company Commander that I could take anything that he ordered me to do.

Several times a week our Company Commander would hold a "white tornado" in our barracks. He would turn over the beds and mess up everything possible. This action really irritated me because it was a stupid and needless harassment that taught nothing and only proved to be very frustrating.

At meal time we were treated pretty much like animals. Get in, eat up, and get out. We weren't supposed to talk and we never had much time to eat. As soon as we were finished eating, we had to run back to the barracks. We often got to taste the foot twice.

From the beginning of boot camp, I looked forward to getting out for a few hours on our fifth weekend liberty. Never did forty hours go so fast!

I was no sooner home than it was time to leave to go back. Probably the worst feeling I have ever experienced was having to walk back through the gate to basic training. I dreaded it so much that I even thought about taking off—going AWOL—but I figured that it would do more harm than good.

The threat that kept me in line throughout boot camp was the possibility of being reverted—going through the same training again. More than anything else in the world, I wanted to get out of boot camp and into a more humane world where I would be treated in a more respectable way. The best and fastest way to do that was to square away—discipline myself to military life.

Basic training was not all bad, however; I did meet a lot of guys and made a few friends. Unfortunately, I knew I'd probably never see most of them again after we got out of boot camp. I also met a few recruits that I was very glad to leave behind. Several arguments took place and a few people pushed each other around, but it never got out of hand. The pressure of basic training can really get to you when you work, eat, and sleep with the same fifty guys for several weeks.

Probably the best time of day was mail call—if you got a letter, that is. After a tiring day, it was really great to hear from someone on the outside. If you didn't get a letter, however, it was very easy to get depressed and really feel low.

The most enjoyable part of boot camp was competing with other companies in track, swimming, and the obstacle course. It gave me a chance to work off some of the excess pressure that I built up every day during basic training. Also, I was pretty proud of my company because we won honor company three weeks in a row—three out of eight was pretty good.

What was supposed to be a highlight of basic training turned out to be a failure. On one of our last weekends, they permitted us to go to the USO. We were all rather excited about seeing girls again, but it turned out that there were three hundred males and twenty-five females. I spent most of the evening reading the current issue of *Playboy*. It was nice, though, just to see civilians and hear music for a change.

Case Study Questions

1. Briefly discuss the possible relationship between the young man's taking of the oath of enlistment to military service and conformity, as demonstrated in the Asch experiment.
2. How did the Company Commander use the group, and its norms, in structuring the interaction of the company during marching and drilling exercises?
3. Was the military's efforts to discipline the recruits in preparation for military life an example of persuasion or propaganda?

SELF-TEST

Multiple Choice

1. Social psychologist Muzafer Sherif concluded from his experiment on apparent movement that:
   a. in a dark room, a stationary spot of light is perceived as moving
   b. human beings cannot judge motion in darkness
   c. judgments were made using mental standards
   d. in a dark room, a spot of light always tends to move four inches
2. The phenomenon that Sherif utilized in his experiments of social behavior is called:
   a. the automation effect
   b. the alpha effect
   c. the beta-trap effect
   d. the autokinetic effect
3. An attitude is composed of all the following components *except*:
   a. an emotional component
   b. a subjective component
   c. a cognitive component
   d. a behavioral component
4. Acting in much the same way as the Freudian defense mechanism of projection, which of the following attitude functions serves to guard us from threats to our self-esteem?
   a. an organizational function
   b. a utilitarian function
   c. a displacement function
   d. none of the above
5. According to social psychology, which of the following would *not* be considered one of the three sources of attitudes?
   a. projected hostility
   b. personal experience
   c. displaced emotions
   d. social influence
6. Some social psychologists have proposed that a major cause of black-white racial hostility is:
   a. a need to conform to the notion of "white" supremacy
   b. the notion that familiarity breeds contempt

c. the notion that lack of familiarity breeds negative attitudes
d. the unconscious redirection of painful emotions

7. The parent-child relationship can best be described as:
   a. a free forum of ideas
   b. a conscious attempt at open-minded exposure to ideas
   c. an intensive course in parental attitudes
   d. all of the above

8. In a study conducted at Bennington College, Theodore Newcomb demonstrated that:
   a. college women are unaffected by social pressure
   b. peer influence became equally as strong as parental influence
   c. the college faculty had a greater influence than either parents or peers
   d. peer influence permanently replaced parental influence with respect to political ideas

9. American children have been found to spend how many hours in front of the television set?
   a. two hours a day
   b. six hours a day
   c. six hours a week
   d. ten hours a day

10. Which of the following most accurately describes the effect of televised violence on the behavior of children?
    a. Televised violence seems to discourage violent behavior in children.
    b. Televised violence seems to have little effect on the behavior of children.
    c. Televised violence seems to encourage violent behavior in children.
    d. Televised violence seems to encourage assertive rather than aggressive behavior in children.

11. The effectiveness of modeling as a process for learning new behaviors seems to be due to:
    a. the presence of external rewards accompanying the modeled behavior
    b. the desire to be like the model
    c. the indirect rewarding of modeled behavior by the model in the form of praise
    d. all of the above

12. In sociological terms, conformity refers to the individual's changing beliefs of behavior to make them agree with those of:
    a. a collection of individuals
    b. another person
    c. a group of persons sharing a common goal
    d. all of the above

13. With the third set of cards in Asch's first study of "visual perception":
    a. the confederates always gave the incorrect answer
    b. the confederates sometimes gave the incorrect answer
    c. the confederates always gave the correct answer
    d. the confederates sometimes gave the correct answer

14. Which of the following factors tends to increase the likelihood of the subject's behavior in the Asch study?
    a. making the task much easier
    b. having a group of close friends serve as confederates
    c. having a more relaxed and comfortable experimental setting
    d. all of the above

15. According to Festinger's social comparison theory, most people:
    a. trust their own opinions when there is no objective means of comparison
    b. seek out other sources of information in order to make a comparison
    c. seek out persons dissimilar to themselves in order to make a comparison
    d. all of the above

16. Conformity will usually occur when the issue or question being decided upon is characterized by:
    a. unfamiliarity
    b. complexity
    c. ambiguity
    d. all of the above

17. Which of the following factors would most likely determine whether or not an attempt at persuasion will be effective?
    a. the consequences, the message, and the audience
    b. the consequences, the communicator, and the message
    c. the communicator, the message, and the audience
    d. the communicator, the audience, and the consequences

18. If you were in a position to advise a political candidate on how to communicate a stand on law and order to the public, you would probably advise the candidate to:
    a. make use of fear-arousing information
    b. portray the community as unsafe and fearful
    c. be careful not to use a message that is too fear-arousing

    d. play down the law-and-order position and highlight another issue
19. Propaganda differs from persuasion because:
    a. propaganda uses more deliberate distortion than persuasion
    b. propaganda is more manipulative than persuasion
    c. propaganda is more self-serving than persuasion
    d. all of the above
20. A favorite campaign tactic of politicians is to:
    a. communicate to the people that they are experts
    b. use positive symbols to support their positions
    c. describe themselves as men of the people
    d. invade the headquarters of the opposing candidate

True-False

1. In the second stage of Sherif's study of social behavior, he found that in a group of two subjects, where one subject had a standard of twelve inches and the other had a standard of four inches, both subjects gradually moved to a standard of eight inches.
2. Generally, attitudes make possible the social life of the individual.
3. For many people, negative attitudes toward other races provide a comforting and organizational sense of superiority.
4. The major source of our attitudes is social influence.
5. More often than not, the parent-child relationship is not a free forum of ideas.
6. In a study at Bennington College, Theodore Newcomb found that after four years of college, students held onto their family's political ideas.
7. During adolescence, the influential power of the family is gradually replaced by the peer group.
8. Due to the learning-through-reinforcement principle, modeling is relatively ineffective without external rewards.
9. The importance of sex as a determinant of modeling is seen in the observation that boys tend to imitate boys and girls tend to imitate girls.
10. In sociological terms, a group is simply a collection of individuals.
11. Given the right set of conditions, a person will conform to just about anything.
12. Studies have found that the more intelligent and self-confident a person is, the less likely he or she is to conform.
13. People are more likely to be convinced by a message that they overheard than by a message directly aimed to convince them.
14. In general, people with low self-esteem are more persuadable than are people with high self-esteem.
15. Persuasion almost invariably carries with it a measure of propaganda.

Completion

1. Social psychologist Muzafer Sherif used the phenomenon called the _____ _____ in his study of social behavior.
2. The transfer of messages from one person to another, or from some media to a person, and its effect upon that person is called _____ _____.
3. The compliant responses of human beings to other human beings is referred to as _____ social influence.
4. In addition to their utilitarian and protective functions, attitudes are said to have an _____ function.
5. The third source of attitudes, and possibly the major source, is _____ _____.
6. The three major sources of influence are parents, peers, and the _____ _____.
7. In the later years of adolescence, the peer group tends to replace the family as the individual's _____ _____.
8. _____ is the learning of new behaviors through imitating other people.
9. _____ refers to the individual changing his beliefs to make them agree with those of a group.
10. According to Festinger's _____ _____ theory, people often doubt the correctness of their opinions and thus seek out other sources of information with which to make a comparison.
11. _____ is the deliberate exercise of influence through the transmission of information.
12. Research indicates that two characteristics that significantly enhance a person's ability to persuade others are _____ and _____.
13. When our freedom is threatened or actually reduced, we try to reestablish that freedom by resorting to the phenomenon of _____ _____.

14. The best defense against excessive influence is to take an _____ rather than a _____ approach to influence.
15. An example of a _____ is the statement: "... kills bugs three times faster than other leading products."

Essay Questions

1. Define the term "attitude." Discuss and provide at least two examples of its three major components. (pp. 288–289)
2. Social psychologists have located three main sources of attitudes. Identify and discuss each of them. (pp. 289–290)
3. Define and discuss the term "conformity." How does it function as a process of social influence? Include in your answer the role of the group. (pp. 296–298)
4. There are certain factors that determine whether or not an attempt at persuasion will work. What are these factors and how do they exert their effect? (pp. 300–305)
5. Support the statement that "The best defense against excessive influence is to take an active rather than a passive approach to influence." (p. 312)

SELF-TEST ANSWERS

Multiple Choice

1. c (p. 287)
2. d (p. 287)
3. b (p. 289)
4. d (p. 289)
5. a (pp. 289–290)
6. c (pp. 289–290)
7. c (p. 291)
8. d (p. 293)
9. b (p. 293)
10. c (p. 293)
11. d (pp. 294–295)
12. c (p. 297)
13. a (p. 299)
14. b (p. 299)
15. b (p. 299)
16. d (p. 300)
17. c (p. 303)
18. c (p. 304)
19. d (pp. 305–310)
20. c (p. 308)

True-False

1. true (p. 288)
2. true (p. 289)
3. false (pp. 289–290)
4. true (p. 290)
5. true (p. 291)
6. false (p. 293)
7. true (p. 291)
8. false (p. 294)
9. true (p. 295)
10. false (p. 297)
11. true (p. 299)
12. true (p. 300)
13. true (p. 303)
14. true (p. 305)
15. true (p. 307)

Completion

1. autokinetic effect (p. 287)
2. social influence (p. 288)
3. direct (p. 288)
4. organizational (p. 289)
5. social influence (p. 290)
6. mass media (p. 293)
7. reference group (p. 291)
8. modeling (p. 294)
9. conformity (p. 297)
10. social comparison (p. 299)
11. persuasion (pp. 300–301)
12. credibility, attractiveness (p. 303)
13. psychological reactance (p. 311)
14. active, passive (p. 312)
15. psuedo-statistic (p. 309)

12 Social Influence: How to Change It

CHAPTER OUTLINE

THE CHAIN OF INFLUENCE
Analyzing a Problem in a Relationship
Description
    Simplicity
    Objectivity
    Specificity
    A sample description
Functional Analysis

CHANGING YOUR SOCIAL INFLUENCE
Setting the Goal
Planning the Interaction
    Avoiding cues for conflict
    Creating cues for pleasant interaction
    "Psyching yourself up" for new responses
Creating New Interactive Chains
    Listening
    Avoiding defensive responses
    Giving clear messages
    Revealing your interpretations
    Being rewarding in general
Two-Sided Change
    Contracts
A Note on Methods
    Punishment
    Dealing with slip-ups

READING

Now You Can Learn to Be Likable, Confident, Socially Successful for Only the Cost of Your Present Education

LOIS TIMNICK

Scrawny kids tired of having beach bullies kick sand in their faces used to send away for Charles Atlas's Dynamic Tension Body-Building Program. Three months of exercise and healthful living, plus $35, the ads said, could turn the puny and paunchy into the he-men who would command respect and get the girls.

These days, the same kind of people are learning to flex psychological muscles. If the popularity of the burgeoning new field of social-skills training is any indication, even a 97-pound weakling can stand up to a bully—and maybe the bully can learn to act differently, too.

Scores of psychologists and teachers—would-be Pygmalions all—believe that "social skills" can be taught just like reading or math, that everyone from preschoolers to prison inmates, schizophrenics to shy college students, juvenile delinquents to alcoholics, can learn how to get along with other people. The unpopular child, these believers note, may be particularly vulnerable to academic problems, juvenile delinquency, and the development of emotional and mental disorders. (It may be just as likely, of course, that whatever causes these difficulties also makes a child unlikable.) A lack of social skills alone may not cause rejection, but at least that lack may be more open to change than factors like physical disability, unattractiveness, having an unusual name, being of a racial or ethnic minority, or having unusual interests.

Social-skills training is now being offered in more than 300 elementary and junior-high schools in California. College catalogs abound in classes on "shyness," "building social confidence," and "social assertiveness," as well as closely related subjects like "personal exploration" and "stress management." The classes provide full-time jobs for psychologists and hot research topics for articles in scientific journals that speak of such matters as the individual who "doesn't self-reinforce himself for his appropriate behavior and tends to catastrophize when he feels he has made an error."

Programs to prevent or correct deficiencies in these areas are springing up throughout the United States, despite lack of agreement on what social skills are, which ones are essential, and how they can best be developed. Some examples:

☐ In Glendora, California, elementary-school students are being trained to sit, stand, and speak "assertively"; to avoid becoming "bullies" or "doormats"; to deal with anger; to make friends; to understand the consequences of their actions; and to solve thorny problems like "Do you tell on a classmate who cheats on a test?"

☐ Students at a Walnut, California, community college can get academic credit for psychology courses that stress "the practical application of psychological principles to problems and circumstances encountered in everyday life." They're also offered self-realization and sensitivity training, as well as noncredit workshops on "putting your best foot forward," "success speak," "loneliness," "the dynamics of self-esteem," "styles of relating," and "creative fighting."

☐ In Pittsburgh, depressed women are learning to make conversation, stand up for their rights, and express affection while avoiding whining, complaining, or speaking in a monotone.

☐ Chronic schizophrenia outpatients at the Brentwood Veterans Administration Hospital in Los Angeles learn or relearn skills involved in everything from how to find a job or apartment to how to carry on a satisfactory conversation.

While the notion of learning to get along better with others seems like a good thing, it is not without its critics, who argue that social-skills training is neither appropriate nor desirable, except for such groups as chronic psychiatric patients. These critics argue that teaching such skills should be the province of the home, not schools or colleges, and that not enough is known about what specific skills make for good social relationships to justify moving ahead with training programs for any but experimental purposes.

Why has social-skills training come to the classroom? Mary Beall, a teacher who is project coordinator for the innovative grade-school program in Glendora, California, says that both teachers and parents complained that behavior problems among their children were increasing. Some children were withdrawn, others were loud-mouthed troublemakers. Many had "unhappy relationships" with their classmates, and still others had learning difficulties, not because of physical disabilities or deep-seated emotional problems, Beall thinks, but simply because they had never learned "successful" ways of behaving. Whether or not the culprits are, as she suspects, television and working mothers, basic social skills were simply not learned at home.

A survey of 3,800 undergraduates at the University of Arizona found that a third were "somewhat" or "very" anxious about dating (37 percent of the men, 25 percent of the women). A similar survey at the University of Indiana found that half the subjects rated dating situations "difficult" (54 percent of the men, 42 percent of the women), and 15 percent of the men and 11 percent of the women in a study at the University of Iowa reported "some fear" of being with members of the opposite sex. Nearly a third of the Iowa students said that they feared meeting new people.

Lest "dating anxiety" be dismissed as irrelevant to academe, psychologist Hal Arkowitz of the University of Arizona points out that dating anxiety is also associated with depression and academic failure, and can lead to an avoidance of the opposite sex and failure to progress to more intimate relationships and marriage. Men—but not women— who do not date frequently tend to have difficulty making friends with people of their own sex and have problems with general psychological adjustment, an Arizona team headed by psychologist William Himadi found.

Clinical psychologist William Skilbeck, acting director of UCLA's psychological and counseling services, says that many young people still haven't picked up social skills by the time they get to high school or college. "Ours is an unusual campus, with sophisticated social norms," he said in an interview. "It's a place where students are [expected to be] successful socially and academically, and not only up on the latest trends, but setting them. If they're oblivious—say from a rural area—they can quickly be pegged as not 'with it.'"

At a competitive school like UCLA it is not unusual to find students with lopsided development—they are accelerated intellectually, but retarded socially. Skilbeck cites a hypothetical student "who's spent 30 hours a week for four years in the library concentrating on his average. He's had no dates, or a handful, and he's hardly even talked to the opposite sex."

Dating anxiety is only part of a more general picture of anxiety. Skilbeck says that he's noticed a change in the kinds of problems for which college students seek help. "The focus in the last two years has been on anxiety-related problems," he says. "Psychosomatic disorders seem to be prominent. Concern for what happens after graduation. Nervousness. Inability to concentrate. The [anxiety] has displaced existential concerns. Today's student is less likely to say 'I don't know the meaning of life,' than 'I have to get into a good graduate school. My parents are counting on it. My grades are going down and I'm a nervous wreck.'"

Accordingly, UCLA offers courses not only in building social confidence, assertiveness, and changing male/female roles, but also in decision-making, procrastination, self-hypnosis, stress management, and relationships with parents. Skilbeck says that his department comes in contact with more than 5,000 students each year, including those who attend informal talks, seek individual counseling, and participate in workshops like the popular "Building Social Confidence." Although in this workshop more men are enrolled than women (perhaps because developing relationships is still seen as a man's responsibility), in everything else women usually outnumber men. Moreover, a surprising number are graduate students.

"Building Social Confidence" takes the approach of cognitive behavior therapy. Groups of eight to 12 students meet for two hours a week. The course includes an individual interview with the group leader ("so if they think they're going to be homecoming queen by the end of the quarter, they can be set straight," according to Skilbeck), short lectures, discussions, videotaped role-playing emphasizing such elements as eye contact and nonverbal signals, practice conversations and rehearsals of hypothetical social situations, tips on such matters as how to spot an approachable person, redefinition of what constitutes a "successful" exchange, and homework assignments like "Establish eye contact with five people you've never met" or "Talk to somebody in the movie line." By the end of the term, the students are supposed to be able to ask people out (and deal with the possibility of rejection), date, and look for a job—all without too much nervousness.

James Curran, a psychologist at Brown University, hypothesizes that social anxiety stems from three sources. The first, he thinks, is a lack of skills. He cites as an example the college freshman from a farm town, an only child who's always been shy around girls and hasn't the faintest idea of what to say or do on a date. A second cause, Curran thinks, is conditioned anxiety. A young woman, for example, may have been taught by her mother to fear men and feel guilty about possible sexual contact. Finally, Curran blames such factors as unrealistic expectations, an overcritical nature, and a misreading of various social cues.

Clearly it is important to identify the cause of the anxiety before trying to treat it. To send a person on practice dates, for example, if he lacks rudimentary social know-how would only allow him to fail repeatedly and become even more anxious. Besides actual instruction in skills, approaches to social anxiety include rehearsals of how to handle everyday problems, relaxation techniques, systematic desensitization, and increasingly difficult homework assignments. Many students, however, aren't socially inadequate but merely inexperienced. They may need simpler forms of practice.

For his master's thesis at the University of Oregon, psychologist Andrew Christensen of UCLA computer-matched 60 men and women (taking into account only sex, height, age, race, and the distance they lived from campus) for a series of "practice" dates. The subjects all said that they dated infrequently. One group provided written feedback on their partners' appearance and behavior, a second simply went on the dates, and a third was put on a waiting list to serve as controls. Practice may not make perfect, but it did increase the students' dating frequency and their comfort in such situations, Christensen found. Members of the group that gave and received feedback from their dates reported three months later that they were dating and socializing casually more often; those that just went on the dates had the lowest pulse rates before each date began, and reported the fewest silences during conversations. Members of this second group were rated by themselves and their peers as the least anxious, and scored lowest on a social avoidance and distress scale. Most members of both experimental groups were dating people outside their own anxious group and enjoying it more.

Some teachers and educational psychologists believe that by the time a student with poor social skills reaches college, courses may provide too little too late. Even by high school the damage may have been done. Some studies have found that 6 percent to 11 percent of elementary-school children have no classroom friends at all, while an additional 12 percent to 22 percent have only one. Jim De Filippi, a Vermont English teacher, writing in *Today's Education,* recently pointed out that after 10 or 12 years, such children may be completely isolated.

"To compound their problem, these students have developed such thick armor in order to survive that they often go out of their way to antagonize and alienate their classmates," wrote De Filippi. "Their defense against loneliness guarantees its continuation and in many cases its intensification." Friendless high-school students usually blame school, not themselves, for their misery, and often drop out, dreaming of a new start in the Army or on a job, only to find that the new situation revives the original problem.

The pioneering group of teachers and psychologists that set up the social-skills course in Glendora, California, decided five years ago that children shouldn't reach adulthood with social strikes against them. The result, developed at a cost of more than $80,000 a year in federal funds channeled through the state's Department of Education, was an elaborate 52-lesson program for grades two through six (with a modified version for special-ed classes). In it, children are taught "social behavior" in two half-hour sessions a week. The Glendora program manages to systematically cover an enormous amount of ground: feelings and emotions, facial signals and body language, assertiveness, criticism, compliments and apologies, listening, being a good friend, social problem-solving, appropriate behavior in different circumstances, cooperation, competition and conflict, and a host of other topics.

Developed by Mary Beall and psychologists Jane Favero and Jule Dombrower, the program has been noncontroversial from the start. Now granted "exemplary" status by California's Department of Education, it has been taught to teachers from more than 300 schools throughout the state. Parents and teachers are enthusiastic. Of 180 questionnaires returned by parents, only two were negative. One mother noted that her second-grader was giving her father some tips on how to approach his boss!

Ben Conner, who has been principal of two Glendora schools that use the program, says that he's seen a marked decrease in behavior problems and an increase in self-discipline. (Teachers are provided with behavioral checklists and tests to assess behavioral changes in their pupils.) But the Glendora team insists that their project is not aimed at behavior management, that it's no tool to control children. Explains Favero: "We try to teach children to think about behavior, to get them to reason, to focus on the ramifications of their actions."

One recent morning in Shirleen Smith's sixth-grade class at Sandburg Intermediate, the subject was three ways of acting and how to make a request. The children were first told to "sit assertively." As the class progressed, two student monitors standing in the back of the room passed out color-coded chips. Anybody who left his hand up while someone was talking, made noise, or tilted his chair back got a red chip for "bully" (aggresive) behavior. Slouching, mumbling, or daydreaming led to a blue chip for "doormat" (passive) behavior. Good posture and confident straightforward answers—even "I don't know"—got white chips for "assertiveness." (In some classes, students cash their chips in for a reward; in this one, the chips themselves are the reward.)

Building on an earlier lesson, Smith asked how bullies, doormats, and properly assertive people would make requests. Bullies "want to fight all the time," "push and make you do things," and are "often very rude," the students explained. One child acted out the part—pounding his fists into his palm, clenching his teeth, booming, "Gimmie that book or I'll beat you up." Doormats, on the other hand, "don't stand up for their rights," "don't look anyone in the eye," and "beat around the bush." A doormat asks, "Gee, you wouldn't want to let me borrow that book, would you?" In contrast, the assertive person "stands up proud," "has good eye contact," and "leaves his hands at his sides." He is not a bully. "You're not afraid of him and you can't stomp all over him," one student said. Another student commented that the assertive person would say, "I would like to borrow that book when you're finished."

Next, the children paired up for a listener/talker exercise to "feel" what it is like when a person you're talking to fidgets and looks off into space. "It makes me mad," said one student. "It makes me feel like I'm not worth anything." Finally, the students discussed requests that they might make at home. One girl, for example, was annoyed by her brother's insistence on a blaring television set. The teacher suggested that she say, "I would like you to turn that down so I can study." "You know what he'd say?" the girl replied. *'Make me.'*"

Before the dilemma could be dealt with, however, the bell rang. Smith lingered to say that the lessons have made a big difference in her class. One bright boy, who became bossy after being elected class leader, changed his attitude. One extremely shy girl now volunteers to answer questions more often, and a couple of kids who learned that the other children considered them obnoxious bullies have toned down their cutting up.

Although the program is fairly new, Favero says that evaluations indicate that the children understand what is being taught and have improved their interpersonal skills and their ability to solve group problems. Their classroom behavior has improved, and the time spent on social-skills training has not slowed their reading progress, she says. She also finds that the students don't day-dream as much, or indulge in other kinds of unproductive behavior, like making up excuses for handing in homework late.

Before and after the social-skills classes, videotapes were made to assess how children presented themselves and how groups of them role-played difficult social situations. In one such situation, two students tell adults that they are sure that two other students took and ate their lunches. The accused students say that they were in fact playing near the lunches, but did not take any. In another situation, two students have been waiting in a long line for lunch. Two other students have to catch a bus and the adult in charge has told them to go to the front of the line. The first two know nothing about the bus.

Before social-skills training, students in these situations threatened, shouted at, and shoved one another. After the training, they tended to discuss their problems more amicably and work out solutions, Favero reports. But a visitor who viewed the before and after videotapes of one group of children answering questions was unsettled by her preference for them "before." Prior to the training, some mugged for the camera or heckled their classmates, while others looked shyly at the floor, shrugging. One tubby and exuberant youngster, when asked his favorite food, tilted back in his chair, paused, rolled his eyes skyward in mock ecstasy and sighed, "Hot dogs—with *tons* of mustard." After social-skills training, however, the children sat quietly with their hands in their laps, answering the questions in a calm, straightforward manner. "Yes," Jule Dombrower agreed, "assertiveness is boring, isn't it?"

That homogeneity, Dombrower and his fellow enthusiasts feel, is a small price to pay for increased ability to get along in a society that values team players over unpredictable eccentrics in the classroom, on the football field, and in the corporate office. Critics say that individuality must be protected at all costs. In a recent article in *Today's Education,* Ruth Bauer, a teacher of English and social studies in Cheshire, Connecticut, describes a socially reticent 6-year-old who wandered the playground, head down, jacket half off his shoulders, shoes untied, hands in pockets. "Is he deep in thought or trying to avoid thinking?" she asks. "Asking him probably wouldn't uncover the answer. Jonathan is bright, but has a speech impediment. What goes on inside seldom gets out. He tried to learn to jump rope with the girls, but is uncoordinated. In class he speaks only when spoken to and then in a whisper. But at age 6, he is a fluent reader.

"One bright fall day, Jonathan topped them all," Bauer recalls. "He left his classmates with their mouths hanging open and their eyes full of admiration. He stood bravely in front of the class and read *Babar and His Children,* by Jean de Brunhoff, from cover to cover. No one commented on his speech defect." Now, several years later, this child is still withdrawn and alone most of the time in his internal world. But Bauer says that she wonders whether there are not some such children who are better "left to themselves, left alone to develop in their own world their own ideas and feelings." Teachers should try to help each child feel comfortable in the world of the classroom, cafeteria, and playground, she agrees, but "the most important task is to help the child develop and maintain his or her individuality. That goal may require teachers to leave some children alone—to be alone."

Other cautious observers point out that "acceptable" ways of interacting differ in various socioeconomic groups. For example, in one study of a working-class school, nonverbal behavior like smiling or giving gifts led to peer acceptance, while in a middle-class school, verbal interaction was more important. What is acceptable also varies by age and ethnic group. In some cultures, for example, it is impolite to look a person straight in the eye.

"Social-skills training frequently assumes that there is a 'right way' to interact with other people, when there may be many," cautions Paula Clayton, a psychiatrist at the University of Minnesota. The result, she suggests, may be the smoothing of rough edges or hammering out of the dents in what should be valued and unique personality styles. Some attention to manners or etiquette should be sufficient, she says, except for people with special needs—the pathologically shy or the incipient juvenile delinquent.

Indeed, psychologists John Gottman of the University of Illinois and Martha Putallaz of the University of North Carolina warn that so far, only peer acceptance and having a close friend have been identified as essential to "social competence." Just what skills and conditions promote these two aspects of social competence "remain largely unidentified at this time," they say.

For example, Gottman and Putallaz write that "there is no evidence, other than intuitive, to indicate that children who interact less frequently with their peers suffer more social-adjustment problems than children who interact more frequently." Nor is there more evidence, for that matter, that being alone can be equated with loneliness. As Ruth Bauer asked: "Must we assume that social integration is inherently good? Do we know for sure that the world of social affability is the best of all possible worlds for all students?"

Perhaps the most common criticism of social-skills training in schools and colleges is that it is sadly trivial—a pastiche of gimmicks and pat statements ("I would like you to stop hitting me"). Often the courses differ little—except that they're considerably cheaper—from one-day or weekend workshops given in hotel ballrooms by itinerant psychologists and psychotherapists who are rife with clichés. A teacher in one "assertiveness training" course in the extension division of UCLA planned to suggest the following conversational openers:

"This car wash seems to do a good job on cars."

"May I light your cigarette?"

"I like listening to your questions in class. Have you been to other classes like this?"

And the prizewinner: "Haven't I seen you somewhere before?"

Much of the excitement in the social-skills training field centers on work with psychiatric patients. Working at the University of Pittsburgh with 125 female outpatients who had nonpsychotic depression, psychologists Alan Bellack and Michel Hersen and psychiatrist Jonathan Himmelhoch compared the effects of four treatments: social-skills training plus a placebo; social skills and amitriptyline (a common antidepressant, better known by the brand name Elavil); the drug alone; and psychotherapy plus a placebo.

After 12 weekly treatments, which were followed by six to eight more treatments over six months, the therapists concluded that each group improved markedly, but that a larger proportion of the patients receiving social-skills training and a placebo improved significantly (42 percent, compared to 32 percent, 23 percent, and 29 percent in the other groups). Only 24 percent of this group dropped out of the program during the initial treatment period, compared to 53 percent of the drug-only group.

The depressives might have lost their social skills out of anxiety, or in the course of a long illness, or during their institutionalization; some may never have had them in the first place. Regardless of the source of their problems, they were taught, with a variety of behavioral techniques, how to start, maintain, and end conversations, refuse unreasonable requests, compromise and negotiate, express annoyance, give compliments, express affection, make apologies and cut out "bitchy" and "sick" talk.

A much broader social-skills project began in Los Angeles last year at the Brentwood VA Hospital. There, at any given time, about 18 chronic schizophrenics and other mentally disabled patients—mostly men—are undergoing intensive and highly structured five-day-a-week social-skills training. In small groups, the men learn to solve day-to-day problems like getting and keeping a job, finding an apartment, and starting and maintaining conversations, preparing meals and using public transportation.

Psychologist Charles J. Wallace is director of the Social and Independent Living Skills program at the hospital, which is funded by the VA and a grant from the National Institute of Handicapped Research. Wallace and his colleagues believe that the patient's lack of social competence may play an important role in the relapse and subsequent rehospitalization of many of them. The SILS program uses videotaped demonstrations, role-playing, problem-solving exercises, practice and homework assignments. It also includes conversational help for the deficiencies in attention and short-term memory that are frequently seen in chronic psychiatric patients. Such patients often flit from topic to topic, or can't remember subjects that they could build on to expand a conversation. They must learn how to find and stick with topics, how to recognize emotions being conveyed by others, how to attend to verbal and nonverbal messages, and how to disclose personal information tactfully.

Whether social-skills training programs improve "social competence" in a general population and beyond the classroom over time remains to be seen. A recent research review of over 100 social-skills training studies suggests that individuals do use these skills while the programs last, but no one knows whether they continue to do so on their own.

The proliferation of social-skills training projects and courses could make for a more civilized society in which more people actually connect. It could also lead to a world of robots—flashing smiles and wishing one another a nice day. It's too soon to tell. But regardless of the merits or shortcomings of the movement, it is growing. No one knows exactly how many psychologists are now teaching social skills or doing research in the area, but the American Psychological Association estimates there may be as many as several thousand. More will no doubt join them soon. Where once only Dale Carnegie trod, now tramples a herd.

Reading Questions

1. Briefly indicate some of the groups of individuals who are being given social-skills training.
2. Describe the nature of the program being used with elementary-school children to teach them social-skills.

3. Comment on some of the objections raised by critics of social-skills training.

RESEARCH STUDY

Investigators: Donald Baucom and Gregory Lester.
Source, date: "The Usefulness of Cognitive Restructuring as an Adjunct to Behavioral Marital Therapy," *Behavior Therapy*, 1986, *17*, pp. 385-403.
Location: Houston, Texas, and Chapel Hill, North Carolina.
Subjects: 24 couples experiencing marital discord.
Materials: Dyadic adjustment scale, marital interaction coding system, Areas of Change questionnaire, Relationship Beliefs Inventory, Irrational Beliefs Test.

Since previous research had demonstrated that behavioral marital training was effective in helping couples whose marriages were distressed, the current study focused on what improvements adding cognitive restructuring would make to this therapy. In behavioral marital therapy, the focus is on helping couples be more positive and reinforcing in their interactions. Cognitive restructuring involves training couples in avoiding blame, developing more realistic understandings of each other's motives, and creating more appropriate and less extreme expectations of each other's behavior.

The couples were each assigned to one of three experimental groups: behavioral marital therapy alone, behavioral marital therapy with cognitive restructuring and no therapy. In the first two groups, the couples were each seen by a therapist once a week for 12 sessions each lasting approximately one and one half hours. In the third group, the couples were asked to wait 12 weeks until they would be provided therapy.

In comparison to the couples waiting for therapy, the couples receiving behavioral marital therapy alone and behavioral marital therapy with cognitive restructuring improved significantly to the point that at least half of the couples were no longer distressed in their relationship. While the degree of improvement between the two therapy groups did not differ, those receiving the additional cognitive restructuring did develop more realistic expectations and assessments of motives of each other. The researchers concluded that for those couples having problems with unrealistic expectations and attributions of motives, the addition of cognitive restructuring to behavioral marital therapy could be beneficial in reducing marital discord.

Research Questions

1. What did the researchers expect to find in adding cognitive restructuring to behavioral restructuring in behavioral marital therapy?
2. What method and procedure did the researchers use in examining the effects of cognitive restructuring?
3. What were the results and conclusions concerning the effects of adding cognitive restructuring to behavioral marital therapy?

CASE STUDY

Self-Control Procedures in Personal Behavior Problems

ISRAEL GOLDIAMOND

MARITAL CASE 1

The husband in this case was a young man, 29, who was working on his master's degree. His wife was taking my course in behavioral analysis, and they both decided that he should come to see me about their marriage, which both wanted to maintain. The issue, as S told me, was that his wife had committed "ultimate betrayal" two years ago with *S*'s best friend. Even worse, it was *S* who had suggested that the friend keep his wife company while he was in the library at night. Since that time, whenever he saw his wife, *S* screamed at her for hours on end or else was ashamed of himself for having done so and spent hours sulking and brooding. Since the events that led to the "betrayal" were an occasion for bringing home the first lesson on the consequences of behavior, we started from there.

Relation of Behavior to Its Consequences

Early discussions concerned the analysis of behavior in terms of its consequences. *S*'s behavior provided stimuli for his wife's behavior. If he wished his wife to behave differently to him, then he should provide other stimuli than the ones which produced the behaviors he did not like. There was considerable analysis of such interactions. This conceptualization

12/SOCIAL INFLUENCE: HOW TO CHANGE IT

of behavior was apparently new to S, who took detailed notes; I have discovered it to be new to many other Ss as well.

Stimulus Change

Altering the consequences of operant behavior will alter the behavior itself. However, this process may take a considerable amount of time. One of the most rapid ways to change behavior is by altering the conditions under which it usually occurs. This is called *stimulus change* or the effects of novel stimuli. If novel stimuli are then combined with new behavioral contingencies designed to produce different behavior, these contingencies are apt to generate the new behavior much more rapidly than they would in the presence of the old stimuli.

As part of the program of establishing new stimuli, S was instructed to rearrange the use of rooms and furniture in his house to make it appear considerably different. His wife went one step further and took the occasion to buy herself a new outfit.

Establishment of New Behavior

Since it was impossible for S to converse in a civilized manner with his wife, we discussed a program of going to one evening spot on Monday, another on Tuesday, and another on Wednesday.

"Oh," he said, "you want us to be together. We'll go bowling on Thursday."

"On the contrary," I said, "I am interested in your subjecting yourself to an environment where civilized chit-chat is maintained. Such is not the case at the bowling alley."

I also asked if there were any topic of conversation which once started would maintain itself. He commented on his mother-in-law's crazy ideas about farming. He was then given an index card and instructed to write "farm" on it and attach a $20 bill to that card. The $20 was to be used to pay the waitress on Thursday, at which point he was to start the "farm" discussion which hopefully would continue into the taxi and home.

Stimulus Control

Since in the absence of yelling at his wife S sulked and since the program was designed to reduce yelling, S's sulking was in danger of increasing. S was instructed to sulk to his heart's content but to do so in a specified place. Whenever he felt like sulking, he was to go into the garage, sit on a special sulking stool, and mutter over the indignities of life for as long as he wished. When he was through with his sulking, he could leave the garage and join his wife. He was instructed to keep a daily record of such behavior and bring it to each session. Sulking time had been reported as 7 hours on the preceding day, and, with occasional lapses, it was reported as dropping to less than 30 minutes before disappearing entirely. The reported reversals and drops were occasions for discussions.

Since the bedroom had been the scene of both bickering and occasional lapses, the problem was presented to changing its stimulus value when conjugality was involved. If this could be done consistently, eventually the special stimuli might come to control such behavior. The problem was to find a stimulus which could alter the room entirely and would be easy to apply and withdraw. Finally, a yellow night light was put in, was turned on when both felt amorous, and was kept turned off otherwise. This light markedly altered the perceptual configuration of the room.

Records

Daily notes of events were kept in a notebook. S took notes of the discussion with E. These notes were discussed at each weekly session.

One of the notions which S held very strongly was that his wife's behavior stemmed from some inaccessible source within her, and that many of his own behaviors likewise poured out from himself. In this context, the final sharp rise in the sulking curve was discussed. "The whole procedure won't work," he said, "my wife doesn't need me as much as I need her." The psychiatric message was that he had no control over his wife, but I chose to ignore this message in favor of a didactic one on the behavioral definition of needs. He was asked how he knew what his wife's needs were. Was he an amoeba slithering into her tissues and observing tissue needs? Was he a mind reader? After my repeated rejection of subjective definitions of needs, he redefined the problem behaviorally, namely, that his wife behaved a certain way less than he did. He said that stated this way it sounded silly, but I said, "No, it's a problem to you and not silly."

What were these behaviors? They apparently included such dependency behaviors as asking him to do things for her. "When was the last time she asked you to do something for her?" I asked. He replied that the previous day she had asked him to replace a light bulb in the kitchen. Had he done so, I asked. "No," he said. He was then asked to consider the extinction of pigeon behavior and took notes to the effect that, if he wished his wife to act helpless, he should reinforce dependency by doing what she asked.

A discussion on needs and personality ensued. "If by personality all that is meant is my behavior," he said, "then my personality changes from one moment to the next, because my behavior changes," he stated.

"I should hope so," I said.

"Well, what is my true personality, what is the true me?" he asked.

"Do you have a true behavior?" I asked.

He reported this as a viewpoint he had never considered; his previous training had been in terms of being consistent to his self, and of searching for "thine own self (to which he could) be true." He took extensive notes.

The next week he came in and stated: "I did something last week that I have never done before in my life. When I teach in classrooms I am able to manage my students, but when I talk to tradespeople I find I am very timid and allow myself to be cheated. Well, last week my carburetor gave out. I knew if I went to the garage they would make me buy a new one even though I have a one-year's guarantee. I sent my wife down to the garage instead. She is a real scrapper. She came back with a new carburetor. It didn't cost us a cent. Why should I have to be all things to all men? In school I control things, but with tradespeople I don't. So what?"

These weekly sessions continued during ten weeks of the summer term. After the initial training, S was assigned homework along with his wife who was taking the course in behavior analysis. The weekly discussions were centered around behavioral analysis and how it might apply to his problems.

During the course of one of the sessions, S started to talk about his childhood and was summarily cut off.

"Shouldn't I talk about this with a psychologist?" he asked. "Isn't this one of the things that interests you? Doesn't it affect me now?"

"Look," I said, "a bridge with a load limit of three tons opens in 1903. The next day, a farmer drives eighteen tons over it; it cracks. The bridge collapses in 1963. What caused the collapse?

"The farmer in 1903," he said.

"Wrong," I said. "The bridge collapses in 1963 because of the cracks that day. Had they been filled in the preceding day, it would not have collapsed. Let's discuss the cracks in your marriage."

At the end of the period, there was no sulking in the garage and the partners were able to commune.

MARITAL CASE 2

This case concerned a young couple who had been married almost 10 years; their sexual relations throughout marriage had been limited to about two contacts a year. Both husband and wife ascribed the difficulty to the husband. Both *S*s were professionals, intelligent, were socially well at ease, highly regarded by their friends and the community. They were Roman Catholic and determined to maintain the marriage, but the wife thought she might be driven into extramarital relations. Both felt that, if only they could get started, the behavior might carry itself.

Husband and wife were seen separately every week, for one hour each. Both were instructed to discuss with me only that which they could discuss with each other, since I would make constant cross reference between the two sessions.

Various procedures were assayed by *S*s, but proved ineffective. Fondling was repulsed. *Playboy* was recommended to initiate amorous activity, but the husband fell asleep reading it. During the lesson on deprivation, the wife stated: "I am at my wit's end as how to shape his behavior. I don't know what reinforcements I have. The characteristic of good reinforcement is that it can be applied immediately and it is immediately consumed. I could withold supper, but that is not a good reinforcer because I can't turn it off and on. I can't apply deprivation, because that's my problem. I don't know what to do."

The husband was a rising business executive who took evening courses and whose time was so tight that he had to schedule almost every minute of his day. We discussed the possibilty of his scheduling his wife in the appointment book for two evenings a week. He thought this might work, But his wife was a bit more dubious. These appointments were kept two weeks in a row, but then lost their control. We then discussed the nature of the control over behavior exerted by discriminative stimuli, of which instructions are one example. There were differential consequences attached to keeping and not keeping the business appointments, but no differential consequences had been attached to meeting or not meeting appointments with his wife. Hence, the instructions lost their control (Ayllon & Azrin,1964).

Both *S*s were extremely well-groomed. Their clothing was always in best array. The wife visited the beautician once a week and the husband went to the barber every other week. In the session following the failure of control by the appointment book, the husband suggested that they might attach the opportunity to visit the beautician or barber as consequences to keeping the appointments. In the event that the appointments were not kept, the visits would not be allowed and could be resumed only when the appointments had been kept. His wife also felt that this would be extremely effective.

The next week, both showed up somewhat bedraggled. Thereafter, they were not bedraggled and the appointments were kept for the rest of that semester, at least.

Case Study Questions

1. How is the psychological principle of reciprocity similar to the process of stimulus change?
2. What is the characteristic of a good reinforcement, and how important is it to the shaping of new interpersonal responses?
3. How did the couple in the marital case in question 2 resolve their sexual problems?

SELF-TEST

Multiple Choice

1. A child psychologist has noted that the best single predictor of what child B will do, with respect to child A, is:
   a. what parent B has done
   b. what child B can do
   c. what child A did to child B
   d. what child B saw child A do to child C
2. The psychological principle of reciprocity is also referred to as:
   a. the two-for-the-road principle
   b. the two-in-the-hand principle
   c. the two-to-tango principle
   d. the two-times-two principle
3. Which of the following rules should not be considered when describing a problem relationship?
   a. simplicity
   b. objectivity
   c. specificity
   d. reciprocity
4. To ensure objectivity, the problem you describe should be:
   a. countable
   b. observable
   c. a behavior
   d. all of the above
5. Which of these is not an important external cue in interpersonal conflict?
   a. situation
   b. attribution
   c. events
   d. your response
6. Whenever you set out to improve a relationship with another person, your goals should be:
   a. higher than they usually are
   b. lower than usual
   c. somewhat ambiguous
   d. particularly modest
7. In order to make a problematic situation less likely to occur, you should include which of the following in your planned interaction?
   a. avoid triggers for conflict
   b. create triggers for pleasant events
   c. psych yourself up
   d. all of the above
8. Which of the following techniques can you use to prevent yourself from backsliding into negative responses?
   a. listening
   b. avoiding offensive responses
   c. avoiding revealing your interpretations and judgments
   d. all of the above
9. Which of the following techniques have psychotherapists been using to show that they hear and value what clients say?
   a. reflection
   b. catharsis
   c. abreaction
   d. direct return
10. If you find yourself in a situation where you simply do not want to hear another person's message, you should:
    a. ignore the message completely
    b. ignore the content and attend only to the feeling
    c. change the topic of the message
    d. listen to it anyway
11. Psychologist Arnold Lazarus has suggested that when confronted by an abrasive sales clerk, you should:
    a. respond in an empathic manner
    b. respond in an aggressive manner
    c. respond in an assertive manner
    d. do not respond and ignore the inappropriate response-stimulus
12. Refusing to listen to another person's emotional cues is an excellent way to:
    a. decrease the frequency of occurrence
    b. let him know that you really care
    c. let him know that you don't care about him
    d. avoid conflicting situations
13. Which of the following is considered a major

cause of negative interactions with others?
a. our habit of responding aggressively
b. our habit of responding defensively
c. our habit of not responding assertively
d. our habit of not responding at all

14. A good way to shortcircuit an argument that you see coming is to:
a. ignore both the zap and the criticism
b. ignore the criticism and respond to the zap instead
c. ignore the zap and respond to the criticism instead
d. respond to both the zap and the criticism

15. Constructive complaining can best be accomplished by making sure that:
a. the complaint is subtle but direct
b. the complaint focuses only on feelings
c. the complaint focuses only on recent events
d. the complaint is witnessed by at least one other person

16. When person A reveals an attribution that turns out to be accurate, this should remind person B to:
a. reform his responses
b. provide constructive criticism
c. provide clearer messages
d. prepare for an argument

17. According to social exchange theory, relationships are based on the exchange of:
a. feelings
b. direct feedback and approval
c. indirect messages and direct complaints
d. rewards and costs

18. Social exchange theory suggests that troubled relationships are characterized by:
a. high levels of punishment and high levels of reinforcement
b. low levels of punishment and low levels of reinforcement
c. high levels of punishment and low levels of reinforcement
d. low levels of punishment and high levels of reinforcement

19. When a person A purposely ignores a zap from person B, this should remind person B to:
a. repeat his communications
b. provide constructive criticism
c. provide fewer messages
d. prepare for an argument

20. A troubled relationship may be defined as:
a. the reciprocal exchange of punishments
b. the reciprocal exchange of problems
c. the careless use of social influence
d. an obvious failure to communicate

True-False

1. It is said that the social lives of most people consists of the direct type of social influence.
2. The psychological principle of reciprocity has also been referred to as the two-times-two principle.
3. Interpersonal problems rarely involve a single casual factor.
4. Your responses to a person set the conditions for the other person's responses.
5. When you set out to improve a relationship with another person, your goals should be high in order to encourage success.
6. Changing your responses to another person is evidence of your refusal to be controlled by the other person's responses.
7. By replacing an old negative response with a new positive response, you weaken the old associations between negative stimulus and negative response.
8. The technique of reflecting shows that you hear and value what the other person is saying.
9. Ignoring a message from another person is a good way of telling him that you don't care what he thinks or feels.
10. Expressing similar feeling while listening to someone comes quite naturally to most people.
11. One of the major causes of negative interactions is the habit that most people have of responding defensively.
12. A good way to shortcircuit an oncoming argument is to ignore the criticism and respond to the zap instead.
13. Communication theorists have pointed out that complaining is not a legitimate way of expressing dissatisfaction.
14. Relationship-contracts guarantee that each party will be rewarded for his or her efforts.
15. Punishment is preferable to reward as a means of changing a relationship.

Completion

1. _____ _____ occurs whenever we think or act in response to the prior action of another human being.
2. We participate in other people's behavior toward us by providing _____ for their responses.
3. The best way to ensure simplicity in your description of a relationship is to pick a problematic _____ in that relationship.
4. When setting out to change a relationship, the goal should be _____.

12/SOCIAL INFLUENCE: HOW TO CHANGE IT

5. Psyching yourself up for changing your responses to another person can be done through _____.
6. One of the best ways to improve your relationship with those close to you is through _____.
7. Briefly restating what another person has just said to you is called _____.
8. One of the major causes of negative interactions is the habit of responding _____.
9. The _____ response is an almost irresistible invitation to an argument.
10. A good way to shortcircuit an oncoming argument is to ignore the _____ and respond to the _____.
11. As long as it remains constructive, _____ ia a legitimate way of expressing dissatisfaction.
12. According to social exchange theory, a number of psychologists have suggested that the problem with unhappy marriages is that there are not enough _____ being exchanged.
13. One of the most reliable rewards is _____.
14. In order to make your approval truly reinforcing to the other person, you should follow four important _____.
15. A troubled relationship may be defined as a reciprocal exchange of _____.

Essay Questions

1. Discuss the principle of reciprocity with respect to its role in social relationships. (pp. 318–320)
2. Discuss the types of variables that are used to fill in the details surrounding a particular behavior. (pp. 321–323)
3. One of the best ways to improve your relationship with others is to listen to them. Discuss the techniques that will make you a better listener. (pp. 327–334)
4. In order to improve a relationship, we have to learn to complain more constructively. Discuss the six common-sensical rules of constructive complaining. (pp. 332–334)
5. Social exchange theory argues that relationships are based on the exchange of costs and rewards. Discuss this notion with respect to improving an unsatisfactory relationship. (pp. 335–338)

SELF-TEST ANSWERS

Multiple Choice

1. c (p. 318)
2. c (p. 320)
3. d (p. 320)
4. d (pp. 320–321)
5. b (p. 323)
6. d (p. 324)
7. d (pp. 324–325)
8. a (p. 326)
9. a (p. 328)
10. d (p. 329)
11. a (p. 329)
12. c (p. 329)
13. b (p. 330)
14. c (p. 330)
15. b (p. 333)
16. c (p. 336)
17. d (p. 335)
18. c (p. 335)
19. b (p. 336)
20. a (p. 338)

True-False

1. false (p. 317)
2. false (p. 320)
3. true (p. 323)
4. true (p. 324)
5. false (p. 324)
6. true (p. 326)
7. true (p. 327)
8. true (p. 328)
9. true (p. 329)
10. true (p. 329)
11. true (p. 330)
12. false (p. 330)
13. false (p. 332)
14. true (p. 337)
15. false (p. 338)

Completion

1. Social influence (p. 317)
2. cues (p. 319)
3. situation (p. 321)
4. modest (p. 324)
5. self-talk (p. 326)
6. listening (p. 327)
7. reflecting (p. 328)
8. defensively (p. 330)
9. defensive (p. 330)
10. zap, criticism (p. 331)
11. complaining (p. 332)
12. rewards (p. 335)
13. approval (p. 335)
14. rules (pp. 335–336)
15. punishments (p. 338)

13
Three Social Problems: Making Contact, Becoming Assertive, and Fostering Intimacy

CHAPTER OUTLINE

MAKING CONTACT
Priming Your Social Skills
   Modeling
   Role-playing
Priming Your Self-Confidence
   Self-talk
   Your clothes
   Shaping
The Contact
   Where to make the contact
   How to open
   Nonverbal behavior
The Follow-Up: More Shaping
For Women Trying to Meet Men
Handling Rejection

BECOMING ASSERTIVE
Do You Assert Your Rights?
   Nonassertiveness and its consequences
   Aggressiveness and its consequences
   Assertiveness and its consequences
Increasing Assertiveness: A Program
   Step 1: Self-monitoring
   Step 2: Modeling
   Step 3: Using imagery
   Step 4: Systematic desensitization
   Step 5: Role-playing
   Step 6: The real thing
   Step 7: Keep at it
   Two pitfalls
The Limits to Assertiveness
   When to squelch assertiveness
   The white lie

FOSTERING INTIMACY
The Search for Intimacy
Making Time
Increasing Self-Disclosure
   Why does self-disclosure foster intimacy?
   How to begin disclosing
   The limits to self-disclosure

READING

How Do I Trust Thee?

JOHN K. REMPEL AND JOHN G. HOLMES

"Trust me, trust me!" the guilty partner begs.

"I trust you, I trust you!" comes the reply, and the relationship, though rocky, goes on. Why? Because trust gives us the ability to rise above our doubts. With it we feel secure—even when we should not—that our most intimate relationships will continue to be a source of fulfillment and joy.

Do you trust your partner? How much? What effect does that trust, or lack of it, have on your relationship? And why does this elusive, ephemeral quality pervade so many aspects of our close relationships?

In an attempt to answer some of these questions, we designed a self-scoring measure of trust in close relationships. Based on our work with this Trust Scale we have developed profiles of people who score high, medium or low in trust. Before going on to the Trust Scale and its interpretation, however, let us explain what we mean by trust.

In a general sense, trust is the degree of confidence you feel when you think about a relationship.

Trust Scale

Read each of the following statements and decide whether it is true of your relationship with your partner. Indicate how strongly you agree or disagree by choosing the appropriate number from the scale below and placing it in the space provided in the left-hand margin.

1 = strongly disagree
2 = moderately disagree
3 = mildly disagree
4 = neutral
5 = mildly agree
6 = moderately agree
7 = strongly agree

Initial score / **Final score**

_____ 1. I know how my partner is going to act. My partner can always be counted on to act as I expect. _____

_____ 2. I have found that my partner is a thoroughly dependable person, especially when it comes to things that are important. _____

_____ 3. My partner's behavior tends to be quite variable. I can't always be sure what my partner will surprise me with next. _____

_____ 4. Though times may change and the future is uncertain, I have faith that my partner will always be ready and willing to offer me strength, come what may. _____

_____ 5. Based on past experience I cannot, with complete confidence, rely on my partner to keep promises made to me. _____

_____ 6. It is sometimes difficult for me to be absolutely certain that my partner will always continue to care for me; the future holds too many uncertainties and too many things to can change in our relationship as time goes on. _____

_____ 7. My partner is a very honest person and, even if my partner were to make unbelievable statements, people should feel confident that what they are hearing is the truth. _____

_____ 8. My partner is not very predictable. People can't always be certain how my partner is going to act from one day to another. _____

_____ 9. My partner has proven to be a faithful person. No matter who my partner was married to, she or he would never be unfaithful, even if there was absolutely no chance of being caught. _____

_____ 10. I am never concerned that unpredictable conflicts and serious tensions may damage our relationship because I know we can weather any storm. _____

_____ 11. I am very familiar with the patterns of behavior my partner has established, and he or she will behave in certain ways. _____

_____ 12. If I have never faced a particular issue with my partner before, I occasionally worry that he or she won't take my feelings into account. _____

_____ 13. Even in familiar circumstances, I am not totally certain my partner will act in the same way twice. _____

_____ 14. I feel completely secure in facing unknown new situations because I know my partner will never let me down. _____

_____ 15. My partner is not necessarily someone others always consider reliable. I can think of some times when my partner could not be counted on. _____

_____ 16. I occasionally find myself feeling uncomfortable with the emotional investment I have made in our relationship because I find it hard to completely set aside my doubts about what lies ahead. _____

_____ 17. My partner has not always proven to be trustworthy in the past, and there are times when I am hesitant to let my partner engage in activities that make me feel vulnerable. _____

_____ 18. My partner behaves in a consistent manner. _____

SCORING

This is how to score yourself: For questions 3, 5, 6, 8, 12, 13, 15, 16 and 17, reverse numbers. That is, if you put down a 1, change it to a 7 and write this in the space provided in the right-hand margin. In the same way, if you scored a 2 change it to a 6, 3 to a 5, 5 to a 3, 6 to a 2, and 7 to a 1. A neutral score of 4 remains unchanged.

When you have reversed the scoring for the items listed above, take the scores for the remaining items and write them in the right-hand margin just as they are. Add all the scores in the right-hand margin to obtain your final trust score.

If you are interested, you can add up the scores for the following questions to arrive at a score for each subscale of trust: Predictability, add 1, 3, 8, 11, 13 and 18. Dependability, add 2, 5, 7, 9, 15 and 17. Faith, add 4, 6, 10, 12, 14 and 16.

But confidence in what? Trust can take on different shades of meaning depending on which aspect of a relationship is being considered. We think there are three fundamental elements of trust.

First, there is the aspect of trust we call predictability. This refers simply to our ability to foretell our partner's specific behavior, including things we like and dislike. A predictable person is someone whose behavior is consistent—consistently good or bad. An unpredictable person leaves us guessing what will happen next. Such volatile people may make life interesting, but they don't inspire much in the way of confidence—and not all their surprises are pleasant. On the other hand, consistency is not enough for confidence to grow. If you have a partner who disappears every time a disagreement looms, you may know what to expect, but it's not something you look forward to. A sense of predictability must be based on the knowledge that your partner acts in consistently positive ways.

For all its value in conducting day-to-day exchanges, predictability is at best a starting point for the development of trust. After all, we predict particular actions, but we trust people. And as relationship grows, we tend to put less stock in specific kinds of behavior and more in the qualities and characteristics of the partner as a person. This is more in line with how most people ultimately understand trust, especially the second aspect of trust, which we call dependability.

The feeling that your partner is a dependable person is based on the emerging sense that he or she can be relied on when it counts. Such judgments depend heavily on how your partner responds in situations in which you might feel hurt or rejection. For instance, you would feel secure in confiding something very personal to your partner if he or she had been a supportive and understanding listener in the past. Paradoxically, we can only be certain that someone genuinely cares when a situation makes it possible for that person not to care. In other words, dependability grows out of a special set of circumstances that involve risk and personal vulnerability.

Both predictability and dependability assume that future behavior will mirror the past. But people change. They mature, their concerns and values shift and they pursue different goals. As this happens, relationships face new stresses and circumstances for which the past is at best an unreliable indicator. There are no absolute guarantees that the hopes and desires we have invested in a close relationship will ever be realized. Yet we make our plans and dream our dreams; and each time we set aside our doubts and continue our commitment to a relationship, we make, to one extent or another, a leap of faith.

Faith, then, is the third and final element of trust. It enables people to go beyond the available evidence and feel secure that a partner will continue to be responsive and caring. Feelings of faith begin with past experiences that show how much our partner cares. These events are the seeds from which confidence grows until, ultimately, the need for a sense of emotional security in the face of an uncertain future leads us to go beyond what the past can tell us.

Predictability, dependability and faith: Each offers a different basis on which feelings of confidence in a partner can be built. The way they are woven together establishes the extent to which we are willing to place our trust in an intimate partner.

HOW TRUSTING ARE YOU?

The Trust Scale is our attempt to measure trust in terms of predictability, dependability and faith. Clearly, such a brief scale cannot capture all the subtleties and nuances in a concept as complex as trust. Nevertheless, the results of two recent studies using the scale have shown it to be a valuable tool for understanding trust in close relationships and have helped us create profiles of people who score high, medium or low on trust for their partner.

The profiles that follow describe typical tendencies and provide a general picture of the patterns people tend to follow, but as with most things in life there are exceptions to the rule. We recommend a certain amount of caution when considering how your score relates to the profiles, since we have certainly encountered people in our research who are involved in successful relationships but have evaluated themselves harshly on the Trust Scale.

Our warnings may be best summarized by the following generalization: Ultimately, you are the best judge of your own feelings. If you have a troubled relationship, your score on the Trust Scale won't make it a good one, and if your relationship is strong, your score won't reveal that there are reasons for serious concern. What this scale can do is provide you with some idea of the characteristics shared by those with scores similar to or different from your own. Much more importantly, it affords the opportunity for you to examine your relationship from a vantage point you may not have considered previously. If completing the scale has raised new issues and offered a fresh perspective on trust, then this will have been its greatest value.

High Trust

If your total trust score exceeds 110, you have described yourself as being a very trusting person. Such people typically feel that they are involved in a very successful relationship and that their love for their partner is very strong. People with high faith scores in particular believe that both they and their partner are motivated by unselfish concerns. Their relationship is seen as valuable in and of itself, and they share a strong sense of attachment and emotional closeness.

Trusting people seem to approach interactions and discussions in a uniquely positive, tolerant manner. First, they expect their partner to behave in a positive way towards them. Even when faced with a conflict or disagreement, they anticipate that their partner will act in a pleasant, accepting, considerate fashion. They take as a given that their partner will be involved and interested in what they have to say. Beyond this, trusting individuals believe that the motives for their partner's actions stem from a compassionate and considerate attitude. We have strong evidence to indicate that these people are using their own emotions as a basis for judging their partner's feelings, though these judgments may not necessarily be accurate reflections of their partner's feelings. In a sense they appear to be projecting their own sense of closeness onto their partner.

How do trusting partners interpret what actually happens during an encounter? As you might expect, they generally have their expectations confirmed. Even folowing a difficult encounter, they tend to see their partner's actions as positive.

Why might this be the case? If we stop to speculate for a moment we can see that trust, and especially faith, may keep us from attaching too much meaning and importance to any particular negative event. If you really trust a person, you are more willing to give that person the benefit of the doubt when things don't look good. This may explain why people who score high on trust seem, at times, immune to evidence that is inconsistent with their beliefs. Even when a partner is clearly doing something negative, it is not taken as evidence of a lack of love or caring. We suspect that such relationships are, on the whole, relatively peaceful, secure and comforting.

Low Trust

People who score below 90 on the Trust Scale fall into the low-trust category. The characteristic profile for such people is fairly simple to describe: It is generally the opposite of the high-trust group. It should come as no surprise that a relationship in which partners have difficulty trusting one another is a relationship in trouble. Of the three groups, these people report the greatest number of problems and are the most poorly adjusted and least satisfied in their relationships. In particular, people scoring low on faith express less love for their partner and are less inclined to see their relationship as one of mutual giving. Their emotional attachment is likely to be rather fragile, and they may fear the risks of being close to and dependent on their partner.

When it comes to specific encounters, these people expect less from their partner. They are more inclined to predict that their partner will act in an angry, critical, distant or defensive manner, at least when the encounter involves conflicts of interest. In addition, distrustful people tend to view their partner's motives less positively. Compared with trusting people, they see their partner as more self-centered, uncaring, intolerant and unresponsive. And they often have their expectations confirmed: Their perceptions of a partner's behavior, and certain motives, are colored in the same dark shades as their initial suspicions.

Again, if we stop to speculate we can see that people who are reluctant to express trust are in no position to risk giving their partner the benefit of the doubt. Lurking close to the surface of most low-trust relationships is a history of broken promises, unmet expectations and emotional disappointments. In other words, there are usually good reasons for the hesitancy these people show. They have taken risks and lost. Is it any wonder that partners in such a relationship are prepared to expect the worst? Is it surprising that the motives would be questioned?

The sad irony is that once trust has been violated, a vicious cycle ensues and trust becomes doubly difficult to establish. Even if a partner "turns over a new leaf" and begins to work at the relationship, it is all too easy for positive actions to be explained away. To be fooled again would just hurt too much. Further, every error, however unintentional, becomes one more piece of evidence indicating that the new efffort is merely a sham and that nothing has really changed. Such a cycle is not hopeless, but for distressed couples, the potential for rebuilding a solid relationship slips away quickly. We present this admittedly extreme scenario in order to emphasize the difficulties couples will confront should trust break down.

Hopeful Trust

The group of individuals scoring in the middle range, between 90 and 110, is perhaps the most interesting group. By most standards these people are involved in successful relationships. In their feelings of love for their partner, the number of problems they report and their marital adjustment, they fall between the trusting and untrusting groups, but in an important way they tend more towards the trusting end. The emotional bonds many of these people feel may be just as intense as those of trustful couples. To a large extent these hopefuls also believe that both they and their partner are involved in the relationship because it is of value in and of itself. Yet somehow they lack the assurance that could allow them to fully accept their partner's demonstrations of unselfish concern without hesitation. In general, one might consider these couples as having relatively good relationships but definitely with room for improvement.

People in this middle range expect their partner to act in a relatively pleasant, helpful and accepting manner, though they are not quite as confident as the trustful group. But when there is a disagreement, they do not expect much; they are no more sanguine than the distrustful group. In contrast to this hesitancy, these people are quite willing to give their partner a break when it comes to evaluating motives: They expect their partner to be motivated by a relatively caring and concerned attitude. It is as if they lack confidence that their partner will actually be there when it counts, but they still hope that their partner's underlying motives consist of caring and concern. That is why we call the people in this group "hopeful."

How do these hopeful people interpret events after a difficult scene? In our study we were intrigued to find that they viewed their partner as more responsive and involved than they expected. In fact the hopeful people did not differ from the very trustful people in their descriptions of their partner's behavior. Interestingly, these positive evaluations failed to alter their perceptions that the underlying motives involved caring and concern.

Why is it that when these individuals saw what they were hoping for, it had no impact on the motives they attributed to their partner? We believe a hopeful person is someone who wants to see the best but is afraid to believe it. These are people who, in general, care for their partner but, for whatever reason, retain lingering doubts about his or her trustworthiness. It is as if they were saying, "Of course my partner will always love me . . . I hope."

We believe that these hopefuls are more ready than either the trusting or untrusting people to read meaning into both their partner's positive and negative acts. They are constantly scanning for clues that their partner cares. They want to be able to set their doubts aside, yet the risk of being wrong may simply be too great to allow them to reach a confident conclusion. In their vigilance they may establish such an exacting set of criteria that any partner would find it almost impossible to live up to them. Their partner's positive behavior is embraced as evidence that the relationship is improving, but since they are not willing to treat this evidence as a clear sign of the partner's underlying motives, it is always weighed against evidence from the partner's negative behavior and compounded by their own anxieties. Ironically, then, hopeful people may actually prevent confirmation of the very conclusion they are hoping to find.

Reading Questions

1. List and discuss the three elements of trust described in this article.
2. Briefly summarize the characteristics of each of the high- and low-trust groups.
3. Rempel and Holmes refer to the middle groups (scores 90 to 110) as hopeful. Discuss why.

RESEARCH STUDY

Investigators: Dennis McGuire and Mark Thelen.
Source, date: "Modeling, Assertion Training, and the Breadth of the Target Assertive Behavior," *Behavior Therapy*, 1983, *14*, 275-285.
Location: University of Missouri, Columbia.
Subjects: 96 unassertive female psychology students.
Materials: Conflict Resolution Inventory, videotapes.

Previous experiments had demonstrated the effectiveness of modeling, instructions, and behavior rehearsal in training unassertive individuals to engage in more assertive behavior. However, there was some question as to the relative added value of including instructions and rehearsals in the training. The present study considered the possibility that the breadth of assertiveness being targeted would make a difference in the relative contribution of instructions and rehearsal to assertiveness training.

Ninety-six unassertive female psychology undergraduates were each assigned to one of four combinations of modeling, instructions, and rehearsal: modeling; instruction and rehearsal; modeling with instruction and rehearsal; no treatment. For each type of training there were two groups, one receiving a narrow definition of assertiveness (simply saying "no") and one receiving a broad definition of assertiveness (expressing feeling, defending rights, etc.). In the groups receiving instructions, information was provided about assertiveness. In the groups receiving rehearsal, the participants rehearsed assertiveness. In the groups receiving modeling, videotaped models of assertive behavior were shown.

The results indicated that what worked best depended on the breadth of assertiveness being trained. With a narrow definition of assertiveness, there were no differences across training groups; however, all three were significantly better than no training. With a broad definition of assertiveness, the group receiving modeling with or without instructions and rehearsal improved their assertiveness significantly over the group trained via instructions and rehearsal. The researchers concluded that the choice of training approaches should depend on what skills breadth is being trained.

Research Questions

1. What was the purpose of this study regarding modeling, assertiveness training, and breadth of target behavior?
2. What was the approach used by the researchers in examining the relationship among these training variables?
3. What were the results of the study and what recommendation did the researchers make?

CASE STUDY

Reducing Heterosexual Anxiety

THOMAS J. D'ZURILLA

Steve was a 21-year-old student in his junior year at Stony Brook. He came in complaining of anxiety and nausea associated with personal contacts with girls. Again, the problem was especially disturbing on dates. Steve was not dating at all at the time of treatment because of this reaction.

This problem dated back about ten years. When he was about 11 years old he began to feel anxious and nauseous when he talked to or thought about a pretty girl that he liked. If he had recently eaten, the reaction would be particularly intense and vomiting would usually occur. The client soon learned to avoid eating for several hours prior to any social contacts with attractive girls to prevent vomiting. However, anxiety and nausea continued. In the case of any unexpected contacts soon after food intake, the reaction again occurred to the degree that the client was forced to remove himself from the situation to avoid vomiting.

Because of this disturbing problem the client had done very little dating until about two years before he came in for counseling when he had tried "going steady." He had attempted to cope with the situation by controlling eating and using "self-hypnosis." The latter involved lying down on a bed, trying to relax, and giving himself hypnotic suggestions taken from a book on hypnotic induction. He had also given himself suggestions to the effect that the anxiety-nausea reaction would not occur. The client employed this procedure before each date for about a month. When this method failed to produce significant improvement, the client gave it up and relied primarily on the procedure of controlling eating.

After about six months of going steady, Steve finally had ended the relationship because of the difficulties involved, even though the steady dating resulted in some reduction in the frequency and intensity of the reaction. During the year and a half before treatment the client never dated the same girl more than three times. He felt that the reaction had greatly interfered with heterosexual development during adolescence and had resulted in a lack of self-confidence in social relationships and feelings of inadequacy. Other problems reported by the client were anxiety associated with taking examinations and disturbing thoughts about possible illness and disease.

Starting Desensitization

After Steve and I explored details of his problem, three problem catagories were identified: formal date, telephone conversation, and informal meetings, such as meeting a girl in a bar and "picking her up." The presence and consumption of food and drink tended to aggravate the anxiety-nausea reaction in these situations. Since Steve was interested in a particular girl, Ellen, she was used in the anxiety hierarchies. The one concerning a date was as follows:

1. Lying in bed in the morning on the day of a date with Ellen
2. Getting out of bed in the morning on the day of the date
3. Eating breakfast on the day of the date
4. Driving home from school for dinner on the day of the date
5. Eating dinner with parents on the day of the date
6. Getting out of the car at Ellen's home

7. Walking up to the door of Ellen's home
8. Meeting Ellen at the door
9. Driving in the car with Ellen on the way to a restaurant
10. Sitting at a table with Ellen in the restaurant waiting to be served
11. Eating with Ellen in the restaurant
12. Sitting in the car with Ellen—you attempt to kiss her
13. You attempt to kiss Ellen, she turns away without saying anything
14. You attempt to kiss Ellen, she verbally rejects your advances

Self-Administered Counseling

At this point the academic semester ended after eight counseling sessions. It was not possible to continue counseling through the summer as planned since Steve had decided to take a job in his home town. It was agreed that he would attempt to apply desensitization principles on his own during the summer and return in the fall to begin formal desensitization treatment.

He was enthusiastic about desensitization treatment and well-motivated to try out a self-control program. First, the client decided that he must try to arrange as many "treatment trials" as possible during the summer. He contacted a girl, Carol, who lived in his neighborhood, and began to see her regularly, nearly every day. His "procedure" was based upon the self-manipulation of three behavioral variables: (1) eating, (2) relaxation and (3) activities associated with the anxiety hierarchies.

EATING TREATMENT

With regard to eating behavior, he started by setting up a three-hour minimum time period between eating a meal and contacts (both phone and personal) with Carol. Gradually, with each success experience, that is, contacts without disturbing anxiety or nausea, he moved the mealtime closer to the time of the contact until he was able to eat a meal with Carol on a date without disturbance. In addition to manipulating time of eating, he also manipulated the amount of food. He began by eating very small portions and gradually increased the amount until he was eating an average portion before and during a date.

RELAXATION TREATMENT

In regard to the use of relaxation, Steve started, by practicing deep muscle relaxation, following the procedures used during relaxation training in counseling, in his home before each date with Carol. He initiated the procedure each time at the first sign of anxiety. In employing this procedure, Steve patterned his self-produced cues after the verbalizations of the counselor during relaxation training; that is, he talked to himself in such terms as "Tense the muscles of your arms," "Relax," "Let go completely," "Notice the contrast," and so forth. In addition to employing complete deep relaxation in this manner, the client used differential relaxation to relax away any tension he experienced during activities just prior to and on the date. After a few weeks of successful dating without a major reaction, the client began to rely entirely upon the latter procedure to maintain control over anxiety.

Confronting Actual Situations

With the regular and systematic use of these procedures, Steve reported that he had completely eliminated the problem with telephone contacts in about two or three weeks. In regard to personal contacts with Carol, progress occurred more slowly but steadily. After about six weeks, he felt that he had the reaction completely under control.

Then a setback occurred. On several occasions he became anxious and experienced nausea at Carol's home. He relaxed himself somewhat in the situation by using differential relaxation with tension-release exercises. Then he moved his mealtime before a date back about 20 minutes, gradually decreasing the time period again on future dates. The client reported being surprised about the effectiveness of a 20-minute change in mealtime. At this point he also returned to practicing complete deep relaxation before a date. He reported that this procedure eliminated the reaction again in a few days. There were a few subsequent relapses following periods of several days when Steve was unable to see Carol for various reasons. In each case he coped successfully with the problem in the same manner as reported above.

After three months the client was able to eat a meal immediately before a date without experiencing disturbing anxiety or nausea and without subsequent relapse. After five months he was eating meals with Carol on a date without any anxiety or nausea.

DEALING WITH A FAILURE

The first setback reported above appeared to be related, at least in part, to considerable anxiety associated with the client's sexual experiences with Carol. At the time of this setback, the client had attempted sexual intercourse with Carol for the first time. This was his first attempt at sexual relations with any girl. Although Carol was cooperative, he became highly anxious and could not maintain an erection. In cooperation with Carol, the client postponed intercourse at this time and began systematically to employ Wolpe's (Wolpe & Lazarus, 1966) self-control procedure for using sexual responses to overcome anxiety and inhibition associated with sexual behavior. (He had become acquainted with this procedure in his abnormal psychology course.) He also used differential relaxation as an aid in the procedure. For one week, sexual intercourse was not attempted. Instead, he and Carol engaged in various kinds of precoital sexual behavior which had lower anxiety-provoking potential until he was getting aroused with a strong erection and anxiety was virtually eliminated. Then intercourse was again attempted with much greater success this time. The procedure was repeated until the problem was completely overcome.

Effects of Counseling

When the client returned in the fall, he described the above procedures and results and expressed confidence in his ability to continue on his own. Therefore, no formal counseling was initiated at this time. In a follow-up interview in January, Steve reported that the problem had been completely eliminated since October and that there had been no further relapses. At the time of the interview he was still going steady with Carol. There was not evidence of substitute "symptoms" or new problems. The client reported feeling much happier in general, more satisfied with life, and more adequate as a person. However, the client's other two problems—that is, test anxiety and disturbing thoughts about illness—remained essentially unchanged even though he made some attempt to deal with these situatuions on his own as well. This failure could be interpreted as reflecting the need for a careful and thorough assessment of the major determinants of the problem behavior before a self-control program is planned and prescribed.

Case Study Questions

1. Was Steve's nondating behavior due to a lack of social skills, or was it a result of learning to inhibit anxiety reactions? What role did operant and respondent conditioning play?
2. What were some of the negative consequences to Steve's aversive reaction to heterosexual contact?
3. What procedure did Steve utilize to overcome his eating problems?

SELF-TEST

Multiple Choice

1. Which of the following would *not* be considered one of the three most common causes of frustration in social life?
   a. being able to establish rapport
   b. being able to make contact
   c. being able to assert oneself
   d. being able to develop intimacy
2. Behavioral rehearsal allows the individual the opportunity to:
   a. practice new skills
   b. try out behaviors in safe situations
   c. get feedback on how he is doing
   d. all of the above
3. The most reliable technique for giving yourself the confidence to initiate contact with others is:
   a. wearing attention-getting clothes
   b. rehearsing with "actors"
   c. observing another's behavior
   d. confronting and talking back to yourself
4. Most people will feel more at ease about starting a conversation with another person if they know:
   a. the content of the conversation beforehand
   b. they will not see that person again
   c. some way of ending it
   d. that they will be successful
5. If you're beginning to develop your contact-making skills, you should select an environment that:
   a. has a large number of the opposite sex
   b. is relatively pressure-free
   c. is fairly close to home
   d. is very popular and well known
6. It is important to remember that people tend to prefer others who:
   a. stare them in the eye
   b. assume a semirigid posture
   c. orient their bodies toward them
   d. all of the above
7. Which of the following activities should a slightly nervous person suggest for her first date?
   a. a romantic dinner date
   b. a thirty-minute date for coffee
   c. a current movie
   d. an evening at her favorite disco

8. Shy women who are trying to meet men should adhere to which of the following hints?
    a. progress at a slow and gradual pace
    b. encourage themselves with frequent self-talk
    c. reward themselves for every small success
    d. all of the above
9. The individual who behaves nonassertively is subjecting himself to which of the following consequences?
    a. emotional harm
    b. social harm
    c. physiological harm
    d. all of the above
10. The individual who behaves assertively can expect which of the following consequences?
    a. increased self-confidence
    b. increased freedom
    c. increased self-respect
    d. all of the above
11. The seven-step program for the gradual learning of assertive behavior includes the optional step of:
    a. modeling
    b. behavioral rehearsal
    c. systematic desensitization
    d. covert imagery
12. The current use of the term "assertiveness" would only include which of the following?
    a. the honest expression of needs
    b. the honest expression of feelings
    c. the honest expression of love
    d. the honest expression of pleasure
13. According to psychologist Robert Weiss, an individual may experience more than one kind of loneliness. Which of the following would be included in his definition?
    a. social loneliness
    b. physical loneliness
    c. cognitive loneliness
    d. existential loneliness
14. Numerous researchers have demonstrated a correlation between loneliness and:
    a. anxiety
    b. depression
    c. ulcers
    d. all of the above
15. Which of the following would be considered accurate with regard to the current search for meaningful relationships?
    a. we seek those that yield total emotional gratification
    b. we seek those that yield a kind of white-hot communication
    c. we seek those that yield a spiritual consummation
    d. all of the above
16. Many psychologists and sociologists feel that the rising divorce rate in America indicates that:
    a. Americans are searching for intimacy
    b. marriage is no longer considered important
    c. marriage is no longer a source of sexual gratification
    d. none of the above
17. According to Carl Rogers, the best route to take if you want to increase your intimacy is to:
    a. increase it with members of a growth group
    b. increase it with members of an encounter group
    c. have a psychologist help you become intimate with others
    d. increase it with people you have known for years
18. What percentage of the American population sits before the television set on an average weekday winter evening?
    a. about 25 percent
    b. about 33 percent
    c. about 50 percent
    d. about 67 percent
19. According to psychologist Sidney Jourard, self-disclosure:
    a. is synonymous with intimacy
    b. enhances friendship
    c. involves a good deal of subjectivity
    d. all of the above
20. A good exercise in self-disclosure, particularly for beginners, is:
    a. expressing similarity
    b. reacting nondefensively
    c. revealing attributions
    d. all of the above

True-False

1. Many people go through life without satisfying their need for others.
2. The norms of our culture generally discourage making contact simply for the sake of making contact.
3. A woman who makes "advances" toward a man is no longer in danger of being mistaken for a prostitute.
4. Most people feel somewhat shy about approaching strangers.
5. When initiating your first contact, you should consider dressing in clothes that have attention-getting qualities.
6. The ideal environment for contact-making

experiments is a gathering organized around some activity other than pairing people off.
7. In order to start a conversation, a well-engineered opener is required.
8. If you avoid making eye contact while engaged in conversation, the other person will probably assume that you are bored.
9. While speaking to another person, your body should communicate a state of moderate tension.
10. In the event that your contact-making efforts are met with a gentle rejection, you should keep on trying and congratulate yourself for staying in there.
11. Assertiveness is nothing more than the behavioral means by which we enact our freedom and responsibility.
12. Numerous researchers have demonstrated that loneliness causes depression and suicide.
13. Looking for causes of depression, Lowenthal and Haven found that the lack of a person to confide in was a crucial cause.
14. The lonelier a person feels, the more intense an intimacy he will seek.
15. The pace of modern life in America tends to encourage easy in, easy out, superficial attachments.

Completion

1. Constructive _____ is the most reliable route to assertiveness.
2. Some psychologists feel that many people are excruciatingly lonely because they lack _____ skills.
3. The larger an individual's circle of acquaintances, the _____ the person's social life.
4. Deliberate _____ is an excellent means of learning how to make contact.
5. The ability to meet other people is not magic; it is simply acquiring a set of _____.
6. The most reliable technique for giving yourself the confidence to initiate contact with others is _____.
7. An excellent method for gradually reducing anxieties about meeting new people is to _____ the contact-making behavior.
8. Much of our communicating is done not through speech but through _____.
9. When you are speaking to another person, your _____ should communicate a state of moderate relaxation.
10. "_____ comes not from thin air, but from experience in which we succeed."
11. _____ means standing up for your personal rights and expressing your thoughts, feelings, and beliefs in direct, honest, appropriate ways.
12. Unnecessary excursions into painful honesty are often simply _____ in disguise.
13. It appears that there are two different kinds of loneliness: _____ loneliness and _____ loneliness.
14. _____ may be defined as a strong attachment, characterized by trust and familiarity between two people.
15. According to psychologist Sidney Jourard, _____ is synonymous with _____.

Essay Questions

1. Identify and discuss at least four of the six suggestions for opening a conversation. (pp. 348–350)
2. Define the term "assertiveness," and discuss the consequences of behaving assertively and nonassertively. (pp. 352–356)
3. Describe the seven-step program designed for learning how to become more assertive. List and describe each step. (pp. 356–359)
4. Define the term "intimacy." How does the American culture work against intimate relationships? How do Americans fill their need for intimacy? (pp. 364–366)
5. Discuss the relationship between intimacy and self-disclosure. Are they really synonymous? (pp. 369–371)

SELF-TEST ANSWERS

Multiple Choice
1. a (p. 343)
2. d (p. 346)
3. d (p. 346)
4. c (p. 348)
5. b (p. 348)
6. c (p. 350)
7. c (p. 351)
8. d (pp. 351–352)
9. d (pp. 353–354)
10. d (pp 355–356)
11. c (p. 358)
12. a (p. 361)
13. a (p. 363)
14. b (p. 364)
15. d (p. 365)
16. a (p. 365)
17. d (p. 366)
18. c (p. 367)
19. a (p. 369)
20. d (p. 371)

True-False
1. true (p. 344)
2. true (p. 344)
3. true (p. 345)
4. true (p. 346)
5. false (p. 347)
6. true (p. 348)
7. false (p. 348)
8. true (p. 350)
9. false (p. 350)
10. true (p. 352)
11. true (p. 355)
12. false (p. 364)
13. true (p. 364)
14. true (p. 365)
15. true (p. 365)

Completion
1. complaining (p. 343)
2. social (p. 344)
3. richer (p. 344)
4. modeling (p. 345)
5. skills (p. 345)
6. self-talk (p. 346)
7. shape (p. 347)
8. body language *or* body nonverbal language (p. 350)
9. body (p. 350)
10. Confidence (p. 351)
11. Assertiveness (p. 352)
12. aggressiveness (pp. 362–363)
13. social, emotional (p. 363)
14. Intimacy (p. 364)
15. self-disclosure, intimacy (p. 369)

14
The Environment: How It Affects Us and How We Can Affect It

CHAPTER OUTLINE

HOW ENVIRONMENT INFLUENCES BEHAVIOR

ENVIRONMENTAL STRESS AND BEHAVIOR
Crowding
   Calhoun's rat experiment
   Population density and crowding
   The human consequences of high population density
Noise
Temperature

THE BUILT ENVIRONMENT AND BEHAVIOR
Rooms
   Beauty and ugliness
   Furniture and seating
Buildings and Neighborhoods
   The Pruitt-Igoe project
   The social amenities of slums
   High-rise and low-rise: Defensible space
Cities
   Crime
   Social indifference
   The other side of the story: Freedom and variety

PERCEIVING THE ENVIRONMENT
Cognitive Maps
Selective Attention
Habituation

ADJUSTMENT AND ENVIRONMENTAL PERCEPTION
Surveying an Environment: A Step-by-Step Procedure
A Sample Environmental Survey
Changing Your Environment

READING

Sound Effects on Behavior

SHELDON COHEN

It was summer, and the weather was sunny: a good day for householders in Seattle to mow their lawns—and for psychologists Kenneth E. Mathews and Lance Canon to conduct a field experiment. As people walked down the street they encountered a confederate of the experimenters' as he "accidentally" dropped several volumes from an armload of books he was carrying. In half of the encounters, a lawn mower without a muffler was running at full throttle nearby; in half, it was turned off. When the lawn mower was off, 50 percent of the passersby picked up the books and handed them back; when it was going full tilt, only 12.5 percent came to the stranger's aid.

Those figures are part of the accumulating evidence that noise can affect human beings in unexpected ways. Studies of how noise affects hearing and other aspects of physical health have been going on for years, but it is only recently that investigators have turned their attention to the psychological effects of noise. Researchers want to know just how irritating noise is to people and just how much psychological harm noise actually causes. The degree of irritation people feel seems to vary greatly, depending in part on how necessary a noise seems to be and how predictable it is. There *are* provocative hints that noise may have an adverse effect on emotional well-being. Recent research suggests that noise can reduce both sociability and sensitivity to the needs of others.

Questions about noise are of more than academic interest. Distracting, unwanted sound is part of our everyday experience. Our homes are full of noisy appliances: air conditioners, vacuum cleaners, dishwashers, refrigerators, exhaust fans. The streets blare with the sound of cars, trucks, motorcycles, and jackhammers.

Even our neighbors, our children, and our spouses are sources of noise. There is reason to believe that noise levels in residential communities have increased substantially during the past 25 years; the Environmental Protection Agency (EPA) estimates that more than 70 million Americans now live in neighborhoods with noise levels high enough to interfere with communication and to cause annoyance and dissatisfaction. In a recent Census Bureau survey, street noise was the most-mentioned neighborhood problem; more than one-third of those surveyed complained about it. And not long ago, the U.S. National Research Council reported that more than 12 million people were thinking of moving because they found neighborhood noise exasperating.

The issue of noise is particularly timely because the Reagan administration's proposed budget provides no funds for the Office of Noise Abatement and Control after mid-1982. The office, a subdivision of the EPA, was created by Congress to coordinate national noise-control efforts, and Congress may refuse to let it die. If it is actually dissolved, however, that could mean relaxed federal regulation of noise sources such as trucks, buses, motorcycles, and railroads; reduced support for research on the effects of noise on health and well-being; and cutbacks in assistance to states and localities trying to develop and enforce noise-abatement legislation.

Before discussing the research that has been done so far, it is important to understand what scientists mean by sound and noise. Sound results from changes in air pressure that are detected by the ear. Noise is a psychological term referring to unpleasant, unwanted, or intolerable sound. It follows that noise is in the ear of the beholder. Thus, even loud sounds may sometimes be judged desirable, while soft sounds may be considered noisy. Your neighbor may enjoy listening to a rock album at a sound level that shakes the foundation of your house, while you find the same sound infuriating. Likewise, the sound of a couple whispering endearments to each other during a theater performance may be barely audible, but other members of the audience may react to it as an intruding noise.

The problem for social scientists is how to measure the extent to which noise disturbs people. One obvious approach is to count formal complaints, which do, of course, reflect annoyance. The difficulty is that not everyone who is disturbed files a complaint. In general, better-educated, higher-income social status people complain most often. It is not that they are more annoyed than other people but that they understand the complaint procedure better and more often expect someone to listen to them. Complaints are thus not an accurate measure of reaction to noise. Most community noise research—that is, studies done outside the laboratory—has therefore focused on the level of annoyance people report in interviews or on questionnaires.

The usual format for surveys is as follows: "To what degree are you annoyed because the noise [of planes, trucks, or some other specified source of sound] interferes with sleep, rest, relaxation; hearing radio and television; hearing conversation; work, study?" Such questions are usually buried in a broad interview concerning satisfaction with neighborhood and community, which avoids making respondents feel that they are *supposed* to complain about noise.

Many interview studies have been done in neighborhoods near airports, highways, and factories. Responses show that the nature of a person's reaction to sound is affected by a wide range of influences, the least surprising of which is loudness. Annoyance mounts with the decibels. (A sound registering zero decibels is the weakest sound that can be heard by a person with good ears in quiet surroundings.) Background sounds up to 50 decibels, the level of an air conditioner, annoy only a few people. Seventy decibels (a vacuum cleaner, for example) irritates a high percentage of hearers, while 110 decibels (a riveting machine) is likely to grate on almost everyone. Complaints are most frequent when there is high intensity sound (jet takeoff at 120 decibels).

But there is considerable evidence that psychological factors—attitudes and beliefs about a noise and its source—are of equal or even greater importance than the intensity of a sound. Studies done near London's Heathrow Airport by sociologist Aubrey McKennel and similar studies in the vicinity of Kennedy Airport in New York by acoustic sociologist Paul Borsky showed that respondents were greatly influenced by what they imagined other people's attitudes to be. Subjects who assumed that pilots, airport personnel, and government officials couldn't care less about those who had to listen to planes were much more annoyed by airport sounds than were people who believed someone cared. Respondents were also more annoyed when they thought the noise was unnecessary, disliked other aspects of their environment, believed that noise was harmful to their health, or feared plane crashes.

Studies of annoyance with traffic noise similarly indicate the important role of psychological and sociological factors. German researchers have found that traffic annoyance increases with worry about accidents; a perception that it is difficult to reduce the noise level; and dissatisfaction with other aspects of the neighborhood. Respondents who believe noise is harmful to their health also report greater annoyance.

A survey by sociologists Craig Humphrey and John Krout at Pennsylvania State University has shown that concern about the economic impact of a noise source is an important predictor of noise annoyance. Respondents who believed that a nearby limited access highway adversely affected the value of their property were more annoyed with the noise than were the people who expected the highway to increase property values. That relationship held no matter how far people lived from the highway. The study also showed that people who believed the road made jobs, religious services, stores, and other services more accessible were less annoyed by the traffic noise than were those not holding that attitude. Both the American and the German researchers found that demographic factors such as age, income, and education were unrelated to annoyance.

A striking study was done by Swedish sociologists Rune Cederlöf, Erland Jonsson, and Stefan Sörensen, who tried to lessen irritation by changing community attitudes toward the source of noise. They sent a group of residents near a Swedish air force base a souvenir book that commemorated the 50th anniversary of the Royal Swedish Air Force and suggested that people living near the base believed the air force to be of vital importance to the country. Surveys conducted several weeks and even years later showed that this group was less annoyed by aircraft noise than was a control group from the same community that had not received the souvenir book. In short, redefining the importance of the noise source drastically reduced annoyance. Thus it appears that the meaning of a noise for a particular respondent is crucial to his or her perception of it.

Although there is no accepted theory of annoyance that explains such findings, many of the psychological factors associated with noise annoyance are understandable if annoyance is viewed as a mild form of anger. According to cognitive theories of emotion, anger occurs when people believe that they have been harmed and that the harm was both avoidable and undeserved. In noisy situations, harm may include threats to health and property values, blocking of valued goals, or simply exposure to an unpleasant stimulus.

If noise caused irritation and frustration, it seems plausible that prolonged exposure can cause or aggravate mental illness. So far, however, the evidence is mixed. Industrial surveys show that exposure to noise increases self-reported anxiety and emotional stress. Workers habitually exposed to very high intensity noise show increased incidence of nervous complaints, nausea, headaches, instability, argumentativeness, sexual impotence, mood changes, and anxiety. German physician Gerd Jansen reported that workers in the noisiest parts of a steel factory had more social conflicts both at home and in the plant. The results of this research are difficult to interpret, however, since the same workers were often subject to work stresses other than noise (for instance, difficult tasks to be done and risks to be faced), which might have precipitated or contributed to the symptoms.

Although a number of studies of the impact of community noise on self-reported mental distress similarly indicate more symptoms among those exposed to noise, the questions in these studies were often worded in a way that seemed to invite people to blame their ailments on noise. For instance, a researcher might ask, "Does this traffic noise give you a headache?" When interviewers do not mention noise as a possible cause of symptoms ("What causes your headaches?" for example), results are inconsistent.

A final group of studies has examined the possible relationship between community noise and admission rates to community mental health centers near London's Heathrow Airport and Los Angeles International Airport. Although some of the studies showed differences between mental-hospital admission rates in quiet neighborhoods and in noisy ones, the differences were so small (between .0001 percent and .0003 percent) as to be trivial. Moreover, critics of the studies say the quiet neighborhoods chosen as controls were not comparable in socioeconomic status with the noisy areas.

A long-range project being conducted by psychiatrist Alex Tarnopolsky and his colleagues at the Institute of Psychiatry in London may help resolve questions about the relationship of community noise annoyance and psychiatric disturbance. Initial reports suggest that respondents who express annoyance with aircraft noise are no more likely to have psychiatric disorders one year later than those who are not annoyed. However, respondents troubled by psychiatric problems at the time they are surveyed are more likely to report noise annoyance than are respondents without psychiatric problems. The implication is that noise does not increase the number of psychiatric cases but may aggravate existing psychological problems.

All of the studies discussed above involved adults only. It is possible that children are more susceptible to noise-induced psychological distress than are adults. David Krantz, Gary Evans, Dan Stokols, and I recently completed a large-scale study of 142 elementary school children living under the air corridor of Los Angeles International Airport. Compared with 120 similar children in quiet areas of Los Angeles, the children near the airport did not perform as well on a difficult task and were more likely to give up in discouragement. In the noisy area, 53 percent of the children were unable to put together a nine-piece jigsaw puzzle within the four minutes allotted to the task, and 31 percent of the children who failed stopped trying even before their time was up. In the quiet area, only 36 percent failed to finish the puzzle, and all but 7 percent of those kept doggedly working at the task as long as they were allowed to. Lack of persistence is characteristic of "learned helplessness," essentially a conviction that there is nothing one can do to remedy a situation or solve a problem. Learned helplessness sometimes develops after people have a traumatic experience in which they cannot control the environment; a sense of helplessness carries over to other situations and is thought to be one cause of depression. Our data suggest the possibility that youngsters living near the airport might have been more susceptible to depression. That is pure speculation, though, without further research.

Recent studies both in laboratory and in community settings have examined the effects of loud noise on social and antisocial behavior in college students and other adults. Although firm conclusions are not yet possible, the research suggests that loud noise can change the way people normally behave toward one another, reducing willingness to help, to be neighborly, and to inhibit aggression.

The researchers mentioned at the beginning of this article— Mathews of Seattle City Light and Canon of the University of New Hampshire—found in a laboratory study that subjects exposed to loud noise were less likely to help people pick up books and papers that they had dropped than were subjects exposed to moderate noise or to none at all. In one part of the lawn-mower experiment, the researchers' book-dropping confederate wore a cast on his arm to see if it would make passersby take pity on him when the books slipped from his grasp. The cast did just that when the lawn mower was silent, but not when it was running. In the first case 80 percent of people picked up the books. In the second, the figure was only 15 percent—a further demonstration of the power of noise to inhibit Good Samaritan impulses.

Studying 2,567 people in the Netherlands, social psychologist Charles Korte and his colleagues similarly found that in both cities and towns, persons in quiet areas with little traffic and few pedestrians were more likely to be helpful than were persons in noisy, trafficked areas. Where it was quiet, 5.5 percent of passersby helped an apparently lost person read a map he was studying with evident puzzlement, and 73 percent agreed to aid a researcher by granting an interview. Under noisy conditions, the figures went down to 1.1 percent and 62.5 percent, respectively.

William Sauser, Carlos Arauz, and Randall Chambers found a lack of sympathy for others when they asked 20 undergraduate subjects to work at a simulated business-management task either in quiet surroundings or while hearing a recording of typical office noises: the sound of typing, ringing telephones, paper rustling, and people moving around. The students evaluated five simulated resumes from job applicants and set starting salaries for each. Subjects working where the noise level reached 70 to 80 decibels recommended a mean salary of $8,989. Subjects in offices registering only 50 to 57 decibels suggested a mean salary of $9,960, almost $1,000 more. (Moral: choose a quiet spot when you ask the boss for a raise!)

It is interesting to speculate about the reasons for decreased helpfulness in a noisy environment. Four explanations come to mind. First, it is probably natural to exchange a few words with a person one is about to help, and people may have sensed that helping would be awkward if noise drowned out their voices. Second, people may have found the noise so unpleasant that their first priority was to get away from it. Third, the noise may have put people in a bad mood, which interfered with their motivation to help.

The fourth possible explanation is a complex one, based on an effect of loud noise that has been established in laboratory research on human performance. Studies by British psychologist Robert Hockey and others have demonstrated that when people are performing a complex task in a noisy environment, they focus their attention on the most important aspects of the task, ignoring everything that is going on around them unless it can help them get the job done. I believe that this attentional focusing is a strategy to cut down on the amount of information they have to process in a noisy situation. In other words, when too much is going on at once, people can't pay attention to everything. Loud noise may be "too much," so people's brains simply may not process—or even perceive—subtle social cues that might otherwise influence their behavior. The arm cast in the Mathews-Canon study was probably such a cue. Under ordinary circumstances, most passersby might have perceived it as a subtle expression of need and come to the rescue. The lawn-mower noise may have made ordinarily helpful people insensitive.

Like planned experiments, surveys of naturally noisy neighborhoods suggest that noise interferes with interpersonal behavior. Donald Appleyard, an urban planner, and Mark Lintell, an architect, investigated the effects of traffic noise on the residents of three streets in a middle-income San Francisco neighborhood. The streets differed in the amount of traffic— light, moderate, or heavy—and, consequently, in noise levels. Residents of the lightly trafficked street were found to have three times as many friends and twice as many acquaintances as residents of the heavily trafficked streets. There was substantially more casual social interaction on the lightly trafficked street than on the other two; on the street with heavy traffic, there was virtually no activity at all. People on the noisiest street reported that it was a rather lonely place to live, while those on the quietest one perceived it as a friendly and sociable area.

Lack of community as well as an unwillingness to use outdoor facilities shows up in other surveys of noisy neighborhoods. People living near a busy airport complain that their friends and relatives refuse to visit them because of the noise. Suburbanites exposed to heavy traffic noise do not make use of decks, patios, outdoor grills, or picnic tables; urban apartment dwellers living adjacent to busy streets are less likely to keep their entryways looking attractive than are their counterparts in quiet neighborhoods. Decreased neighborliness in the midst of noise probably occurs for the same reason decreased helping does: communication difficulties caused by noise, desire to get away from the noise quickly, a bad mood, and a tendency to concentrate on one's own problems.

Evidence on the relationship between noise and aggression is sparse but consistent. Laboratory studies clearly indicate that while loud noise itself is not sufficient to cause aggression, noise intensifies a predisposition to behave aggressively. In a study by psychologists Edward Donnerstein and David Wilson, an experimental confederate intentionally angered half of the subjects by telling them they had done poorly on a laboratory task and by giving them a number of painful shocks. The confederate gave the remaining subjects a positive evaluation and only one shock. Subject and confederate then switched roles, with the subject now in the role of shock-giver. As we would expect from our knowledge of conditions that lead people to act aggressively, angry subjects administered more intense shocks to the confederate than did subjects who were not angry. Moreover, when a recording of loud noise was played during the shock session, angered subjects administered even more severe shocks. But the noise did not affect the intensity of the shocks given by the unprovoked group.

In real life, noise sometimes appears to lead to extreme violence. A middle-aged mother recently strangled her neighbor's four-year-old daughter and later told the police that she had done it because the girl made too much noise and disturbed her two teenage sons, who were studying for school examinations. The child's murder occurred only one month after a 47-year-old worker was convicted of stabbing his neighbor's wife and her two daughters to death because "they played the piano too loudly." Several months ago, my hometown newspaper reported the story of a man who was apparently angered by a gas company crew using a jackhammer in the street in front of his house. The man approached the workers, asked them to be quiet, and then went home. The workers told police that they had begun to work again when they heard a shotgun blast and saw the man standing on his porch with a gun aimed at them. Of course, these are not everyday occurrences; they exemplify extreme reactions to noise by people who must have serious psychological problems to begin with.

The research up to now is far from complete concerning the effects of noise on human beings. There are data linking noise exposure to heart disease, but the evidence is not conclusive. Some studies suggest that noise can impair the ability to do certain tasks well, but the findings are inconsistent and open to different interpretations; as yet, we do not know how a specific noise will affect performance in specific circumstances.

Despite the gaps in our knowledge, we do have enough information to formulate community noise policies. On the one hand, individual attitudes toward a noise and its source are probably as important as noise intensity in determining response to sounds. Thus it is reasonable to expect large individual differences in reaction to any noise source. Does that make laws limiting the intensity of noise beside the point? Not at all. We know that intensity remains an important factor, with increases in loudness almost always resulting in increases in the percentage of affected residents. Noise-elicited annoyance and disruption of interpersonal activities can be a serious threat to the quality of life; increases in intensity result in increased risk of psychological harm.

The role of noise research in setting public policy is only just beginning to be established. The fact that loud noise can damage hearing is widely accepted, but until recently, few if any public officials accepted as fact the idea that noise can do psychological harm. In a recent landmark court case, however, several residents of the area surrounding Los Angeles International Airport sued for compensation from the city of Los Angeles for loss of property value and for mental and emotional distress caused by airport din. Not only were they granted compensation for loss of property value, but the California Supreme Court also affirmed their contention that jet noise interferes with daily life and causes "a sense or feeling of annoyance, strain, worry, anger, frustration, nervousness, fear, and irritability." Moreover, the court didn't even demand medical proof that the residents had suffered impaired hearing or other physical injury. Thus, the court made it official in the eyes of the law, as well as in the minds of psychologists, that noise is a nuisance.

Reading Questions

1. What is meant by the term "noise"? How has noise been measured?
2. What are some of the factors that determine the impact of a noise?
3. Discuss the effects of noise on human beings that have been found in the research that was described.

RESEARCH STUDY

Investigators: Andrew Baum and Glen E. Davis.
Source, date: "Reducing the Stress of High-Density Living: An Architectural Intervention," *Journal of Personality and Social Psychology*, 1980, *38*, 471-481.
Location: Washington College.
Subjects: 67 female first-year undergraduate college dormitory residents.
Materials: questionnaires and 12 anagrams on index cards.

A good deal of attention has been given to the problem of crowding. Generally, studies have found crowding to be a complex situation resulting in discomfort, withdrawal, and other unpleasant effects. Much of the research on crowding has focused on helping individuals cope with its effects. In the present study, the environment was modified in order to reduce the sensation and effects of crowding. The experimenters believed that if the number of persons who were likely to interact was reduced, group formation would be facilitated and individuals in those groups would be more comfortable with those around them.

Using a college dormitory as the setting, the researchers compared the effects of crowding in a long corridor area in which 40 students lived with the effects in a short corridor area in which 20 students lived. These two settings were compared with a second long corridor area that had been divided in half, leaving 20 residents in each half, with a barrier (architectural intervention) between the halves.

The subjects represented a random group of those living on these corridors. They were surveyed at the beginning of their residence and after five weeks and twelve weeks of dormitory residence. They were asked how crowded and hectic they found dormitory life to be as well as how much control they felt they had over social interactions.

In addition to the surveys, an observer visited the corridors regularly and recorded the amount of social behavior and the number of doors to rooms that were open. Finally, each subject was surveyed and tested in a laboratory setting to determine her degree of social withdrawal and her ability to perform a complex task (solving anagrams).

The researchers found that the residents on the bisected long corridor and the residents on the short corridor behaved and responded similarly. The behavior and responses of these groups differed from those of the residents on the long corridor. The residents on the bisected and short corridors engaged in more social interaction, showed more local group development, felt they had more control over their surroundings, and exhibited less social withdrawal than the residents on the long corridors.

On the basis of results, Baum and Davis concluded that the architectural intervention of bisecting the long corridor had a definite effect in reducing the sensation and effects of crowding. They also concluded that the reduction in residential group size brought about by this intervention led to better group development, thus reducing symptoms of stress, withdrawal, and helplessness.

Research Study Questions

1. Discuss the issue addressed by this research and the investigators' approach to studying it.
2. Describe the design of the study.
3. What were the results of the study? Briefly discuss group development in relation to crowding.

CASE STUDY

Murder on the Street

GEORGE KALUGER AND MERIEM FAIR KALUGER

Tuesday, June 17, is a day I will never forget. That was the day I witnessed an actual murder. After dinner my brother left the house, my mother went to sit on the porch, and, as usual, I proceeded to clean the kitchen. It was a typical June evening, and the children were playing outside, running up and down the street.

After washing the dishes, I went to the porch with my mother. All of a sudden a man (I'll call him Larry) came running down the street. He was being chased by two teenagers (Sumpter and Al). At first I thought they were just playing with each other, but later Larry came back down the street and collapsed in my neighbor's front yard. There was blood covering his chest. After Larry fell, Sumpter ran up to him and stabbed him several times. Each time the knife plunged into Larry's body, I could feel the sharp pains. As Sumpter and Al began to walk away from Larry's mutilated body, I heard Sumpter shout over his shoulder: "That's what you get for f—king with my mother!"

Mrs. Dexter, the owner of the yard, told me to call the police, because she was too shocked to move. My mother and I ran inside, called the police, and told them what had happened. By the time I returned outside, Larry was dead.

When the police arrived they pronounced him dead and took him to the morgue. Men from the Crime Lab were sent out later to take pictures of where Larry had lain. Then detectives came around to ask questions.

My brother and his friends had returned from playing basketball; they all were sitting on the front steps. I was the only one who had witnessed the murder. When the detectives came to our porch, I wasn't sure if I could answer their questions or not. The one detective asked: "Did anyone here see what happened?" No one answered. Then he explained how nothing would happen to us if we told him what had occurred. Still no one answered. The silence was broken when one of the boys told the detectives that everyone was at the basketball court when Larry was killed, and nobody saw anything. The detectives left and started asking other people in the neighborhood what happened.

The reason I didn't volunteer any information was that I was scared. I feared that some harm would happen to me, because one of Sumpter's friends was sitting on our front steps; he would certainly tell if I told. I knew that Sumpter and his friends would find some way to hurt me. One of our neighbors told the detectives what had happened; she identified Sumpter, and he was arrested the next day.

Later I found out the reason behind Sumpter's act. Larry had been seeing Sumpter's mother for several years, and Sumpter's brothers and sisters never liked him. Earlier Tuesday afternoon, Larry and Sumpter's mother began to argue and Larry started hitting her. Sumpter didn't find out about it until later that evening, but when he did he began searching for Larry. He found him around the corner from our house and stabbed him three times. Larry tried to run away, but Sumpter and Al caught him and eventually killed him.

This incident had a deep psychological effect on me because, until this day, I am wondering whether or not I should have been the informer. This probably will remain on my conscience for the rest of my life.

Case Study Questions

1. In what way was Larry's violent death similar to the Kitty Genovese incident of 1964 (hint: bystander apathy)?
2. According to social psychologist Philip Zimbardo, the anonymity of city life encourages crime. How does fear influence the chances of recognition and anonymity?
3. What role did subjective reality play in the incident of June 17 involving Larry's murder? Which of the three factors of subjective reality had the greatest impact on Larry's murder?

SELF-TEST

Multiple Choice

1. The interacting unit of organisms and their environment is referred to by scientists as:
    a. a symbiosystem
    b. an organvironment
    c. a unisystem
    d. an ecosystem
2. The environment helps to create behavior in all the following ways *except*:
    a. the environment establishes the ego
    b. the environment puts constraints on behavior
    c. the environment elicits behavior
    d. the environment molds the self
3. The results of John B. Calhoun's experiment

with rats suggest that overcrowding will cause human beings to:
   a. establish territorial boundaries
   b. become hypersexual
   c. increase cooperative social behavior
   d. all of the above
4. When autopsies were performed on the rats in Calhoun's experiment, it was found that many of them:
   a. had enlarged adrenal glands
   b. had enlarged detrussor muscles
   c. had enlarged sex organs
   d. had an enlarged hypothalamus
5. The psychological definition of population density is best exemplified by which of the following situations?
   a. standing room only at a basketball game
   b. "full house" at a jazz festival
   c. twelve persons in an eight-person elevator
   d. all of the above
6. The psychological condition of population density is characterized as being:
   a. a subjective state
   b. an objective state
   c. a state of equality
   d. a state of wish-fulfillment
7. The condition of high population density seems to have a noticeable effect on:
   a. interpersonal attraction
   b. self-esteem
   c. intelligence-test performance
   d. perceptual ability
8. Recent research has indicated that the crucial determinants of social pathology are actually:
   a. poverty and crowding
   b. crowding and ethnic group membership
   c. ethnic group membership and poverty
   d. temperature and crowding
9. The least number of negative after-effects would be produced by which of the following situations?
   a. having a subway pass under your home every ten minutes
   b. living under the erratic landing pattern of a busy airport
   c. living across from the community's fire and emergency siren
   d. living above a couple who enjoy loud music
10. In a test of social perception, two investigators found that photographs of people's faces received the highest rating:
    a. in an ordinary room
    b. in an ugly room
    c. in a pretty room
    d. in a painted room
11. Sociofugal space would tend to be created by which of the following seating arrangements?
    a. having seats face one another
    b. having seats placed side by side
    c. having seats placed back to back
    d. having seats placed one behind the other
12. The Pruitt-Igoe Project refers to:
    a. a government study of the effects of classroom size on learning
    b. the reclamation of Pruitt Lake in Igoe County, Illinois
    c. a St. Louis apartment complex
    d. a university study of environmental planning
13. The Kitty Genovese incident, which occurred in New York City in 1964, is an extreme example of:
    a. bystander intervention
    b. bystander apathy
    c. bystander separation
    d. system overload
14. According to social psychologist Stanley Milgram, the Kitty Genovese incident was the result of:
    a. bystander intervention
    b. bystander apathy
    c. bystander separation
    d. system overload
15. The mental picture of an individual's environment is referred to as the person's:
    a. perceptual reference
    b. mental design
    c. cognitive map
    d. internal set
16. The psychological process of selective attention involves which of the following criteria?
    a. the magnitude of habituation
    b. the degree of cognitive consistency
    c. the extent of divergent discriminability
    d. the extent of convergent discriminability
17. People will come to accept, without complaint, various unacceptable environmental conditions due to the principle of:
    a. divergent discrimination
    b. convergent discrimination
    c. habituation
    d. cognitive consistency
18. An individual can come up with the psychological "tone" that the environment conveys to her by:
    a. adding up the psychological messages of her environmental survey
    b. adding up the physical features of her environmental survey

c. adding up the behavioral consequences of her environmental survey
   d. adding up the emotional consequences of her environmental survey
19. An individual can come up with the net impact that the environment has on her responses by:
   a. adding up the psychological messages of her environmental survey
   b. adding up the physical features of her environmental survey
   c. adding up the behavioral consequences of her environmental survey
   d. adding up the emotional consequences of her environmental survey
20. The column of the environmental survey that tells you which aspect of the environment is threatening to you is:
   a. the psychological messages column
   b. the physical features column
   c. the behavioral consequences column
   d. the emotional consequences column

True-False

1. Although our actions, emotions, and thoughts constitute an interaction with the environment, only our thoughts can be separated from it.
2. The rats in John Calhoun's experiment gradually displayed a breakdown in social behavior.
3. Crowding is the psychological state of stress that always results from high population density.
4. When women were put into crowded classrooms and asked how they felt, they reported feeling aggressive.
5. Recent research suggests that the crucial determinants of social pathology are actually poverty and crowding.
6. Recent research has indicated that predictable noise produces fewer negative after-effects than unpredictable noise.
7. It is possible that the civil disorders of the 1960s were due in part to heat.
8. The built environment encompasses only those settings that have been slightly modified by human beings.
9. Sociopetal space encourages interaction by arranging seats that face one another.
10. Airport seating arrangements are notoriously sociopetal by design.
11. The major cause of the failure of the Pruitt-Igoe Project was the lack of sociofugal facilities.
12. Semiprivate, sociopetal spaces tend to promote a strong sense of local identity.
13. It is the process of habituation that leads people to accept, without complaint, unacceptable environmental conditions.
14. By adding up the behavioral consequences column of your environmental survey, you will come up with the net psychological impact of your environment.
15. In general, people do not notice the degree to which their behavior is being manipulated by the environment.

Completion

1. Environmental psychology is concerned with the _____ between the human being and his environment.
2. Scientists call the interacting unit of organisms and their environment an _____.
3. Stress is defined by psychologists as a sense of threat accompanied by _____ efforts aimed at reducing that threat.
4. Autopsies of the rats in Calhoun's rat experiment showed that many had enlarged _____.
5. The environmental condition of high population density is considered to be a(n) _____ state.
6. Recent research suggests that the crucial determinants of social pathology are actually _____ and _____ membership.
7. The _____ environment, in contrast to the _____ environment, includes all settings that have been designed and created largely by humans.
8. _____ space tends to discourage interaction by placing seats side by side.
9. According to researcher Oscar Newmann, _____ space is a residential building small enough that the residents can control it through informal precautions.
10. The Kitty Genovese incident is an extreme example of what is called _____ _____ .
11. Social psychologist Stanley Milgram has suggested that the Kitty Genovese incident was the result of system _____.
12. When we look at our physical surroundings, we are seeing a(n) _____ _____ reality made up of three factors.

13. An individual's mental picture of an environment is referred to as a _____ _____.

14. The process whereby we screen out the stimuli we do not want to see is called _____ _____.

15. The tendency to become less aware of and less responsive to a stimulus once we have had repeated exposure to it is called _____.

Essay Questions

1. Describe John B. Calhoun's famous experiment with rats, and discuss its implications for human behavior. (p. 380)
2. Discuss the human consequences of high population density. (pp. 381–384)
3. Discuss the causes for the failure of the Pruitt-Igoe Project. How can these be applied to future project development? (pp. 390–393)
4. Define bystander apathy, and discuss its relevance to the Kitty Genovese incident that occurred in New York City in 1964. (pp. 394–395)
5. Discuss the relationship between anonymity and crime. What does this relationship suggest about city living? (p. 394)

SELF-TEST ANSWERS

Multiple Choice

1. d (p. 378)
2. a (pp. 378–379)
3. b (p. 380)
4. a (p. 380)
5. d (p. 381)
6. b (p. 381)
7. a (p. 381)
8. c (p. 384)
9. a (p. 384)
10. c (p. 388)
11. b (p. 389)
12. c (p. 390)
13. b (pp. 394–395)
14. d (p. 395)
15. c (p. 397)
16. b (p. 398)
17. c (p. 400)
18. a (p. 405)
19. c (p. 405)
20. a (p. 406)

True-False

1. false (p. 377)
2. true (p. 380)
3. false (p. 381)
4. false (pp. 382–385)
5. false (p. 384)
6. true (p. 384)
7. true (p. 385)
8. false (p. 387)
9. true (p. 389)
10. false (p. 389)
11. false (p. 392)
12. true (p. 392)
13. true (p. 400)
14. false (p. 405)
15. true (p. 406)

Completion

1. interaction (p. 377)
2. ecosystem (p. 378)
3. coping (p. 380)
4. adrenal glands (p. 380)
5. objective (p. 381)
6. poverty, ethnic group (p. 384)
7. built, natural (p. 387)
8. Sociofugal (p. 389)
9. defensible (p. 393)
10. bystander apathy (p. 394)
11. overload (p. 395)
12. subjective (p. 396)
13. cognitive map (p. 397)
14. selective attention (p. 397)
15. habituation (p. 399)

Application Chapter A

Intimate Adjustment: Love, Sex, and Marriage

CHAPTER OUTLINE

SEX-ROLE DEVELOPMENT
The Biological Contribution
The Social Contribution
Learning Sex Roles
Living with the Stereotype
   Becoming a man
   Becoming a woman
   Becoming androgynous

LOVE
What Do Psychologists Say?
Why Do People Fall in Love?

SEX
The Sexual Revolution
   Gay Liberation
   Why the change?
   Teenage freedom
The Counter-Revolution

MARRIAGE
Why Marry?
Assumptions and Adjustments
Divorce
Alternatives
   Living together

READING

Another World

LAUREL RICHARDSON

Beyond the primary world of husbands and wives, marriages and families, children and houses is another, second world, one shrouded in secrecy and stigma: the world of the Other Woman. Though there has been a great deal of scientific research on extramarital relationships, there has been virtually none from the perspective of the single woman. The contours of such relationships have been ignored and rendered invisible and the women in them mute: the second sex in a second world.

Relationships between single women and married men are nothing new, but they seem to be much more common today. Recent reviews of the research literature by Ira L. Reiss and Anthony Thompson indicate that from 40 to 50 percent of all married men report having had affairs.

More than 15 percent of all husbands say they have had a series of affairs, and nearly 70 percent of married men younger than 40 expect to have an extramarital relationship. Considering the permissive attitudes that young adults have about sex these days, researchers such as Gilbert Nass and Roger Libby predict that between one-half and two-thirds of all husbands will have an extramarital liaison before age 40.

What makes this state of affairs possible, of course, is a supply of willing women. Most are single, both because of the growing numbers of unmarried women (there are 34 million in the United States today) and because single women generally have more free time and energy than do their married counterparts.

Consider these statistics: One out of every five women today has no potential mate because there are simply not enough single men to go around. A 25-year-old single woman faces a serious undersupply of available men to start with, and the situation gets worse the older a woman gets. Divorced men are much more likely than divorced women to

147

remarry (and they tend to marry younger women), so that there are more than twice as many single women as there are single men in their 40s. Indeed, a woman who divorces at 35 today is likely to remain single for the rest of her life. Caught in a demographic bind while seeking greater autonomy, more and more single women are opting for involvement with married men. They are the new Other Women.

Prior to my investigation, virtually all research on the subject had dealt with spouses' extramarital experiences and how they affected their marriages. No one had looked into the experiences of the single women and the consequences for them. I decided to do in-depth interviews with single women who were, or had once been, involved in long-term liaisons with married men. For eight years, I met and talked with approximately 700 Other Women (they are not hard to find), received letters from another 300 and did a detailed study of 55, asking them how their relationships began, were sustained and, in some cases, ended.

Today's Other Women generally have a different agenda than did women who became mistresses in the past. Today's woman wants to finish her education, build a career, recover from a divorce, raise her children, explore her sexuality. Getting married is not necessarily her primary goal. Indeed, she may see marriage or a marriage-like commitment as a drain on the time and energy better spent achieving other personal goals. Yet she may still want an intimate relationship with a man. As an Other Woman, she believes, she can have both.

The growing numbers of female professionals, more highly educated and economically independent, are especially likely to get involved with married men. The shortage of suitable men hits the 25-to 40-year-old group particularly hard. In addition, these women have come of age during a period of sexual liberation and expansion of women's opportunities and expectations. Sexual activities that were problematical for early generations are less so for these women. Similarly, they view the work world with greater confidence in themselves, their abilities and their career accomplishments. Seeing marriage as something for the future, they organize their lives around professional goals. These career women find themselves spending a great deal of time working with men, most of them married. Two out of every five management and executive positions are now held by women, many of whom travel on business and frequent the same gyms and social clubs as their male counterparts. Unlike in times past, when the opportunities for enduring affairs were limited by social circumstances, today's business climate facilitates such liaisons.

Despite women's progress in the working world, many of the married men that single women meet at work are still their occupational superiors. Because women often see powerful men as desirable, and because women's security and advancement may depend upon compliance with their supervisors' wishes, strong forces are at work facilitating a liaison. This is an old, familiar pattern, one that sometimes leads to charges of sexual harassment. But according to the Other Women I interviewed, another trend is emerging—the involvement of women with men who are their occupational peers.

Hired to work with men as equals, professional women are often uncertain how to label the good feelings associated with camaraderie at work. As one woman described a fellow research intern, a married man with whom she eventually had an affair, "He wasn't competitive or arrogant. And I didn't feel like he was trying to get me into bed. I didn't know how to interpret it." Thus today's career woman can be intrigued by the positive feelings associated with being treated as a professional equal, just as women once were intrigued by male wealth and power.

The opportunities for single women and married men to meet through work, play and the daily rounds of their lives are indeed legion. And the chances that these encounters will be transformed into more intimate relationships are good, even if a woman at first views the men around her simply as mentors, colleagues and friends. With this socially acceptable relationship as a rationale, her erotic attraction may grow free of guilt or undue expectations. The lengths to which some women go in refusing to recognize the potential for intimacy are amply illustrated by a social worker who told me she really believed her supervisor's car broke down, forcing them to spend the night in a motel. And she was convinced that his request for a single room with two beds was simply a matter of saving money.

Once the relationship becomes sexually intimate, the lovers usually find ways to conceal the liaison. Although the woman may be able to accept herself in the role of the Other Woman, she knows that many others won't. If she does well in her career, she might be accused of "sleeping her way up." Her feminist friends may disavow her. She may even get fired for being involved with a married man. While keeping a mistress may be approved and even applauded in some circles, being a mistress seldom is.

If the Other Woman works with her lover, one favored strategy is what I call "cloaking." Like a spy or a member of a secret organization, she acts as if the time she spends with her married lover was strictly business. By not altering the usual routines, she can see him fairly frequently and openly—or at least that is what many of the women in my study believed. One woman routinely stays late at the office with her lover and accompanies him on business trips, just as she had before their affair began; another, a teacher, continues to spend considerable public time preparing classes with her lover, a member of her teaching group. Both believe their romances are totally camouflaged by the cloak of routine work activity.

Many of the women whose lovers are not coworkers use a compartmentalizing strategy to conceal the relationship. By completely separating the time spent with their married lovers, they believe they can carry on other activities as usual. Some women—especially those involved in long-distance relationships—view this as having the best of both worlds, giving them control over their work and their private relationship. As one woman commented, "Because I know I can close the door when he leaves—because the relationship does not control my whole life—I can give and get more from it and from everything else in my life." What these strategies often do, of course, is prolong the relationship; believing her affair is effectively concealed, the woman becomes more deeply embroiled than she ever intended.

Contrary to the stereotype of a kept mistress, sex is not the primary activity in these relationships, nor is it what keeps women involved. Rather, it is the talking together, the listening, the sharing of secrets and the mutual vulnerability. Within their time-bound private world, the lovers avoid the heavy bargaining and escalating expectations that attend regular romances. Once they have violated the rule of social acceptability, it is easier to resist other fundamental assumptions about how men and women should behave. And since none of her friends or family are judging or testing the relationship, the woman is freer to imagine the relationship as "ideal" and her lover as "special." Based on the testimony of the Other Women in my study, this special atmosphere deepened their involvement more than they had originally intended.

Some career women I talked to said that their liaisons helped relieve major conflicts in their personal and professional lives. Many women still feel insecure in their roles as professionals and top-level managers. Some fear that their femininity will be compromised; others fear that they are frauds, incapable of doing the work that their high-level positions entail. Although a woman can get some guidance and reassurance from female mentors and colleagues, most of those I interviewed still placed a higher value on a man's judgment and approval.

In a relationship with a married man, I was told, a woman can risk expressing her fears and showing her inadequacies without the risk of exposure to others. She can be vulnerable and weak, a luxury she denies herself in her professional role. When the married man listens and offers support, he also strengthens the woman's emotional attachment, increasing the probability of a long-term affair. As one executive woman commented, "I hadn't realized how powerful a force he would be in my life because I hadn't realized how much I needed a safe harbor. A place where I didn't have to know everything and make all the decisions. That's what swept me off my feet."

Having her lover as supervisor, mentor or colleague sometimes offers other advantages, especially to women in traditionally male occupations, where knowledge and skills still rest largely in the hands of men. One management trainee, who became involved with her supervisor, told me, "I know he gave me special help and attention he wouldn't have otherwise. That's why I've been able to move up so fast." Another woman, a graduate student who was romantically involved with her adviser, considered her relationship as professionally advantageous to her. Her adviser "hyped her dissertation" and introduced her to important people in the field.

Such advantages are often outweighed by high costs. The relationship may make much heavier demands on her than she expected. The Other Woman is, after all, the second woman in her lover's life. Because his free time away from family obligations largely determines their time together, the Other Woman gradually loses control of how her time is spent.

One bank vice president, a divorced woman who managed a staff of 50, chose not to remarry because she wanted control over her time and life; she thought a married man would be ideal. In retrospect, however, she saw a "fatal flaw in the relationship." As she explained, "The flaw was that he really was in charge, even when I thought I was. When it finally came down to it, he thought I should stop what I was doing when he came over, even when he knew I had deadlines to meet. He really did not respect the importance of my work to me." Another woman, a dentist, found herself not scheduling noontime appointments because "sometimes he shook time loose" at midday. Still others hang around their homes at night or on weekends waiting for a call.

Why does the Other Woman, so independent in many aspects of her life, arrange her time to fit the schedule of a married man? His marital obligations are only part of the answer. Men, it appears, take charge of these relationships early on because the women assume they will. At first, they told me, they find it exciting to be called and accept the attention happily; once they have accepted male initiative in the relationship, they sacrifice control over life's moments, moments that stretch to hours, days, months and years. It is an insidious entrapment that is only later recognized as a major sacrifice of independence.

Some of these women lose dreams as well as time. When they find that they cannot manage these secret affairs as well as they thought, when the relationships begin to damage other areas of their lives, the women suffer a loss of self-esteem; they are unable to hold onto the ideal image of themselves as women with mastery and control.

The banker mentioned earlier described the situation this way: "Worst was the energy drain, the psychological energy that went into keeping the relationship at bay, and then dealing with the unexpected hurt. It ended up being very costly to me, to my career and my life in general." This woman and others like her blame themselves for poor judgment; when they cannot use the relationship to achieve external goals, they see themselves as personal failures.

There is a second kind of disappointment these women commonly report. They go into the relationship viewing it as an opportunity to experiment with new selves, to try new identities, and it turns out to be nothing of the kind. Indeed, because of all the limitations on these relationships, growth may be stifled. One woman, for example, who had what she called a "history of emotional aloofness," thought her liaison would help her change that pattern. Instead, she reported, "I've become what I most dislike in men—cold, calculating, unfeeling. I'm not sure I'll ever be able to be a really loving, giving person."

Being the Other Woman appears to be a workable solution for many contemporary single women. Some in my study are quite successful in limiting their emotional involvement and in making the relationship dovetail nicely with the pursuit of other goals. They come through their liaisons (or continue in them) feeling empowered and clear about the kind of relationships they want with men. They manage in one way or another to maintain a sense of independence throughout the relationship. But then there are those who are hurt and disappointed, not unlike their earlier counterparts, the kept mistresses. They lose control over their feelings, become totally invested in the affair and end up deriving more pain than pleasure.

Because of the demographic, cultural and social forces at work, single American women will continue to get involved with married men. The ubiquity of these relationships is what sociologist Emile Durkheim referred to as a social fact—like marriage, divorce and suicide. It persists not just because it fulfills women's needs alone; it fulfills husbands' needs as well. In fact, the prevalence of the Other Woman phenomenon can be understood best in terms of the social functions it performs for men as a class.

What do men get from the ready availability of single women? First, of course, is the continuing supply of new sex partners. But there is much more than sex, which as I have said is not the major activity in these affairs. The relationships offer married men an opportunity for intimate female friendship—a person to listen to their grievances and a safe person to be vulnerable with. They also offer men an opportunity to relive their young manhood and, finally, the opportunity to control two worlds—the primary world of wife and children and the second, secret world. Sexual gratification, self-esteem and power. Strikingly, these are the very elements of male prerogative that have been challenged for the past 15 years by the women's movement.

Since it is in the men's interest to have a ready supply of available women, I believe Other Womanhood will come to be considered a simple fact of life. If the stigma lessens, even more women are likely to consider it an option. That is not to say that the role will be condoned. The fact that the relationship is secret and not socially acceptable is precisely what gives the man rein on his affair.

For the most part, then, the widespread phenomenon of the Other Woman will contribute to and support the status quo: male privilege, female distrust of other women and divorce, with its attendant social and economic liabilities for women. The "deviant" world of the single woman and married man is not so deviant after all, because the Other Woman in the end strengthens and perpetuates the social and cultural bulwark of male privilege.

Reading Questions

1. According to the article, increasing numbers of single women are having affairs with married men. Why?
2. Why is the increase in the number of single women having affairs with married men seen as diminishing feminist progress?

3. How do you see this "trend" affecting the future of male/female relationships?

RESEARCH STUDY

Investigators: Marilyn Coleman and Lawrence Ganong.
Source, date: "Love and Sex Role Stereotypes: Do Macho Men and Feminine Women Make Better Lovers?" *Journal of Personality and Social Psychology*, 1985, *49*, 170-176.
Location: University of Missouri, Columbia.
Subjects: 100 male and 136 female students in introductory classes in family living and human development.
Materials: Bern Sex Role Inventory, Scale of Feelings and Behaviors of Love, Balswick Expression of Emotion and Emotion Scale.

Conventional wisdom has traditionally held that men are more interested in sex and women are more interested in love in a relationship. Studies of these differences have had mixed results, suggesting a lack of clear differentiation between the sexes in their approach to relationships. More recent work on sex roles indicates that one individual's perception of his or her sex role is a more significant factor in how relationships are viewed. This study thus looked at the relationship between an individual's sex role orientation and his or her feelings about his or her behaviors related to love in a relationship with another. The researchers expected that there would be a definite relationship between sex role and love. In addition, they expected that individuals who tended to display sex-role characteristics of both sexes (sex-role androgyny) would experience love differently from individuals who displayed traditional stereotyped sex roles.

Students enrolled in introductory classes in family living and human development were recruited to participate in this study. They had to be currently in a love relationship with someone of the opposite sex. They were asked to complete a battery of questionnaires that included a scale measuring their sex roles, one measuring their feelings and behaviors about love, and a scale describing their experience and expression of emotion.

The results from the study indicated that sex roles did play a large part in the feelings and behavior of love of both sexes. Sex was not a major factor. Sex-role socialization appears to be important in the expression of love for both sexes. Further, when this sex role socialization is of a more traditional type (either masculine or feminine), individuals are less expressive of love than when the sex-role orientation of the individual is androgynous (reflecting sex-role characteristics of both sexes). The authors suggest that the reason for this is that the androgynous sex role allows for greater flexibility and adaptability in relationships.

Research Study Questions

1. What approach to studying males' and females' expression of love was used in the study and how was it different from previous approaches to this issue?
2. Who were the participants in this study and what did they do for the investigator?
3. What were the results of the study and what conclusion was drawn from these results?

CASE STUDY

Dressing Up

The following is a transcript of an interview with the parents of a seven-year-old boy:

Mother: Well, my husband doesn't feel there's a problem as much as I do.... When I really realized there was a problem is when he was four years old and he wanted to put a picture of a little girl by his bed. He cut the picture out of a magazine. It was a very pretty girl. I didn't think anything of it and said go ahead. And when I went to tuck him in bed he said, "Mommy, if I look at her hard enough, will I turn into her?"

He leans toward feminine type of behavior. He follows me around constantly with the baby; he likes her ruffled panties, and he comes in when I comb her hair. He loves the little bows. He's very interested in female things. His natural singing voice is a deeper voice, but he prefers to use a high voice.

Stepfather: I feel it's just that most of his life he was thrown into playing with girls. Wherever he lived he had nothing but girls to play with. Competing with girls is very easy, and he liked it. When we moved, he got thrown in with a bunch of boys, and competing was a lot harder. Without girls he didn't want to compete because the boys are too rough.

Mother: He gives up playing with boys for a girl. If he had his choice and no one would ridicule him, he would go in the room and play with the girls and be more comfortable.

Stepfather: At four years old they were playing with dolls; he never picked up a ball, knew how to throw a ball.

Mother: He didn't have any kind of relationship at all with his father. . . . My mother and I were actually competing for him. She wanted to be his mother, and I wanted to be his mother. She would take him for the day and he would go visit her girlfriends, and he would sit with the women at the table . . . he was a little old lady with the little old ladies. I can honestly say I just didn't know how to relate to a boy. I played with him. I didn't realize I was playing with him like a girl . . . I realize now I was playing with him as a girl.

Doctor: How do you mean?

Mother: Combing his hair a lot, dressing him twenty times a day, telling him how pretty he was all the time. When he started wearing pants I called them bloomers. . . . The first time I went to see his kindergarten teacher, she said he played in the girls' corner all the time, and she had a really hard time getting him with the boys.

Stepfather: He always acted a little bit feminine. He played so placidly. When the other boys would come over to the house, he wouldn't play well with them. He would always kind of back off; and if they hit him, he would come and hide behind my legs rather than hit them back. He was wanting more to be with the girls or wanting to be with the women and not play rough and tough.

Mother: If he could get into the makeup, he'd put the makeup on. If he could get into my clothes, he'd put them on from when he could first start putting something on. He always leaned more toward copying me than anyone else . . . he would just follow me around the house copying everything that I do.

Doctor: How far back did his interest in getting into your clothes go?

Mother: As early as he could start putting something on himself. He would take scarves, and underwear he loved to put on . . . he was taking something of mine and putting on shoes, whatever. He loved jewelry. He used to love my wigs.

Doctor: How did you feel about the behavior?

Mother: In the beginning I laughed at it; it was funny and cute. My mother laughed at it and in a way encouraged it. We didn't think it was anything . . . a phase; it was cute and we laughed.

Doctor: Did he at any time improvise or make up women's clothes from other materials?

Mother: Yes. To this day he wears my husband's old pajamas, and he loves to wear just the tops . . . it's like a little dress . . . I remember his taking scarves and using them to make dresses.

Doctor: You mentioned his interest in wigs. When did he begin to show that interest?

Mother: From day one . . . I would take my wig and prop it on his head. As a young baby if I was wearing a wig I would take the wig off and put the wig on him . . .

Stepfather: 99% of the books that he reads . . . little girl books . . . Jane went . . . Jane baked a cake . . .

Doctor: Does he imitate characters from books or television when he would role play?

Stepfather: Yes. Women. Girls.

Mother: I have to be completely honest. This son, when he was one, was my life, my whole world. I found something to pour it all out in, a possession and ownership. His brother, at one, I was indifferent too. It wasn't mother love; it was smother love.

Stepfather: From the time I came into the picture, all I heard from her is, "I wish I had a girl. I wish I had a girl. I love to buy girl clothes. Oh, how nice it would be to have a girl." She'd sit and talk to her sisters about how it would be to have a girl, and he hears all that stuff. I think his desire to change into a girl was to please her.

Mother: He had this head full of curly hair, and many times he got mistaken for a girl, which I think he kind of enjoyed. Then when I bought him a christening dress instead of the pants, everyone told me they would have preferred pants. But I preferred the dress and did it my way.

Doctor: Did you buy other clothing that people commented on?

Mother: I would buy him little sunsuits; they had elastic, people told me they're for girls. But I still feel I would rather see a boy with the elastic around the legs.

Stepfather: It was a standard joke . . . you and your sister would laugh how you dressed him as a baby like a girl and you would say, "Oh, he's getting more like a girl every day," and they'd laugh. And he'd walk in.

Mother: He's already been called names. His brother calls him a faggot.

Discussion of Dressing Up

From the report of the parents, there is clear evidence of a conflict in gender identity early in the life of this child. There was a wish to be a girl, as well as behavior by his mother that could be seen as feminizing. He asked his mother if he would turn into a girl if he looked hard enough at a picture he had cut out of a magazine and placed by his bed. He is preoccupied with female stereotypical activities. He prefers to play with girls at school and in the neighborhood, plays in the doll corner at school, enjoys wearing his mother's clothes, jewelry, and wigs, and improvises female clothing from his stepfather's pajamas. When imitating characters from books or television, he always takes the female role.

This is the characteristic picture of Gender Identity Disorder of Childhood as seen in a male. When this disorder is diagnosed in a female, the desire to be a male, because of a profound discontent in being a female, needs to be distinguished from the desire merely to have the cultural advantages associated with being a man.

Case Study Questions

1. What were some of the indicators of the seven-year-old boy's problem with his sex-role identity?
2. How did his mother contribute to the problem of identity?
3. What problems do you expect this boy will have as he gets older?

SELF-TEST

Multiple Choice

1. Major physical differences between males and females are due to:
   a. socialization
   b. hormones
   c. chromosomal abnormalities
   d. none of the above
2. Margaret Mead's studies proposed that each society, in regard to masculine and feminine behavior:
   a. follows a biologically determined pattern
   b. works out its own definitions of behavior, and enforces them through socialization
   c. haphazardly defines sex-related behavior with each generation
   d. seems to disregard the behavior of different sexes
3. If males and females enacted the same roles in every society, this would support the theory of:
   a. biological determinism
   b. socialization theory
   c. feminist theory
   d. liberation theory
4. The theory that proposes that behavioral differences between sexes are due to both biology and sociology is:
   a. biological determinism
   b. bi-causal theory
   c. interactionism
   d. social conditioning theory
5. A behavior that is *not* an example of sex-role socialization is:
   a. giving a football to a boy
   b. playing "dolls" with a girl
   c. encouraging a girl to feed her dog
   d. dressing a baby girl in pink dresses
6. Removing sexism from the media does not include:
   a. featuring women as police officers and lawyers in TV programs
   b. using female news commentators
   c. adding examples of competent female figures in textbooks
   d. showing only men in powerful, prestigious roles, such as doctors and police officers
7. Many American women are unable to develop independence and confidence because:
   a. they are not encouraged to participate in activities that teach independence and achievement
   b. they are simply incapable
   c. women are seldom interested in independence and challenges
   d. none of the above
8. Recognizing and expressing both the "masculine" and "feminine" traits in ourselves is known as:
   a. self-security
   b. androgyny
   c. stereotyping
   d. sex-typing
9. Which of these are *not* one of the three components of love, according to Rubin?
   a. attachment
   b. sexual need
   c. intimacy
   d. caring
10. What were some of the signs of the "sexual revolution"?
    a. more premarital sex, acceptance of homosexuality, and sex used in advertising
    b. a stronger moral code
    c. more stable marriages
    d. wider discrimination against homosexual persons
11. What are some causes that precipitated the sexual revolution?
    a. more stringent attitudes in other areas, like religion
    b. the availability of novels
    c. increased divorce
    d. changes in traditional attitudes, along with convenient birth control devices

12. According to research cited in the text, premarital sex for women:
    a. decreased in the sixties and seventies
    b. decreased in the sixties, but shot up in the eighties
    c. increased in the sixties and early seventies, but dropped to around 50 percent
    d. has remained steady for the past thirty years
13. What has been a critical factor in the sexual "counterrevolution"?
    a. widespread sexually transmitted disease
    b. concern over lack of birth control methods
    c. babies with congenital deficiencies
    d. all of the above
14. American men and women today seeking a relationship seem to be looking primarily for:
    a. economic security
    b. tax breaks
    c. intimacy and personal growth
    d. sexual satisfaction
15. Who is more likely to report happy marriages and positive feelings about marriage?
    a. single men
    b. married women
    c. married men
    d. there is no difference between the sexes in such reports
16. Why might women experience dissatisfaction with their role of housewife in a marriage?
    a. chores can be dull
    b. there is no direct financial reward
    c. societal value of this role is low
    d. all of the above
17. What are some of the common results of divorce on individuals who undergo it?
    a. emotional problems and excessive drinking
    b. psychosis
    c. health problems
    d. both a and c
18. What characteristics seem to predispose a marriage to last even less than the median length of seven years?
    a. partners have high income
    b. partners have low income and little education
    c. partners have at least college-level education
    d. partners have high income and college education
19. What are some tips listed in the text designed to help a marriage survive?
    a. recognize that good marriages often undergo fluctuations and allow for this
    b. try to get married if others are urging you to do so, regardless of your own feelings
    c. bargain with your spouse only as a last resort
    d. view all changes with alarm—a good marriage should be completely stable at all times

True-False

1. There is no basis for the theory that socialization affects sex roles.
2. Socializing little boys to be macho, emotionally restrained, and competitive leads to a healthy self-image, as well as a healthy body.
3. Companionate love is probably the basis of most good marriages.
4. Traditionally, the function of sex has been procreation.
5. Availability of birth control dramatically affected the percentage of both women and men engaging in extramarital sex.
6. According to the text, premarital sexual behavior of a person is a good indicator of his or her extramarital behavior.
7. Males and females enact about the same roles in all societies.
8. Sexually transmitted diseases, particularly AIDS, have created alarm and probably contributed to changing attitudes toward casual sex.
9. It is a good idea to attempt to communicate with your partner about sexual desires.
10. In a survey of 4,000 married men and women, love, need for companionship, and desire to establish a home were the top three reasons given for marriage.
11. Availability and similarity also play a role in whom one chooses to marry.
12. Only about 20 percent of married women now work outside the home, according to the U.S. Bureau of the Census, 1980.
13. Divorce is difficult and lonely, but rarely leads to depression or other health problems.
14. Americans have the highest divorce rate in the world.
15. Age, income, and education are three factors that do not seem to affect likelihood of divorce.

Completion

1. The major physical differences between men and women are due to mixes of secretions called _____.
2. Psychologists are interested in knowing which differences between men and women are _____ and which are learned through socialization.

INTIMATE ADJUSTMENT: LOVE, SEX, AND MARRIAGE

3. Expressing both the traditionally "masculine" and "feminine" traits in ourselves is known as _____.

4. Rubin concluded three differences between love and liking, based on his survey. These are _____, _____ and _____.

5. _____ _____ is probably the basis of most good marriages, according to the text.

6. Walster suggests two steps involved in the development of love: _____ and _____.

7. For a long time, our culture viewed the primary function of sex to be _____, so sexual activities that could not lead to legitimate offspring were considered wrong.

8. With the sexual revolution of the '60s and '70s, the goals of sex became _____ and _____.

9. This view was challenged by the widespread occurrence of _____ _____ _____.

10. _____ has become increasingly accepted since the advent of the sexual revolution, and some companies have made it a point to have nondiscrimination policies concerning this group.

11. The sexual revolution has been attributed to the fact that important _____ _____ were being challenged at this time, and to the availability of birth control.

12. _____ is essential for a happy sex life with a regular partner, according to the tips in the text.

13. _____ and _____ seem to play a large role in whom we will choose to marry.

14. One way in which couples are working out problems is by modifying their _____ about each other.

15. _____ have the highest divorce rate in the world.

Essay Questions

1. Discuss the question of whether sex-linked behavior is biologically determined or sociologically learned. Use examples from the text. (pp. 412–415)
2. Discuss the consequences of the negative approach to sex-role development for men. Do they seem positive or negative? (p. 414)
3. What is androgyny? How do people who see themselves as androgynous differ from people who do not? (pp. 414–415)
4. What were some of the outcomes of the sexual revolution of the '60s and '70s? (pp. 419–421)
5. What are some important things for marriage partners to be aware of? (p. 426)

SELF-TEST ANSWERS

Multiple Choice
1. b (p. 412)
2. b (p. 412)
3. a (p. 413)
4. c (p. 413)
5. c (p. 413)
6. d (p. 413)
7. a (p. 414)
8. b (p. 414)
9. b (p. 416)
10. a (p. 420)
11. d (p. 421)
12. c (p. 422)
13. a (p. 422)
14. c (p. 423)
15. c (p. 423)
16. d (p. 424)
17. d (p. 424)
18. b (p. 425)
19. a (p. 426)

True-False
1. false (p. 413)
2. false (p. 414)
3. true (p. 417)
4. true (p. 419)
5. false (p. 421)
6. true (p. 422)
7. false (p. 412)
8. true (p. 423)
9. true (p. 423)
10. true (p. 423)
11. true (p. 423)
12. false (p. 424)
13. false (p. 424)
14. true (p. 425)
15. false (p. 425)

Completion
1. hormones (p. 412)
2. innate (p. 412)
3. androgyny (p. 414)
4. attachment, caring, intimacy (p. 417)
5. companionate love (p. 417)
6. physiological arousal, labeling (p. 418)
7. procreation (p. 419)
8. self-expression, pleasure (p. 419)
9. sexually transmitted disease (p. 422)
10. homosexuality (p. 420)
11. social institutions (p. 421)
12. communication (p. 423)
13. availability, similarity (p. 423)
14. expectations (p. 424)
15. Americans (p. 425)

Application Chapter B

Adjustment and Maladjustment in Adulthood

CHAPTER OUTLINE

WORK
Changing Views of Work
Work and the Individual
Women and Work
Career Change
The Future of Work

CHILD-REARING
Choosing Parenthood
Learning New Skills
The Child-Care Crisis
Choosing Child Care

MIDLIFE AND AGING
Midlife: Prime or Decline?
Traps and Empty Nests
Social Changes
Aging
The Physical Signs
The Stresses of Aging
Dealing with Age

ABNORMAL PSYCHOLOGY
Defining Abnormal Behavior
The Classification of Abnormal Behavior
The "Neurotic" Disorders
The Psychotic Disorders

READING

The Nine-to-Five Dilemma

DENNIS MEREDITH

Kathryn has a new baby, but she also has a challenging 9-to-5 job in a large corporation, and the combination is proving almost unmanageable. The corporation offers no day-care, so she and her husband must find their own. They have interviewed dozens of babysitters and still cannot find one who is reliable and capable. As a result Kathryn misses work often and when working is plagued by worries about her child.

Marie and Ken, with three children, have become master jugglers. After being on a waiting list for two years, they have managed to enroll their 3-year-old son in a church-run school three days a week. He spends the other two days with a neighbor who cares for children. The couple's daughters, ages 11 and 8, take care of themselves after school and sometimes watch the 3-year-old in emergencies. But just one sneeze and the juggling act is disrupted.

The day-care center won't accept sick children, and if the older children are ill, the parents don't want to leave either of them at home alone.

These parents have problems, but at least they can afford day-care. Barbara, a maid, has to take her new baby to her employers' houses. Her older daughter used to come along to mind the baby and help with the work, but now that she's in school, Barbara has to combine housework with child-care. Some of her employers are not particularly happy with this arrangement, and Barbara fears losing her jobs.

All of these parents are caught up in a dramatic alteration in the way we rear our children. The majority of children no longer grow up in the traditional family of a male bread-winner and a female homemaker and child-raiser. Economic need and the desire for challenge outside the home have led unprecedented numbers of mothers of young children to join the work force during the past decade.

Almost half of all mothers with young children work, according to the Bureau of Labor Statistics. The current total is 8.2 million women, and nearly 200,000 more are joining the work force every year.

In surveys, most working women with young children say they would prefer to continue working, even if they didn't need the money. And many women at home with children say they would work if they could either find or afford child-care. Some predictions are that 80 percent of families will have two working parents by the end of the century.

As this trend continues, more and more working parents will be thrust into the frustrating and sometimes frightening business of finding day-care for their children. They can choose from a confusing number of alternatives, usually expensive and sometimes unreliable. And they must keep on re-solving their day-care problems, as underpaid, overworked sitters and day-care center workers leave and as children grow and change.

The compromises parents make in juggling careers and rearing children often cause them to worry that they are less fit parents. They have heard that they are damaging their children's development, weakening the mother-child bond and even exposing their children to abuse or disease.

Both business and government are making some progress toward aiding working parents, but it's a "good news-bad news" situation. More than 2,000 companies now offer some form of day-care assistance, but this is still a very low percentage of companies in this country.

On the other hand, tax credits for child-care now total more than $3 billion annually. And there is a rising tide of interest in Congress. Approximately 20 child-care bills were submitted during the last session.

But the tax credit is threatened by changes in the income-tax code, and the federal government has not shown full commitment to solving the problems of child-care.

The most fundamental problem is that leaders in business and government, as well as the public, still tend to believe that the traditional family predominates. It's a widespread misapprehension, says University of Virginia psychologist Sandra Scarr, author of *Mother Care/Other Care*. "The traditional-family, which now makes up 11 percent of our families, is still a major myth," she explained at a recent symposium on day-care. "We believe that is what most American families are like. When we survey the general public [about] the typical American family, we still get a description that includes two parents, two children and a white picket fence." Americans' concept of the family doesn't include many of the current forms, including single-parent families and the working poor, Scarr says.

It is clear that for both financial and personal reasons the surge of women into the workplace is going to continue. So the question becomes not, is day-care more detrimental than parent-care, but what kind of day-care is the best.

Research on day-care itself has now entered a new phase, experts say. The first studies simply compared the effects of mother-care with high-quality center care, and concluded that day-care neither harms nor helps children. Now researchers are sharpening their focus, attempting to evaluate different forms of day-care.

At one end of the spectrum is the middle-aged woman down the block who cares for an infant and three toddlers in her home. At the other end is the nursery school that has three teachers with Montessori training, serves 25 children from 2 to 4 years old and boasts a well-equipped playground.

But parents cannot transfer the special warmth of the sitter's home to the nursery school nor bring the more elaborate play equipment and the staff of the nursery school to the conveniently located sitter's home. And these are only two of many options from which parents must choose. They may also find sitters willing to come to their home, or they may look into day-care centers that offer a variety of services.

For parents of children 2 years old and older, the results of day-care research offer both relief from guilt and some guidance. Psychologists have found clear evidence that older children of working parents can develop just as well socially and intellectually as those whose mothers are at home. In fact, in some cases day-care may be better than home care. For disadvantaged children it may offer enrichment they can't get at home.

Unfortunately, for parents of infants, day-care research offers neither such certainty nor such comfort. So few studies have been done and their results are so controversial that the effects of infant day-care remain agonizingly murky.

"The first wave of research made everybody feel pretty sanguine," says Edward Zigler, a psychologist at Yale University who has just completed a review of the research with psychologist Tom Gamble.

Although early studies concluded that there were not many problems with day-care, the studies were all conducted in high-quality settings and were not very representative, Zigler says. "The second wave of studies shows that there seem to be some problems in mother-infant attachment with babies in day-care."

One such study was reported by psychologist Brian Vaughn of the University of Illinois at Chicago. He and his colleagues found that about 50 percent of babies in sitter-care were insecurely attached to their mothers, compared with 30 percent of babies under mother-care.

Attachment is "the degree to which the baby is able to use the mother or other caretaker as a source of support and security in unfamiliar settings," Vaughn explains.

"If there's a balance (between attachment and exploration) the child is motivated to find things out about the world and when his resources get exhausted, he returns to mother for a sort of psychic refueling."

Vaughn cautions that his findings "don't mean that all children in non-maternal or day-care groups have an insecure attachment, it's just that the probability is higher." He also points out there are consequences associated with any type of child-care, including mother-care.

Zigler, former head of the federal Office of Child Development, has called infant day-care "the psychological thalidomide of the '80s," a remark he now qualifies.

"When I said that, unfortunately people didn't hear what I was saying," Zigler explains. "They thought I was saying that mothers of infants were not to work. What I'm saying is that mothers are working, and they will continue to work, and we have to make sure that we have infant day-care of good quality."

Parts of the country permit a level of care that Zigler considers detrimental. For example, in many states a woman can take care of as many as eight babies in her home. Zigler believes any single adult trying to take care of the psychological and physiological needs of eight babies must in some way be neglecting the children.

For Scarr, the debate over infant care is colored by what she calls "the cult of motherhood." It's a cult that obscures the fact that high-quality day-care can yield happy, well-adjusted babies, she says.

Studies have shown that high-quality infant care is not necessarily damaging to either the child's emotional development or to the parent-child relationship, according to Scarr. What is crucial is that infants have a consistent and warm relationship with their care-givers.

"We know that children are attached to their fathers and most fathers are not home all day with their children. So, why should we be surprised that working mothers can have the same kinds of relationships with their children?" In fact, Scarr argues, an infant may thrive on intense relationships with more than one care-giver. "After all, how bad can it be to have more than one person in this world that you can trust?"

If there is a consensus regarding infant day-care, it's that care of one baby by one sitter (the alternative most preferred by parents) is probably the most desirable. Since babies largely ignore other children, having playmates is not as important. Most vital, the experts agree, is that infants have warm, consistent, nurturing relationships with all their care-givers, both sitters and parents.

Once children are ready to begin socializing, parents have more day-care options open to them. Many psychologists believe that day-care for children older than 2 or 3 does no harm and, in fact, can be very helpful.

One recent study claiming that children of working mothers can develop perfectly well was presented at last summer's meeting of the American Psychological Association. The psychologists, Adele Gottfried of California State University at Northridge, Allen Gottfried of California State University at Fullerton and Kay Bathurst of the University of California, Los Angeles, began their study of 130 children seven years ago when the children were 1 year old.

The children were mostly from white, middle-income families that included both employed and homemaking mothers. About one-third of the mothers were employed at the beginning of the study, and 56 percent were employed by the time the children reached the age of 5. While the California researchers did not include day-care as a specific factor in their study, children of employed mothers were far more likely to be in day-care.

After testing the children's intellectual, physical and social skills, the researchers concluded that the children of employed mothers developed no differently than the children of unemployed mothers. A child's development "really has nothing to do with maternal employment," Adele Gottfried says. "Mothers who are employed can provide the same kind of environment as mothers who are not employed. And they can be good environments or bad environments."

Psychologist Alison Clarke-Stewart, then at the University of Chicago, and her colleagues investigated what happens to children in various day-care environments. They studied 80 children in the Chicago area in a variety of day-care settings, including the children's homes, day-care homes, nursery schools and full-time day-care centers. The researchers interviewed each child's parents and caretakers, tested children's intellectual abilities and observed how the children reacted to their mothers, peers and strangers.

They also noted the physical environment, listing

toys such as tricycles, adult objects such as plants, hazards such as razor blades and open stairways and dirty conditions such as unwashed dishes and open paint cans.

They recorded whom the children spent time with, what types of encounters these were (teaching, touching, kissing and hitting) and what caretakers said to children. For example, the command "Put the toy down" was listed as directive, while "Put the toy down because you're going to hurt somebody" was coded as explanatory. After analyzing the results, the researchers characterized each setting.

Sitter-care in the child's home, used by about one-third of working mothers in the study, was typically given by older women with no professional training and limited education. The child's home was usually adult-oriented with fewer creative toys and more hazards than at a day-care center. While the children cared for at home were hugged, kissed, helped and talked to more often, they had little peer contact, particularly with more skilled older children. The only playmates were siblings, and there was little visiting with other children. More time was spent alone watching TV, and there were few structured activities.

Care at a sitter's house was used by another one-third of working mothers. The women who ran these day-care homes were younger, usually in their mid-30s. They were better educated than in-home sitters but had no professional child-care experience. These homes were similar to the child's home in that they were adult-oriented and contained hazards and messes.

"A day-care home is fundamentally a home, even when it is stretched to take in more children or to provide service for a fee," says Clarke-Stewart, now at the University of California, Irvine. The major difference was that day-care homes provided more social stimulation. Most had about five children, all around the same age.

The women who ran nursery schools were typically in their early-30s and were child-care professionals with formal college training in child development. As might be expected, there were few hazards, more adults and a wider variety of playmates for the children. There were fewer direct contacts between children and caretakers but more group and structured activities. Thus, the center offered more opportunities for education and socializing.

Full-time day-care centers were similar to nursery schools but included meals, naps and more free-play periods. The only difference was that the teachers were slightly younger and had held their jobs for less time than had teachers at nursery schools.

The researchers found that each type of day-care affected children differently. "Children attending nursery school programs scored consistently higher across the board, but especially higher on cognitive ability, social knowledge and sociability with the adult stranger," Clarke-Stewart says. "Least advanced were children with sitters in their own homes. These children never scored highest on a test and they were significantly more likely than children in day-care centers to avoid their peers. Children in day-care homes scored highest on sociability with the unfamiliar peer but lowest on independence from their mother."

Many parents choose home day-care because they are attracted to the idea of the warmer home environment, but Clarke-Stewart found that such warm environments may not challenge a child as much as other day-care alternatives do. "We found the greater the hugging and kissing, the worse the kids were doing, she says. If you're helping and touching and cuddling 3- or 4-year-olds, it's not pushing them into developing faster."

Although day-care centers had many positive effects on children, Clarke-Stewart cautions that a super center won't automatically produce a super child. "Children were not randomly assigned to the day-care programs in which we observed them," she points out. "Their parents deliberately selected these programs for them." Parents from more highly educated backgrounds may have chosen some programs because of the educational opportunities they offered.

But in the end, Clarke-Stewart believes that the support, stimulation and good genes parents give their children are as important as the type of day-care they are in. "Children do not live by day-care alone, no matter how fitting its form and fine its functions."

A recent study led by psychologist Kathleen McCartney at Harvard University also showed that center quality can have a positive effect on a child's development. She and her colleagues, Scarr and psychologists Deborah Phillips and Conrad Schwarz, studied 166 families with children in Bermuda day-care centers.

Bermuda was an ideal place to study day-care centers because the huge majority of Bermuda children are in day-care and the researchers were able to find nine centers that varied widely in quality, staffing and programs. The researchers tested and interviewed children in the centers to measure their intellectual, language and social skills, as well as their emotional adjustment. They also interviewed center directors and families, observed how children and teachers talked to one another and collected background information on the families.

Other concerns were how well the caregivers met the children's needs and interacted with them, how well the centers were furnished for the children and the quality and quantity of intellectual and social activities.

Neither the age at which the child began day-care nor the amount of time spent in group care affected intellectual or social development. However, children in the better centers did better on all tests of intellectual and language skills and showed better social development. And according to McCartney, "Both parents and caregivers agree that children in higher-quality day-care centers are more considerate and more sociable than children in lower-quality centers."

Quality, of course, will be an issue as parents make decisions about day-care, but much remains to be resolved. Legislators will continue the day-care debate and psychologists will do more studies. Their efforts, however, will be hindered by the moving nature of the target—the American family. The question of how our society should support its families in rearing their children is a devilishly complex issue of economics, government, social engineering, psychology and opportunities for women. But despite these complications, it is already clear that there are many ways to rear happy, effective children. Although all of them represent hard work and hard choices for parents, they can all be equally valid.

Reading Questions

1. The article differentiates between child-care for those over two and child-care for those under two. What has the research shown about each?
2. What are the major issues to be dealt with by parents in selecting day-care for their children?
3. Given the increasing numbers of parents in need of quality day-care for their children, how can business and government provide assistance?

RESEARCH STUDY

Investigators: Abby King, Richard Winett, Steven Lovett.
Source, date: "Enhancing Coping Behaviors in At-Risk Populations: The Effects of Time-Management Instruction and Social Support in Women from Dual-Earner Families," *Behavior Therapy,* 1986, *17,* 57-66.
Location: Virginia Polytechnic Institute and State University.
Subjects: 56 women currently employed at the university.
Materials: Time-management questionnaires; Bandura Self-efficacy Scale; LaRocco's Social Support Scale; Stress, Mood, Productivity Inventory; Stressful Conditions Questionnaires; Life Events Checklist.

It has been recognized that women from dual-earner families experience a large amount of stress due to the combined demands of their work and home. This overload of demands creates time shortages and an inadequate support network, all contributing to the stress experienced by the women. The purpose of the study was to determine the effectiveness of time-management training and provision of social support on perceived stress in women from dual-earner families.

The investigators recruited women employed at the university to conduct this study. Of the fifty-six who participated, one-fourth were trained in time management and were assisted in developing and utilizing a social support group from their research group. One-fourth of the women only received training in time management. One-fourth only received assistance in social support and the remainder were put on a waiting list.

For all participants, scales regarding time management, self-efficacy, social support, and perceived stress were completed.

As a result of the time management training, participants in the groups receiving this training spent more time engaged in activities that were positive and important to the women. They also demonstrated greater knowledge of time management as well as greater effectiveness in its use. Those in groups in which social support was provided indicated greater enjoyment of the group as well as increased knowledge concerning the value and use of social support. The investigators concluded that there was a clear benefit for women in a stressful lifestyle to receive such training and its impact was most direct on those behaviors (time management and social support) on which training was focused.

Research Study Questions

1. According to the investigators, what contributes to the feelings of stress experienced by women from dual-earner families?

2. What kinds of training did the various groups receive and how did the training they received vary from group to group?
3. As a result of the training, how did the women benefit? In short, what were the specific findings of the study?

CASE STUDY

The Workaholic

The patient is a 45-year-old lawyer who seeks treatment at his wife's insistence. She is fed up with their marriage: she can no longer tolerate his emotional coldness, rigid demands, bullying behavior, sexual disinterest, long work hours, and frequent business trips. The patient feels no particular distress in his marriage, and has agreed to the consultation only to humor his wife.

It soon develops, however, that the patient is troubled by problems at work. He is known as the hardest-driving member of a hard-driving law firm. He was the youngest full partner in the firm's history, and is famous for being able to handle many cases at the same time. Lately, he finds himself increasingly unable to keep up. He is too proud to turn down a new case, and too much of a perfectionist to be satisfied with the quality of work performed by his assistants. He finds himself constantly correcting their briefs, displeased with their writing style and sentence structure, and therefore unable to stay abreast of his schedule. People at work complain that his attention to detail and inability to delegate responsibility are reducing his efficiency. He has been through two or three secretaries a year for 15 years. No one can tolerate working for him for very long because he is so critical of any mistakes made by others. When assignments get backed up, he cannot decide which to address first, starts making schedules for himself and his staff, but then is unable to meet them and works 15 hours a day. He finds it difficult to be decisive now that his work has expanded beyond his own direct control.

The patient discusses his children as if they were mechanical dolls, but also with a clear underlying affection. He describes his wife as a "suitable mate" and has trouble understanding why she is dissatisfied. He is punctilious in his manners and dress and slow and ponderous in his speech, dry and humorless, with a stubborn determination to get his point across.

The patient is the product of two upwardly mobile, extremely hard-working parents. He grew up feeling that he was never working hard enough, that he had much to achieve and very little time. He was a superior student, a bookworm, awkward and unpopular in adolescent social pursuits. He has always been competitive and a high achiever. He has trouble relaxing on vacations, develops elaborate activities schedules for every family member, and becomes impatient and furious if they refuse to follow his plans. He likes sports but has little time for them and refuses to play if he can't be at the top of his form. He is a ferocious competitor on the tennis courts and a poor loser.

Discussion of The Workaholic

Although the marital problem is the entry ticket, it is clear that this fellow has many personality traits that are quite maladaptive. He is cold and rigid and excessively perfectionistic. He is indecisive, but insists that others do things his way; his interpersonal relationships suffer because of his excessive devotion to work. It is hard to imagine a more prototypical case of Compulsive Personality Disorder!

The additional notation of the V code Marital Problem is not made in this case since the patient's marital problems are clearly symptomatic of his mental disorder.

Case Study Questions

1. What was the reason for this person's being seen in therapy? What was his real problem?
2. What are the man's attitudes toward work and how does he act at work?
3. What about this man would make him difficult to work or live with?

SELF-TEST

Multiple Choice

1. A person's work may be a central anchor of his/her:
   a. success
   b. finances
   c. identity
   d. thoughts
2. The idea that working is a moral obligation is part of the:
   a. American code
   b. Protestant ethic
   c. American ethic
   d. moral ethic

3. Another part of this ethic says that _____ is a sign of moral deficiency:
   a. idleness
   b. wealth
   c. selfishness
   d. overwork
4. Why do many Americans continue to work even when they do not have to for financial reasons?
   a. to provide daily patterns, relationships, and self-esteem
   b. they are required to work by law
   c. only as a means of self-expression
   d. none of these are reasons
5. We begin forming attitudes and interests that will affect our choice of a job:
   a. only after beginning high school
   b. as teenagers
   c. when we begin college
   d. as children
6. Career choice is affected not only by interests, but also by:
   a. sex
   b. social class
   c. race
   d. all of these affect our career choices
7. According to U.S. Bureau of Labor statistics, women now occupy how much of the country's labor force?
   a. over two-thirds
   b. less than 10 percent
   c. almost one-half
   d. about 33 percent
8. Why are women still affected by the same income gap of forty years ago?
   a. they are incapable of success in high-status positions
   b. women are never ambitious
   c. many women now in the work force were not educated with high-paying positions in mind
   d. women have no desire for high-status jobs
9. Although most people make changes in their work patterns at various times in their lives, the major change in work pattern for almost all workers is:
   a. retirement
   b. promotion
   c. resignation
   d. being fired
10. Because many people now seek fulfillment as well as financial security from their jobs, some industries have attempted to:
    a. require psychiatric sessions for workers
    b. "rehumanize" the workplace
    c. allow the most compatible workers to work together
    d. replace most workers with computers
11. If you enjoy your job, but are unhappy with some of the conditions, it is a good idea to:
    a. demand changes immediately and aggressively
    b. quit altogether
    c. force the employer to fire you
    d. use your influence to try to make changes
12. The prevalent attitude toward having children in the United States seems increasingly to be that:
    a. it is wrong to have children
    b. although children can be fulfilling, family planning is wise and it can be appropriate to choose not to have children at all
    c. children only interfere with personal goals, but are necessary for economic reasons
    d. none of these
13. Child-care outside the home has become a critical issue because:
    a. both parents often work for financial reasons
    b. most people are no longer interested in their children
    c. many women desire work outside the home today
    d. both a and c
14. In child-rearing, the authors suggest:
    a. remembering to allow children leeway for personal oddities
    b. being alert to factors you may dislike in child-care situations
    c. being aware of repeating patterns from your own childhood, even if they are not constructive
    d. all of these are suggested
15. Midlife is a time of emotional stress in which one chooses between the two approaches of:
    a. generativity and self-absorption
    b. changing jobs or remaining stable
    c. having children or remaining childless
    d. both a and c
16. Many aging people must deal with the stress of:
    a. negative attitudes of society toward the aged
    b. physical problems
    c. poverty and loneliness
    d. all of the above
17. Any behavior ranging too far from the norm is considered abnormal. This is known as:
    a. mental aberration
    b. mental disorder
    c. statistical rarity
    d. deviation of the abnormal
18. An overwhelming fear of something that the

person actually realizes does not pose a great threat is known as:
   a. obsessive-compulsive disorder
   b. hallucination
   c. general anxiety
   d. phobic disorder
19. The main difference between a neurotic and a psychotic person is that:
   a. neurotics have little contact with reality
   b. psychotics have little contact with reality
   c. there is no real difference
   d. neurotic persons are catatonic
20. When studying psychological disturbances, it is important to remember:
   a. not to glibly label yourself or others with diagnostic labels
   b. that treatment is available for those who do feel they may have a serious psychological problem
   c. to point out to others symptoms they may display of psychological disorders
   d. both a and b are important points to remember

True-False

1. The ideas of the Protestant ethic have had little effect on the American views of work.
2. Because of the 1964 Civil Rights Act, women no longer suffer from unequal pay at any time.
3. Most people change work patterns several times in their lives.
4. "Rehumanizing" the workplace has included new work schedules, flex time, and efforts to include workers in company decisions.
5. In the past, many families wanted more children so they could help with the farmwork.
6. Spock's approach to child-rearing is now considered by psychologists to be the best method.
7. All day-care facilities are excellent, and parents do not need to exercise much care in choosing an appropriate facility these days.
8. Extramarital sex seems to be fairly common in midlife.
9. Intellectual functioning does not necessarily decline with old age.
10. Almost all elderly people become swamped with despair, dwelling on past failures, losses, and disappointments.
11. One of the worst problems old people face is the social attitude that they are completely different from young people.
12. The personal discomfort criterion of abnormality is helpful in all cases, especially for socially disruptive behaviors such as rape.
13. Anxiety disorders are a category of neurotic disorder characterized by unreasonable and disabling fear.
14. A psychotic person has a distorted view of reality. He may have hallucinations or delusions.
15. Schizophrenia means the same thing as split personality.

Completion

1. Work gives us a sense of _____.
2. The success of women now entering the work force in high status jobs should cut down on _____ against women in the work world for future generations.
3. _____ of women still hold typically low-status female jobs.
4. According to Spock's _____ view, children are basically innocent and good.
5. The increased birth rate in the U.S. after World War II is known as the _____ _____.
6. Today's average couple has less than _____ children.
7. _____ _____ or family day-care is usually inexpensive but difficult to regulate.
8. When choosing day-care for your child, it is important to take note of the caregivers, the _____, and the planned activities.
9. Age-appropriate jobs and privileges are good for children's _____ _____.
10. _____ is the capacity to develop a concern for others. This is important for good adjustment.
11. Only _____ of the aged are senile, according to a recent estimate.
12. Norm-violation, statistical rarity, and personal discomfort are three ways of defining _____ _____.
13. The _____ _____ _____ is a system of classifying problem behaviors.
14. _____ disorder is a term used to describe disorders that do not rob the person of contact with reality.
15. _____ _____ is a rare pattern of behavior in which a person alternates between periods of mania and depression.

Essay Questions

1. Discuss the role of the Protestant ethic in the attitudes of Americans today. (p. 430)

ADJUSTMENT AND MALADJUSTMENT IN ADULTHOOD

2. What are some changes occurring in the world of work today? (pp. 433–434)
3. What are some of the problems involved in being a parent today? What are some solutions? (pp. 434–437)
4. What are some of the difficulties that occur with aging? (pp. 440–441)
5. What are some types of "neurotic" disorders given in the text? Types of psychotic disorders? (pp. 444–446)

SELF-TEST ANSWERS

Multiple Choice

1. c (p. 430)
2. b (p. 430)
3. a (p. 430)
4. a (p. 430)
5. d (p. 431)
6. d (p. 431)
7. c (p. 431)
8. c (p. 431)
9. a (p. 432)
10. b (p. 433)
11. d (p. 433)
12. b (p. 435)
13. d (p. 436)
14. d (p. 438)
15. a (p. 439)
16. d (p. 441)
17. c (p. 443)
18. d (p. 444)
19. b (p. 444)
20. d (p. 445)

True-False

1. false (p. 430)
2. false (p. 431)
3. true (p. 432)
4. true (p. 432)
5. true (p. 435)
6. false (p. 435)
7. false (p. 436)
8. true (p. 439)
9. true (p. 441)
10. false (p. 441)
11. true (p. 441)
12. false (p. 443)
13. true (p. 443)
14. true (p. 444)
15. false (p. 445)

Completion

1. identity (p. 430)
2. discrimination (p. 431)
3. 80 percent (p. 431)
4. permissive (p. 435)
5. baby boom (p. 435)
6. two (p. 435)
7. home-based (p. 436)
8. setting (p. 437)
9. self-esteem (p. 438)
10. generativity (p. 439)
11. 8 percent (p. 441)
12. abnormal behavior (p. 443)
13. Diagnostic and Statistical Manual (p. 443)
14. neurotic (p. 443)
15. bipolar disorder (p. 445)